The Culture of Tourism,
the Tourism of Culture

The Culture of Tourism, the Tourism of Culture

Selling the Past to the Present in the American Southwest

EDITED BY HAL K. ROTHMAN

UNIVERSITY OF NEW MEXICO PRESS **I** ALBUQUERQUE

PUBLISHED IN COOPERATION WITH THE CLEMENTS CENTER
FOR SOUTHWEST STUDIES AT SOUTHERN METHODIST UNIVERSITY

Library of Congress Cataloging-in-Publication Data

The culture of tourism, the tourism of culture : selling the past to the
present in the American southwest / edited by Hal K. Rothman.— 1st ed.
    p. cm.
"Published in cooperation with the Clements Center for Southwest Studies at Southern
Methodist University."
    ISBN 0-8263-2928-4 (cloth : alk. paper)
    1. Heritage tourism—Southwest, New.   I. Rothman, Hal, 1958–
II. William P. Clements Center for Southwest Studies.
    G156.5.H47 C86 2003
    338.4'79179—dc21

                                                          2002155307

Design: Melissa Tandysh

⚊ CONTENTS ⚊

— LIST OF ILLUSTRATIONS —

LIST OF TABLES

⟶ LIST OF CONTRIBUTORS ⟶

WILLIAM L. BRYAN, JR. received his Ph.D. in Natural Resource Planning and Conservation from the University of Michigan in 1971. After running a regional management consulting group for cause-oriented, non-profit organizations for years, he and his wife, Pam, co-founded Off the Beaten Path in 1985, a custom travel planning service for people traveling to the Rockies, Southwest, and Alaska. Bill is currently Off the Beaten Path's chairman and is involved in a variety of start-ups in the area of responsible travel in the rural West.

ERIKA MARIE BSUMEK is an Assistant Professor in the Department of History at the University of Texas in Austin. Her book, *Indian-made: The Construction and Consumption of Navajo Identity, 1860–1940* will be published by the University Press of Kansas. She teaches and writes about the history of the American West, American Indian history, race, ethnicity, and consumerism.

LEAH DILWORTH is Associate Professor of English at Long Island University's Brooklyn campus. She is the author of *Imagining Indians in the Southwest: Persistent Visions of a Primitive Past* (1996) and the editor of the forthcoming volume, *Acts of Possession: Collecting in America.*

SUSAN GUYETTE, PH.D., is the owner of Santa Fe Planning & Research. She practices cross-cultural planning and writes textbooks on planning method. Her current areas of expertise include tourism, cultural preservation, economic development, and evaluation.

PHOEBE S. KROPP is an Assistant Professor in the Department of History at the University of Pennsylvania, where she teaches courses on the American West, culture, environment, and public memory. Her book on Southern California's "Spanish fantasy past" is forthcoming from the University of California Press. She is also currently at work on a project about the history of family camping in the United States.

CHAR MILLER is Chair of the Department of History and Interim Director of the Urban Studies Program at Trinity University. He is author most recently of the award-winning *Gifford Pinchot and the Making of Modern Environmentalism* (Island Press, 2001). Miller is also editor of *On the Border: An Environmental History of San Antonio* (University of Pittsburgh Press, 2001), and *An Environmental Atlas of the United States and Canada* (Routledge, 2003).

SYLVIA RODRIGUEZ is an Associate Professor in the Department of Anthropology at the University of New Mexico. Her research interests deal with interethnic relations in the U.S. Southwest with ethnographic emphases on the Upper Rio Grande Valley. She has published articles on tourism, land and water issues, and ritual performance. Her book, *The Matachines Dance: Ritual Symbolism and Interethnic Relations in the Upper Rio Grande Valley* (University of New Mexico Press, 1996), was awarded the 1997 Chicago Folklore Prize.

HAL K. ROTHMAN is Professor of History at the University of Nevada, Las Vegas, and author of, among numerous books, *Neon Metropolis: How Las Vegas Started the Twenty-First Century* and *Devil's Bargains: Tourism in the Twentieth-Century American West*, which won the 1999 Western Writers of America Spur Award for best contemporary non-fiction work.

MARGUERITE S. SHAFFER is Associate Professor of History and Director of the Program in American Studies at Miami University. She is the author of *See America First: Tourism and National Identity, 1880–1940* (Smithsonian Institution Press, 2001). She is currently working on a book entitled *Popular Environmentalism*.

RINA SWENTZELL is a native of Santa Clara Pueblo. She holds an M.A. in architecture and a Ph.D. in American Studies from the University of New Mexico. A weaver and potter, she also lectures and writes about Pueblo architecture, culture, and art. Her books include *Younger-Older Ones* (2001), *Children of Clay* (1992), and, co-authored with J. J. Brody, *To Touch the Past: The Painted Pottery of the Mimbres People* (1996).

DAVID WHITE, PH.D., is an anthropologist with experience in historic preservation, cultural resource management, tourism planning, and ethnographic research. He owns and operates a consulting firm, Applied Cultural Dynamics, in Santa Fe, New Mexico.

CHRIS WILSON is J. B. Jackson Professor of Cultural Landscape Studies at the University of New Mexico School of Architecture and Planning. He is the author of *The Myth of Santa Fe: Creating a Modern Regional Tradition* (1997) and *Facing Southwest: The Life and Houses of John Gaw Meem* (2001). He is currently editing a book about the historic plazas of New Mexico, their potential for revitalization, and the adaptability of that civic form for contemporary community design.

INTRODUCTION

TOURISM AND THE FUTURE ⟶

HAL K. ROTHMAN

In the summer of 1999, I led the American Orient Express train tour of the national parks. At $5,000 a berth, this was a specialty experience that took travelers on a ten-day trip that began in Denver. It continued to Salt Lake City, down through the Utah parks, out to Death Valley, and around to the Grand Canyon. From El Tovar Hotel at the Grand Canyon, we rode the train to Acoma, the Sky City of the Acoma Indians, and finally finished in Santa Fe. The train was a refurbished 1940s luxury train, with small berths and shared showers in a style long gone from American society. Glorious five-course meals in the beautiful dining car and entertainment in the club cars and observation car transcended limited personal space. The train offered both past and present, a luxury tour reminiscent of an earlier America, a cultural experience, really, as well as a combined train and bus tour through the national parks of today. It gave its travelers an image of the past in the train and showed them the spectacular national parks, an affirmation of American culture in themselves, as they were wined and dined with the best that post-modern America has to offer.

First and foremost, the American Orient Express offers a deluxe experience. The needs of the passengers—what they sought, what they wanted, and what they expected—were paramount. They'd chosen a mode of travel with powerful cultural overtones, but they had not in any way agreed to shed the trappings of class, context, and position. The train took them back in time but provided them the soft edges of an experience with the rough corners thoroughly planed. A sleeping-car porter turned down the beds; he left water in the ubiquitous plastic bottle. This wasn't the 1940s at all—it was the 1990s in 1940s costume, which was better than the old days ever could have been. It might even have been better than real.

The train was filled with people in their sixties and seventies, people who could very well have traveled on such a train in its heyday. They were of a different America than me, people who could remember a nation of small towns and farms, who knew of places like Bucklin, Kansas, and Pesotum, Illinois. That lonesome whistle meant freedom and adventure to them as did the automobile to their children. Once it spelled out the names of places they'd never seen, experiences they only dreamed of. Now it brought back memories.

They moved comfortably on the train, part of a culture that was raised with the shared space of club cars and dining cars. Within one day of boarding the train, I understood the need for manners in a society that shared space; after more than forty years of living, I'd finally found a reason to be polite! In postmodern America, where we insult each other in traffic and think of it as communication, the older virtues that made a world where people stood, walked, sat, and chatted in common space have fallen by the wayside. On the train, where everyone lived in a ten-by-seven compartment, the ability to negotiate public space was critical. Everyone had to be able to deal with people they didn't necessarily like; they had to abide by a code that allowed people to disagree without disagreeing, to deflect unwanted conversation or attention without giving offense. It was a skillful dance, where disapproval was established by a turn of the head or a reorienting of the shoulders, certainly not with words, mild or harsh. Here was a lesson to younger America, a vision of a past where interactive skills were essential to the persistence of community in a world in which only the wealthiest could separate from the rest. Space and privacy in that world conveyed status; in ours, only time allows that distinction.

The most overwhelming feature of the train was service. The entire ethos of the train stemmed from a world where labor was cheap. In part because of the price and equally because of the age of the travelers, the train staff spent most of its time performing little tasks that made the trip not only special but also memorable. This attention was the personification of enlightened self-interest; I learned only later that the staff depended on tips as a crucial part of their income. Besides train staff, waiters, porters, and cooks among them, the train company hired not only lecturers like me but also tour guides who transferred people from the train to buses and other conveyances, arranged for hotel rooms and meals on the nights we were not on the train, and otherwise handled the day-to-day arrangements. Like the tours

Japanese companies provide their countrymen in the United States, nearly every aspect of the train travelers' experience filtered through one or another of the service people.

Here was a form of cultural tourism, a package of events and experiences in a setting that was made comfortable for its audience. Travelers got to experience culture, and many of them got to relive an earlier time in their life through the mechanism of the train. One man told me that he traveled home on a similar train with his severance pay from the military at the end of World War II. Another couple told how they'd honeymooned on such a train in 1947. Clearly culture and personal history—some might say nostalgia—melded. This was a trip in the present and the past simultaneously.

This intersection has a lot to show, for the American Orient Express is a harbinger of the future, a window into the complexities of cultural tourism. Cultural tourism has come to mean a great deal more than education about the past. It also includes status markers like a labor-intensive luxury experience, memory—nostalgia to some—and a definition of what's important that stems from an ideal of high- and lowbrow cultures, of knowledge worth having. It has also become a cash cow, a way to sustain when other economic strategies fail. The train fused the elements that make cultural tourism an integral part of the future not only of tourism, but also of the economy of the American Southwest and of the restructuring of the economy of much of the nation. It mirrored a process long evident throughout the region, a story that combined imagery, accouterments, and experience in an effort to persuade the public that in fact what they'd experienced was different from the norms of daily life. The combination of age, wealth, service, and cultural symbolism of the train portends a future with plenty of possibilities and equally many challenges. The train carries us through more than the Southwest. It illustrates many of the essential challenges of promoting culture in a changing age.

In the past decade, tourism has become one of the major buzzes in American society. It became important quickly, coming from nowhere as the nation went through the first stages of an excruciating shift from an industrial to a postindustrial economy. The combination of Vietnam War–era inflation and the OPEC oil embargo brought postwar prosperity to a screeching halt and unmasked the aging of American industrial infrastructure. Industrial America was forced to compete against newer facilities and cheaper labor overseas, and the result was disastrous. Between 1974 and 1997, the real value of American wages declined every year for twenty-three successive years. The nation even lost entire industries. Once the United States made televisions. The last place in the nation to assemble them was the Zenith plant in Springfield, Missouri. By 1998, the same building housed the mail-order inventory for Bass Pro Shops, a recreational tourist entity that catered to the tastes of blue-collar America. As electronics and other industries disappeared, communities and regions sought a panacea, something to replace the lost jobs in the figurative widget factory, the ones that paid the bills for families and filled tax coffers, the dollars that hired new teachers and repaved torn-up roads. In many places, there were few alternatives—stories of retraining programs for forty-five-year-old steelworkers who'd been in the mill since they turned eighteen and, in the words of Bruce Springsteen, "got a union card and a wedding coat" abounded—and as county commissioners and city officials scratched their heads, they cast about for a way to sustain their communities and themselves. Tourism seemed a ready-made panacea: it rarely required tax abatements or givebacks, and it seemed to provide jobs and opportunities. Even better, people got paid for being themselves.

When the rest of the nation looked for models of how tourism worked, they looked to the Southwest. The mythical Southwest had long been the locus of American tourism, the panoramic dreamscape of the nation. The Southwest's weird and spectacular scenery and divergent cultures, from the petrified forests of Arizona and the festive Mexicano nature of San Antonio to the solitary cliffs of the Colorado Plateau and the Navajo Nation, promised difference and in that difference authentic experience. You could be yourself in the Southwest, Americans wholeheartedly believed; you could become whoever you wanted to be, and in the process you could feel the past of the nation, could see the American pageant before you. You could be part of the past, free of the indignities of the oppressive present. When others looked at models for tourism, especially cultural tourism, as an economic engine, no region had done it better than the Southwest. From Santa Fe to Santa Barbara, from San Antonio to Las Vegas, the Southwest has been a landscape for visitors, a place where people can see the past as they want it to be, take a piece of it with them, and feel their distance from the norms of the mainstream. Here's a landscape that works—because it isn't what it claims to be; it's a softer, manipulated, more valued version of the realities of the region.

This particular look at the Southwest skewed its evolution, transposed a past awkwardly with the present. The region had been in transformation since the end of World War II. Tourism had long been the shadow industry in the region, seemingly ephemeral to states that for years made their living in timber, ranging, agriculture, and mineral extraction. In the quarter century that followed the end of World War II, a combination of economic innovation, access, and technology brought millions to visit the region and almost as many to live there. All of a sudden, tourism catapulted to enormous significance: the long history of visitation turned into a torrent of cars, backpackers, operagoers, skiers, mountain bikers, and history buffs. Even states like California, the core area for the West, began cultural tourism initiatives. California has the twelfth-largest economy in the world. Its interest in cultural tourism affirmed this new importance and, at the same time, made it the subject of scrutiny as a model for similar endeavors.

Tourism grew in importance as the seeds of a new, connected future were taking shape. The catalyst of this transformation came from a minuscule piece of silicon called the microchip. This little chunk of information-processing material caused the radical, inexorable, fundamental, and overnight transformation of the basis of the world economy; it created a transformation every bit as great as the Industrial Revolution, a divide across which people peered with great trepidation. The Microchip Revolution, the constellation of changes associated with the rise of this funny little piece of equipment, changed life as people knew it. Microchips created the so-called Information Age, in which knowledge and the ability to manipulate it genuinely became power, and it dramatically increased the range and significance of the service economy.

Without the microchip, all the revolutions of the past twenty years, in everything from manufacturing and banking to health technologies and elite job choice, simply could not have taken place. This transformation created large amounts of wealth and equal amounts of consequences. Cyber-transactions now move capital around the globe, creating what the noted cultural critic Christopher Lasch recognized as a transnational class of monied individuals who are in essence stateless in their sense of national obligations. This boundary-free wealth has few obligations to people and places, and its incredible mobility may even constitute a threat to the stability of individual places and national economies. The tremendous exporting of manufacturing to developing countries, from the maquiladora corridor in Mexico to the Far East, where Michael Jordan inspected Nike factories and Kathie Lee Gifford got in so much trouble, is only one poignant example of a trend that has profound implications for anyone dependent on a paycheck. The result has been that some skills—especially white-collar, information-based skills—have gained in value, while other skills have been stripped of value. "Foreman says these jobs are going, boys," sang Bruce Springsteen, the bard of the dispossessed, in the early 1980s, "and they ain't coming back," and right he was. What replaced them was a dispossession of the old American working class, the lunch-bucket and hard-hat brigade who voted Democratic and sent their children to college to eventually turn into Republicans.

Like all its predecessors, this new revolution picks winners and losers. Some sectors of the economy fare marvelously. The educated, the highly skilled upper end of the service sector—everyone from attorneys to consultants of all stripes—find opportunities galore at fees that reward their choice of career. The technically proficient—and here skilled health care professionals stand out, along with the denizens of Silicon Valley—also benefit greatly. They are their skill; they sell their knowledge, and it is transferable from the equipment of one employer to another. These two groups lead the pack. Wageworkers of all kinds, agricultural workers, and the semiskilled and unskilled bear the economic brunt of this change. Their skills have simply lost value, and many have been consigned to the scrap heap of economic history. Stocking bottles in a 7–Eleven never had the upward mobility of industrial work, not to mention the job security, wages, or benefits.

In the end, this revolution has changed the way life progresses in the United States. We don't work as we did even fifteen years ago; PCs and the Internet created access and information transfer in ways that seemed like science fiction in the 1970s. We no longer rely on the sources of capital that once drove the American economy. The junk bonds of the 1970s, themselves an innovation, have become the derivatives, a computer generated sort of splitting and matching, of the 1990s. We don't do the same tasks in the same ways, and we barely experience the constraints that once placed limits on the way business was done.

The transformation has been powerful and comprehensive. It has diminished not only the market value of American resources but a significant piece of the national mythology as well. The United States was built on two premises: cheap labor, often provided by immigrants and family members, and cheap natural resources. Labor hasn't been cheap in the United States since before World War II, and the formerly cheap natural resources are both more expensive and less necessary in a global economy. Although it may be premature to declare the end of the natural-resources-based world economy, it is clear that the ways in which resources are organized, used, and the purposes to which they are put have dramatically changed—especially in the First World. The changing economy and a changing culture put a premium on experience—precisely the entity that tourism and travel could provide—that was new in its scope and scale. In a society charged with questions of race and ethnicity, the Southwest became a canvas for the nation, a place to visit in anticipation of working out the complex tensions at the core of a diversifying nation. No better landscape, no better demography existed on which to paint American dreams. Nowhere did the United States offer a clearer image of a multiracial past; nowhere did that image draw Americans more completely into a mythic past. The nation had treated the Southwest as a dreamscape for more than a century, psychically taming the landscape and its people in a way that the public culture of tourism, the set of signs and symbols that the tourist landscape gives off like radiation, wholly embraced. The result was a script for change without change, a cultural tourism that genuflects to a mythic past as a way to minimize and finally erase tension.

In this new world of individual expression, experiences became currency and entertainment, replacing conventional culture. This equation had enormous ramifications for the country, but especially for the Southwest. On the canvas made of America dreams of expansion and the creation of order, the rise of culture as commodity sent hundreds of thousands streaming to the Southwest, the most mythic region of the nation and the destination of the greatest number of tourists. Not only did visitors seek to find themselves and to solve their qualms about a changing society both then and now, they also sought to possess the amorphous culture of the self. The Old Southwest promised self-realization in a world of inauthentic and fabricated experience. Even you, Greg Brady of *The Brady Bunch*, could befriend an Indian boy of the same age and with your family be adopted into his tribe. Only here could you see mythic Indian people making the crafts that gave you credibility. Only here did Spanish seem like an indigenous language, not an overlay as in *West Side Story*. Against the backdrop of the American Indian and Hispano past, cultural tourism attained great cachet.

And no wonder. Much of the physical landscape of the region, its public symbolism, the construction of its roads, trails, and even cities reflected a process that took cultural history, planed off its rough edges, and placed it in a neat little wrapper that was intelligible to the traveling classes. Even one hundred years ago, Americans saw in the reflected mirror of a constructed Southwest a canvas on which to paint their social tensions. New Mexico excelled at that process, often at the expense of its natives; California obliterated a past but kept its symbolic vestiges in names, roads, and trails, and entire industries devoted to the creation of "authentic" goods—souvenirs, really—and the assigning of status to them developed with a flourish. The poverty of the region, its difference from humid-clime America, its browns and golds instead of green, made a persuasive setting for a nation in love with its self-designated mission that needed precisely the space, close in but illustratively far away, that allows cultural dissent. The presence of seekers from Charles Lummis through Mary Austin and Mabel Dodge Luhan and on to Georgia O'Keeffe confirmed that here was space that was different, but not so different that the ways of American life, the contentions to high culture, to literary publishers, to art museums, did not hold sway.

Cities like San Antonio embraced this new conception of a manufactured past, recognizing in it a future that they could not find in any other activity. Without industry, with low wages and masses of unskilled and semiskilled workers, San Antonio sought a package for its attributes. Along with Santa Barbara and Santa Fe, San Antonio became one of the earliest cities to package an exotic but smoothed past for the consumption of a public who seemed likely to pay for little else from it. Tourist cities morphed from there. Las Vegas became the first city in the world entirely devoted to tourism. Even vaunted California joined the game in the 1990s with its cultural tourism initiative that left smaller cities complaining of the dominance of Los Angeles, San Francisco, and San Diego. A full generation before much of the rest of the nation recognized anything but conventions as having an impact on regional economies, southwestern cities understood the value of tourism and catered to it with a subtle determination to make it pay.

By the time of the Microchip Revolution, this construct was set in stone in the Southwest. Tourism and the soft corners of culture described the place of the Southwest in American iconography, and generations of southwesterners, Native, Latino, and Anglo, were accustomed to the dance of tourism. The serving of outsiders at the expense of locals had gone from sacrifice to custom to way of life. People complained about it, but they recognized it as essential to their existence. If the tourists weren't going to mail in the checks and just stay home, the Southwest would have to deal with them, their needs, their litter, their mythic misconceptions of the places they visited. Tourism offered an embrace, a close hug, that sometimes squeezed the air out of the Southwest.

⌒

The future of tourism in some ways looks very bright. In the Southwest especially, the changes in American culture and demography speak to a future full if not inundated with tourists. In a world where trees are more valuable as scenery than as timber, places with long histories of providing surface experience stand to do very well. In states like Nevada, Hawaii, and New Mexico, long histories in tourism speak to the potential of the industry.

A new world is dawning, one that will change cultural tourism and especially the places that depend on it. The baby boomers, the largest birth cohort in American history, are reaching the onset of retirement. These are the wealthiest group of people in human history, in no small part because of the run-up in the stock market of the 1990s, and they will also be the recipients of the biggest cross-generational transfer of wealth in human history as they inherit from their parents. The nation will have an older, more affluent population in far better health than any people of its age in human history. As the new century dawns, they are hitting precisely the stage of life where cultural tourism, the reach for a past not necessarily their own, will become important to them. They'll travel in ever growing numbers to see the places they associate with their own personal history as well as those important to their construction of their nation and its heritage. They'll need not only gasoline and meals but rooms and tour guides, IMAX theaters and medical care. They'll demand amenities; this is the most self-indulgent cohort yet to travel through American life. And more than anything, they'll require parking lots for their recreational vehicles. From now until about 2040, when the last of the baby boomers reach the logical end of their traveling years, all cultural tourism providers have to do is figuratively build parking lots—provide more and better amenities to the ever increasing number of retirees who search for the past as recreation and enlightenment. It's a dream for museum professionals and park rangers, people who deal with the visitor populations of today.

If only it were this easy. There's a flip side, far more difficult to negotiate. A quick look around American society shows a culture without continuity. There's a fault line in American culture that I call the MTV line. If you came to maturity before 1982, when MTV came on the air, you're part of one culture with a widely shared set of signs and symbols. You're likely to know who Abraham Lincoln was, that the Civil War was in the nineteenth century, and that presidents before John Kennedy weren't necessarily telegenic. If you're a little older, you're likely to have traveled somewhere by train and, if you're male, to have been conscripted and fought in a war. If you crossed that line after 1982, you come from a different world, visual and postliterate. It's a spectator culture, one where you watch and change channels if you're dissatisfied with what you see, where you put a value on your ability to choose and to experience without effort.

This is what John Seabrook of *The New Yorker* has called "Nobrow," a culture of neither high nor low, when all comes together in a manifestation of the self. Nothing's better anymore, and maybe that's a good thing: the glassware at Target is as good as that from the best houses; the knockoffs are better than the real watches. It's a world where, as Seabrook tartly puts it, "culture and marketing are as cozy as Mickey and Minnie."[1] Everything has become mainstream, creating independent sets of signs and symbols to describe culture.

For the young this has been particularly telling. Coming from a specta-tor youth culture, they understand the world in different terms, genuflect at different statues, and generally respond to a parallel set of cues to the world. What these young people—and all who subscribe to their culture—know and how they learn it is different from the world of "culture" with a capital C. Spoon-fed from an "I'm OK—You're OK" motif, they crave experience, not in the authentic terms of Livingston or Stanley, not in the quest for knowl-edge of Humboldt, but in the self-indulgent, "experience is a mirror for my desire" terms of postindustrialism. In this frame, it is experience, culture with a video camera that makes the self important, that gives meaning to exis-tence. It is the process, the act of doing, not the knowledge acquired, that is the grail here.

Culture has become a script that places the visitor at the center. Riding around Las Vegas, backpacking in the wilds of Chaco Canyon or southern Utah, and sitting in the IMAX have come to have the same meaning. It's not that the people on the other side of the MTV line don't know the dif-ference between inauthentic and authentic; it's very simply a problem of communication: the denizens of the old have not given sufficiently good rea-sons for their definition of authenticity. From the signs and symbols around them, they've shaped their own view of culture, and it follows their dictates, not those based in the historical and cultural past. It's a new culture, and its adherents regard their symbols as their guidelines; in it Dr. Dre is more impor-tant than Abraham Lincoln, Thomas Jefferson's possible liaison with Sally Hemings more significant than the Declaration of Independence and his life-long struggle with the institution of slavery.

For cultural tourism, this is a whole new world, one in which the Rock and Roll Hall of Fame is more important than Civil War battlefields. Cultural tourism as it is currently practiced sells learning, reverence and dismay at the past, immersion in the values of society. Unlike its counterparts, recreational and entertainment tourism, both wrapped up with the self in different ways, cultural tourism is about more than individuals and their needs. It affirms culture . . . but what culture and under what circumstances?

This distinction turns out to be as hard for the baby boomers as for the MTV generation. It reflects more than the transformation of culture; it is also the transformation of what culture means. Cultural tourism is supposed to do more than reflect the self; that is its promise and its value. In a "me, me, me, now, now, now" culture, its audience is necessarily the smallest. Even for those in midlife, most likely to inquire about the context of the world around them, most likely to see themselves in a quest for enlightenment—not about the self, but about society—the persuasiveness of self-indulgence persists. Like the MTVers, the baby boomers pull away from a culture of sacrifice—hey, we're on vacation after all!—and toward messages that affirm the self even under the guise of learning.

The American Southwest has long experienced these issues and the transformations they embody. One of the first loci of the power politics of identity, one of the first regions of the country whose objects became commodities of authenticity, a place that turned itself over to tourism while industry still ground forward, giving it cities as different as San Antonio and Las Vegas devoted to tourism in different forms, a part of the country where daily life and mythology melded, often to the disadvantage of daily life, the Southwest experienced the cataclysmic transformation at the root of the tourist economy before the rest of the nation. Its cultural tourism and the issues that still swirl around it instruct a nation increasingly consumed with visiting itself in the figurative mirror of affirmation.

Notes

1. John Seabrook, *Nobrow: The Culture of Marketing, the Marketing of Culture* (New York: A. A. Knopf, 2000).

ETHNIC/SEXUAL PERSONAS IN
TRICULTURAL NEW MEXICO ⟶

CHRIS WILSON

You find yourself on foot in downtown Albuquerque. Perhaps you're in town for a conference, or in from the suburbs for a night out, or just killing an hour before returning your rental car and flying home from a relaxing week in Taos or Santa Fe. You cross a parking lot left in the wake of urban renewal, skirt a nearly empty civic plaza, approach high-rise offices, and there they are on the sidewalk: nine larger-than-life bronze figures.

Facing you, a seven-foot-tall Anglo-Texan developer instructs a Hispanic foreman in the day's work. Or is the developer's outstretched finger pointing the way to the future? So familiar is the iconography of contemporary cloth-ing and gesture that we read the figures' identities unconsciously: one in a suit coat, tie, creased pants, cowboy boots, and the kind of hat that LBJ liked to wear; the other in a work shirt, rumpled jeans, and round-toed boots—his hard hat held deferentially at his side, his bushy mustache recalling Juan Valdez, fictional Colombian coffee-bean picker of TV commercial fame. Behind them, a young, upper-middle-class family on vacation or perhaps a Sunday outing gaze at an Indian mother and daughter dressed in carefully coordinated traditional costumes. Beyond this cluster, a boy in a T-shirt, shorts, and brand-name basketball shoes does a wheelie on his skateboard, while a thirty-something Anglo businesswoman in a blazer and skirt strides purposefully past the others.

This piece, titled *Sidewalk Society,* is the work of Glenna Goodacre, the noted Texas-born sculptor who has made Santa Fe her home. In selecting these components, she consulted with the BetaWest Corporation, builders

Figure 1.1. *Sidewalk Society*, Glenna Goodacre, corner of Third and Tijeras, Albuquerque, 1990.

Photo by Kirk Gittings.

of the Hyatt Regency Hotel in front of which it stands, and representatives of the city of Albuquerque, which paid the quarter-million-dollar cost.[1] As a result, this 1990 piece was intended for tourists as much as for local consumption and reflects the interaction between tourist image making and civic identity that has been a central cultural dynamic in New Mexico for over 125 years.

New Mexico's public ideology of triculturalism holds that the state consists of three separate ethnic groups living together in harmony, be they Pueblo Indians, Mexicans, and Americans—the terms first used—or Native Americans, Hispanics, and Anglos—the terms most often employed today. The primary visual manifestation of this rhetoric—found in both public art and tourism promotional literature—is a set of ethnic personas. Occupying the middle ground between racial stereotypes and mythic archetypes, these popular cultural types—like the iconography of the saints before them—are recognizable through attributes of costume, arts and crafts, skin color and facial type, tools and modes of transportation. When linked to assumptions about technological progress, occupational status, and, above all, gender roles, these images also encapsulate and endorse a particular vision of social hierarchy.

This interaction of political rhetoric with popular tourist imagery began in the 1870s at the point when the colonization of the Southwest shifted from the first, military phase of conquest to the second, romantic phase. When New Mexican territorial officials were asked in 1874 to assemble exhibits for the upcoming centennial exposition in Philadelphia, they thought first of precious minerals and agricultural produce but soon added Pueblo pottery, moccasins, and a large number of Navajo blankets, including one woven for the occasion, reading "1776 / USA / 1876." Indian fighter Major José D. Sena objected to this recognition of the Navajo, who had been at war with his people only ten years before. But others felt, in the words of Santa Fe's newspaper, *The Daily New Mexican*, that "the handiwork of the Indians will show in pleasant contrast with the products of science and civilizations." From that exposition to the present, traditional handcrafts have served as emblems for indigenous groups, and, by contrast to modern technology, have placed them below Anglos in the social hierarchy.[2]

Local boosters also framed their arguments for statehood in historical and cultural terms, which they hoped would appeal to easterners' romantic interest in the Southwest. Veteran New York state politician L. Bradford Prince, for instance, who arrived in 1878 to serve as territorial secretary and later as the appointed governor, dedicated his 1883 book, *Historical Sketches of New Mexico*,

> TO THE PUEBLOS, Still representing in unchanged form the aboriginal civilizations . . . ;
> TO THE MEXICANS, Who in generosity, hospitality, and chivalric feeling, are worthy sons of the conquistadors . . . ;
> TO THE AMERICANS, Whose energy and enterprise are bringing all the appliances of modern science and invention to develop the almost limitless resources which nature has bestowed upon us;
> TO ALL, AS NEW MEXICANS, Now unitedly engaged in advancing the prosperity, and working for the magnificent future of the Territory.[3]

That same year, Prince helped organize the Tertio-Millennial Exposition at Santa Fe, which personified this new ideology with an opening parade of Indians (including, according to the *New Mexican*, "the oriental and innocent looking Zunis, of the Sixteenth century") as well as reenactments of the Spanish reconquest of Santa Fe in 1693 and the U.S. occupation of the territory in 1846.[4]

Apparently Prince was familiar with nineteenth-century colonial rhetoric, for the basic elements of triculturalism were present from the inception of this ideology: a chronology of conquest and technology justifying social hierarchy, the consignment of Pueblo Indians to the past, the linking of contemporary Mexicans with Spanish conquistadors, and the association of Americans with military conquest, science, and capitalism.[5] In response to nineteenth-century fears of miscegenation, Prince and other boosters of statehood also emphasized that the three groups were not intermarrying (when in reality they had already mixed to a considerable degree).

At the same time, *Harper's, Century, Frank Leslie's,* and other illustrated magazines published romantic images of Navajos, Pueblo Indians, Spanish conquistadors, and, to a lesser extent, contemporary Mexican Americans. As early as 1878—two years before the arrival of the railroad in New Mexico—Santa Fe curio dealer Jake Gold began to market Navajo and Mexican rugs, Apache baskets, and Pueblo pottery. Empress Eugenie, the Spanish-born wife of Napoleon III, had created an international vogue of Spanish filigree jewelry in the 1860s, and Santa Fe jewelers recruited Mexican silversmiths in the early 1880s to satisfy the tourists' expectation that they could purchase filigree in Spanish New Mexico.[6]

By comparison to the importation of a full-blown filigree jewelry industry, the adaptation of the Navajo blanket into rugs and wall hangings appropriate for home decorating proceeded over the three decades following the centennial blanket. Through the eighteenth and early nineteenth century, Navajos adapted aesthetics and weaving technology from Pueblo Indians and Spanish colonists, Saltillo trade blankets with designs derived from Moorish weaving, and U.S., British, and German yarns and fabrics. A classic cultural hybrid, Navajo weavings were used as saddle blankets, worn over both shoulders in lieu of coats, and over one shoulder by women as dresses.[7]

The introduction of calico, velveteen, denim, and other industrially produced fabrics in the 1860s and 1870s spelled the end of the so-called Classic phase of Navajo weaving. Some weavers sought new markets by dyeing their hand-spun wools with intense commercial colors. The vibrating contrasts of red, yellow, orange, and lime green against blue, black, and white backgrounds earned these blankets the name Eye Dazzlers.[8]

As mass-produced blankets continued to displace local weaving, trading post owners such as Lorenzo Hubble of Ganado, Arizona, guided Navajo weavers to a new tourist market. Hubble and most tourists shared an Arts and Crafts preference for natural materials, hand craftsmanship, and an earth-toned palette—all understood as antidotes to the social alienation of the industrial city. In a similar vein, the nineteenth-century cult of domesticity viewed women as nurturers of the young and the primary defenders of civilization, who might make their homes into oases of refinement amid the relentless transformations of the capitalist economy. Arts-and-Crafts furnishings in one's parlor became signs of cultivation and refuge. Accordingly, Hubble and other trading post operators awarded higher prices to weavers who adopted earth-toned colors and approved patterns, and by early in the twentieth century, the production of Eye Dazzlers ceased.[9]

While cultural entrepreneurs such as Jake Gold and Lorenzo Hubble cultivated tourist crafts ad hoc, the Santa Fe Railway initiated the systematic promotion of tourism in the late 1890s. The railway's advertising department acquired paintings of Pueblo and Navajo Indians, the Grand Canyon, and stark southwestern landscapes primarily from the Taos and Santa Fe art colonies. These appeared in travel brochures and annual calendars distributed to as many as three hundred thousand depots, schools, and homes across the Midwest and Southwest. The railway's California Mission Revival depots and Fred Harvey House hotels created romantic, trackside enclaves for tourists. Their flagship complex in Albuquerque, begun in 1901, included the largest Harvey House—the Alvarado Hotel—along with a Mission-style depot, an Indian building housing museum exhibits and a large curios shop, and an Indian village boasting pseudo-Pueblo and Navajo hogans. Lorenzo Hubble not only supplied blankets to the Fred Harvey Company, he also recruited Navajos—notably Elle and Tom of Ganado—to demonstrate their crafts at Santa Fe Railway installations.[10]

Elle came to national attention in 1903 when she wove a red, white, and blue blanket for President Teddy Roosevelt. For twenty years, she and Tom resided in the heart of Albuquerque, in that Indian village just north of the Alvarado Hotel. As with the suppression of commercial dyes in Navajo weaving, the postcard and travel images of Tom and Elle at their hogan edited out the surrounding reinforced concrete warehouses. Like other Navajo women, Elle had abandoned the handwoven shoulder dress for a velvet blouse, full skirt, silver belt, and necklace—a costume tourists now considered traditional. Most photographers posed Elle with Navajo children, usually girls. Although usually identified as her children, she had none, and these were likely those of other craft demonstrators or Tom's grandchildren from an earlier marriage. The rise of tourism during the first quarter of the twentieth century expanded the repertory of ethnic images and arts, while also purifying them of evidence of the modern world—whether commercial dyes

The Santa Fe
Magazine

Mary Pickford
At Albuquerque

March 1917

Figure 1.2. Elle of Ganado (far right) with Mary Pickford in front of the Indian Building, Alvarado Hotel complex, Albuquerque, cover of *Santa Fe Magazine*, March 1917.

or concrete warehouses—and more often than not also editing out Indian men and adding children for the women, which served to feminize the popular conception of native America.

This antimodern symbolic repertory was at first only loosely linked to New Mexico's rhetoric of triculturalism, however. The joint Museum of New Mexico and School of American Archeology (later renamed the School of American Research), established at Santa Fe in 1909, collaborated with the Santa Fe Railway in promoting tourism, encouraging crafts revivals, and patronizing the local art colonies. After the granting of statehood in 1912, the museum defined the Santa Fe style (more accurately termed the Pueblo Spanish Revival) for government buildings and to remake that city into a tourist destination.

Most important for our topic, the museum staff actively linked ethnic personas to civic ideology through historical pageants on the Fourth of July in 1911 and 1912, a set of three murals in the Palace of the Governors, and the modern Santa Fe Fiesta, begun in 1919. Each pageant episode, mural panel, and fiesta pageant day celebrated one of the three cultures. Traditional clothing and tourist arts placed Pueblo Indians in a timeless past, Spanish conquest reenactments provided more assertive roles but still consigned Spanish Americans to past glories, while mountain men, Santa Fe Trail merchants, the occupying U.S. Army, and industrial technologies represented the advent of the modern political and economic order. Parades that linked advances in transportation to particular ethnic groups implicitly justified social hierarchy: Pueblo Indians on foot and Spanish colonists with horses, burros, and two-wheel carts, followed by Santa Fe trail wagons, the U.S. cavalry, stagecoaches, a railroad locomotive float, and, finally, civic and business leaders riding in recently arrived automobiles.[11]

In this spirit, the museum staff encouraged key Indian contacts to adjust their clothing to create an image attractive to tourists.[12] Beginning with the first archeological excavations on the Pajarito Plateau in 1907, museum director Edgar Lee Hewett drew laborers primarily from the nearby Tewa-speaking villages of Santa Clara and San Ildefonso. Santiago Naranjo of Santa Clara, for instance, first guided Hewett on horseback reconnaissances of the plateau, then served as excavation camp cook. Pueblo men typically had worn white cotton shirts over baggy breeches with calf-high, button-up moccasins in the mid-nineteenth century but by the early twentieth century had adopted work clothes including store-bought shoes or boots, denim pants or overalls, cotton shirts, and broad-brimmed felt hats.

Tewa workers were easily distinguished from the few Mexican workers on the Pajarito excavations, however, by their silver earrings and long hair—

Figure 1.3. Julián Martínez at the Pajarito Plateau excavation, 1912.

Photo by Jesse Nusbaum, Museum of New Mexico (MNM) #61768.

braided or tied with yarn—and their practice of wearing their shirts out over their pants. As a key cultural intermediary and the chief organizer of Indian participation in the early Santa Fe Fiestas, Santiago Naranjo exchanged his work clothes for beaded moccasins, a cotton shirt worn out over fringed buckskins, and, on some occasions, a feathered headdress. He thereby became a suitable subject for an early Santa Fe Railway poster.[13]

The museum had a particular impact on the revival of Pueblo pottery—the leading tourist craft produced near Santa Fe. Like Navajo weaving, pottery production had declined in the late nineteenth century because of the availability of mass-produced pots and pans. Then early in the twentieth century, the craft was revived and adapted to the tourists' desire for earth-toned, arts-and-crafts souvenirs to be used in home decoration (and as tokens of connection with Native Americans, in the popular imagination, living in harmony with nature). One of the laborers at the Pajarito excavations in 1907, Julián Martínez of San Ildefonso, and his wife, María, had already demonstrated pot making and traditional dances at the 1904 St. Louis world's fair while on their honeymoon. María had learned the traditional female craft of pottery from her

Figure 1.4. Unidentified person, Julián and María Martínez, and their son, Popovi Da, April 1936.

Photo by T. Harmon Parkhurst, MNM #28933.

aunt. But at San Ildefonso, a day-school teacher encouraged several young boys to take up painting, most importantly Crescencio Martínez, who taught Julián to paint after the fair. During the Pajarito excavations, Julián and other Tewa workers had the opportunity to study unearthed pots, wall murals, and rock art. Hewett and museum pottery expert Kenneth Chapman encouraged Julián and María to reproduce prehistoric, polychromatic designs for sale, and, as a matter of archeological curiosity, to reproduce the glaze of some unusual black pot shards.[14]

When the museum opened in Santa Fe's Palace of the Governors in 1909, Julián was employed as janitor, and María and their children lived with him in rooms behind the museum. Julián succeeded in duplicating the black pottery in about 1910 and spent his free time studying the museum's pottery collection, while the couple also demonstrated pottery making in its court-yard. In 1916 they lived at the Painted Desert Exhibit at the San Diego world's fair, again demonstrating pottery making, with María shaping the pots and Julián painting them. Only in 1918 or 1919 did Julián begin experi-menting with black-on-black pottery, perfecting black matte painting on glossy, highly polished pots by 1921. In this process, Julián also adapted a water serpent motif he had seen in the Pajarito rock art. So popular was the Martínezes' black-on-black style that they produced little polychromatic pot-tery after 1925, and the new style became the trademark for both the San Ildefonso and Santa Clara Pueblos. When the Martínezes were the first at Santa Clara to purchase an automobile, Julián added his trademark serpent motif in black matte paint over the standard Model T glossy black finish.[15]

During these years, the Martínezes also refined their clothing and pub-lic personas through interactions with tourists and the museum staff. Julián typically wore work clothes at the museum but added a beaded vest or an Indian blanket when posing for photographs. By the late 1920s, after he and María had moved back to Santa Clara and their pottery had become famous, he had acquired a Plains Indian costume like Santiago Naranjo's. By com-parison, María's everyday clothing and that of other Tewa Pueblo women in the first part of the twentieth century remained more traditional and there-fore required little alteration to satisfy tourists and museum photographers. Most wore high-wrapped white moccasins and woven cotton belts like their great-grandmothers, although they replaced the old style of dark, handwo-ven dresses worn over one shoulder with colorful calico now worn over a contrasting calico blouse. For special occasions, they added mass-produced fringed shawls, silver or beaded earrings, and squash-blossom necklaces.[16]

By the 1930s, most Tewa children were being dressed in store-bought shoes, calf-length dresses for the girls, and overalls or jeans for the boys. From the tourist perspective, women were always dressed for the camera, while men and children could often be persuaded to pose with a blanket wrapped around their shoulders to disguise their contemporary clothing. Julián and María's son, Popovi Da, like other San Ildefonso boys of his generation, wore contemporary clothing and a short haircut during his youth. But after World War II, when he had begun to paint his mother's pots and to run a pottery and general store at the pueblo, he sometimes posed next to the village kiva wearing beaded buckskins, moccasins, a velvet shirt, a silver concha belt, and a squash-blossom necklace. His hair, nevertheless, remained short, and he wore no headdress or earrings. Just as often, however, he can be seen posing at special functions—with his mother and the actor Vincent Price in Santa Fe, for instance—wearing a stylish business suit.

Julián and María's work was highly collaborative: she shaped and fired the pots; he painted them. Both were more amenable than other Pueblo Indians to working as pottery demonstrators and living for long periods away from their village. Although the historical record is somewhat con-tradictory, Julián appears to have been largely responsible for the develop-ment of the black-on-black style. Why, then, is María given far greater credit for their work, frequently to the total exclusion of her husband? Perhaps, in part, because he died in 1943, while she lived until 1980 (and took first her daughter-in-law, Santana Roybal, and then her son, Popovi Da, as her painting partner). Perhaps the romantic yearning for authentic, unchanging preindustrial crafts also favored the suppression of Julián's innovations in pottery-glazing technique and serpent iconography. Like other Tewa men, Julián had abandoned traditional farming and gathering practices to work in the modern cash economy—on the railroad in Colorado after his marriage, as a laborer in archeological excavations, as the museum janitor, and at Los Alamos at the outbreak of World War II. María and other Pueblo women, by comparison, spent more time at San Ildefonso raising children and dressing more traditionally. Above all, the Anglo-American tendency to feminize images of Pueblo Indian cultures as a domestic antidote to rapid industrialization probably accounts for the apotheosis of María rather than Julián.[17]

If traditional costumes fulfilled tourist expectations and placed Indians in the romantic past, contemporary Anglo social authority came clothed in the business suit. Since its development by London tailors in the late 1700s, the dress suit with vest and tie has been the uniform of modernity, signifying sobri-ety, rationality, and utility. It has conferred status not only on businessmen (such as the developer in Goodacre's sidewalk sculpture), government officials, and professionals, but also, in our context, on curio dealers, the Museum of

New Mexico staff, and the Anglo artists of Taos and Santa Fe, who often inflected the basic uniform with a cowboy hat or a scarf in place of a tie.[18]

The contrast of their dress suits to María and Julián's traditional clothing signified the larger dichotomy between their professional training and the Martínezes' limited formal education and between their mastery of the Renaissance and academic conventions of realism and the Martínezes' nonrepresentational craft, all of which implied the evolutionary superiority of Anglo culture. If money is the ultimate measure in a capitalist society, the $250 to $2,000 paid for major works by Anglo artists such as Joseph Sharpe and Irving Couse during the 1920s compared to the $15 to $20 that María and the famous Hopi potter Nampeyo earned for their best, signed pots makes the relative cultural hierarchy only too clear.[19]

Coincident with the Southwest tourism boom following World War I, women received the right to vote, began entering the workforce in large numbers, and made major changes in their clothing. Gone were the corseted waists and voluminous ruffled skirts that made women seem frivolous creatures of

Figure 1.5. Carlos Vierra, Datus Myers, Sheldon Parsons, Theodore Van Soelen, Gerald Cassidy, and Will Shuster, Santa Fe artists in the gallery of La Fonda hotel, 1933.

MNM #20787.

fashion throughout the nineteenth century. Under the particular influence of designer Coco Chanel, working women donned tailored jackets and narrow, knee-length skirts, an echo of the sober business suit. Pants even became permissible for the first time, primarily as upper-class touring and sportswear.[20]

When Erna Fergusson started her Koshari Tours company in 1921, her preferred uniform consisted of tall lace-up boots, riding breeches, a man's khaki shirt, a tie, and a stiff-brimmed Stetson. Only her concha belt outside a loose-fitting suit jacket differed from what a forest ranger or well-heeled male tourist might wear. After she sold her business to the Fred Harvey Company in 1925 and stayed on to manage it as Indian Detours, the guides' costumes were feminized by the sort of squash-blossom necklace, concha belt, and velvet blouse associated with Elle of Ganado, worn with knee-length tweed skirts, walking shoes, stockings, and floppy, soft-brimmed hats. Santa Fe's fall fiesta presented a particular opportunity for historic costumes and ethnic cross-dressing as Anglo women became Indian maidens and Spanish señoritas and men became conquistadors, coolies, cowboys, or mountain men. Apart from the fiesta, Anglo women were more apt than Anglo men to adopt native dress and jewelry.[21]

Most Spanish Americans—the third of New Mexico's tricultural mix—adopted contemporary clothing styles during the second half of the nineteenth century: store-bought dresses or homemade approximations for women and, depending on occupation and social class, work clothes or business suits for men. Unlike Pueblo and Navajo women, whose clothing constituted an everyday exoticism, contemporary Spanish-American clothing offered little fodder for tourist image making.[22]

But beginning in 1911, organizers of the modern Santa Fe Fiesta drew images of conquistadors from romantic novels and illustrated magazines. Hollywood clichés of señoritas and caballeros dressed for a fandango were soon in evidence during fiestas and at emerging Spanish tourist sites such as the village of Cordova. Throughout the 1920s, the romance of conquistadors and señoritas left contemporary Hispano farmers and migrant laborers largely invisible to tourists and neglected by government policy makers.[23]

Documentary photographers working in support of Franklin D. Roosevelt's New Deal during the 1930s created more realistic images of the contemporary Spanish Americans of New Mexico, while other federal programs sought to promote economic development, education, and health care.[24] One initiative fostered Spanish arts and crafts to produce supplemental income from the tourist market as pottery and blankets already did for many Pueblo and Navajo families. Although Spanish filigree jewelry had gone out of fashion by the time of World War I, local Hispanic weaving and wood carving had begun to revive at the end of the 1920s with the support of arts aficionados centered in Santa

Figure 1.6. *Knees and Aborigines*, John Sloan, 1927.

Fe. WPA manual arts programs also sought to revive traditional embroidery, furniture, and quilt making.

Although known to a small group of collectors, few if any Spanish-American revival artists developed public personas, and none entered the standard tourist iconography. This may be attributable to the stronger tourist interest in Indians, although the fact that most Hispanic folk artists were male may have made them (like Julián Martínez earlier) more difficult to romanticize. The Hispanic folk artists who appear in a few remaining photographs typically wear tattered work clothes. To cast them in historical garb—say, the costume of a conquistador—would have strained plausibility. Similarly, the desire of Hispano leaders to distance themselves from Mexican immigration following the 1910 Revolution made the sombrero and poncho unpalatable. Meanwhile, the WPA's emphasis on the manual arts projected most Spanish Americans into the working class, while Indian schools emphasized established tourists arts, and the predominately Anglo schools of railroad new towns focused on business, science, and the liberal arts.[25]

Across the country, the New Deal monumentalized local history and cul-

Figure 1.7. Fiesta group in front of the Fine Arts Museum, Santa Fe, about 1935.

Photo by T. Harmon Parkhurst, MNM #117680.

Figure 1.8. *The Spanish-American's Contribution to the Civilization of This Area,* by Kenneth Adams, 1937–1938.

Zimmerman Library, University of New Mexico.

tures through regional-style buildings and allegorical murals in courthouses, post offices, and schools. Those painted in 1938 in the PWA, New Deal library on the University of New Mexico campus in Albuquerque constitute the foremost distillation of the visual iconography of triculturalism. Initiated by university president James Zimmerman and funded by a grant from the Carnegie Corporation, they were painted by Kenneth Adams, a member of the Taos Society of Artists and artist-in-residence at UNM from 1942 to 1963.[26]

The first mural on the left, described in President Zimmerman's funding proposal as "the Indian showing his work as artist," depicts dark-skinned Navajos, Apaches, and Pueblo Indians in traditional costumes; an Apache tepee and a multistory pueblo; sheep and corn; and a full array of traditional tourist crafts, including a Navajo blanket, an Apache basket, a squash-blossom necklace, and Pueblo pots. The lack of contemporary artifacts places Indians in the past, while the use of traditional symbols offers them up as objects of tourist interest.

The second mural represents "the Spanish-American's contribution to the civilization of this area in agriculture and architecture," signified by wheat and rectangular fields, an adobe wall, and the Ranchos de Taos church. The three laboring figures wear contemporary clothing, while mass-produced metal buckets, a trowel, and a plow further position Spanish Americans in a contemporary, if rural, setting.

The third mural, described as "The Anglos, with their scientific contributions," introduces two researchers gazing into microscopes illuminated by electric lights and a doctor in surgical gown, mask, and rubber gloves, who steadies a toddler standing on a counter with both hands as though holding a shiny trophy. Behind them, the sun, earth, moon, and stars evoke astronomy and scientific control of the physical world. The Spanish Colonial–style rosettes on the researchers' tables, which duplicated those carved on the circulation desk below the murals, explicitly connected science and Anglo culture to the university.

In the final mural, "The union of all three races in the life of the Southwest," day dawns over a future of harmony and equality among the three races, set in a landscape of mountains, desert, stylized Pueblo fields, rectangular Spanish fields, forest reserves, and reservoirs. The three male students— one for each culture—wear generic pants and shirts.

Despite President Zimmerman's laudable desire to "reflect the spirit of democracy by representing the cultures of the three races as socially equal," the murals convey racial and gender hierarchies in a variety of ways. All but one of the women, for instance, kneel or sit, while all but one of the men stand. In terms of ethnicity, a majority of the figures in the Indian and Spanish panels are female, while the majority in the Anglo panel is male. Zimmerman and Adams deployed the sort of technological chronology used at the great world's fairs and in Santa Fe Fiesta parades, which implicitly justify racial hierarchy: Indians practice preindustrial handcrafts; Spanish Americans possess the sort of tools mass-produced since the first Industrial Revolution of about 1800; and Anglos contribute scientific instruments, electricity, and germ theory medicine, which emerged in the second Industrial Revolution at the end of the 1800s. The skin pigment hierarchy of the murals is reinforced by a subliminal dichotomy between dirt and cleanliness seen in the contrast between earthen pueblos and mud plastering, the sterile precautions of the surgical mask and rubber gloves, and the hyper-Aryanism of every Anglo figure, all of whom have blue eyes and blond hair. In the final panel, the Anglo holds the central, authoritative position, indeed, is the only figure in the series with open eyes. That the baby set amid symbols of modern technology at the center of the previous panel is the only child in the murals implies that the future belongs to Anglo descendants.

These ethnic and gender hierarchies became painfully transparent following the civil rights movement. The final panel was defaced with splattered paint twice in the early 1970s, and students repeatedly protested for their removal through the early 1990s. Many argue (including me) that they should be preserved as historical artifacts and an object lesson of the subconscious prejudices that can be embedded even in a populist program.[27]

Civic leaders have employed this tricultural formulation throughout the twentieth century, for instance, when Governor Thomas Mabry, in his 1949 inaugural address, noted that "members of three races have lived together in harmony and understanding through the long years" or when Joaquin Ortega, director of UNM's School of Inter-American Affairs, wrote in 1942 of New Mexico's "three cultures—Indian, Hispanic, and Anglo-Saxon—developing in parallel lines." A knowledgeable scholar such as Ortega would admit elsewhere that "biologically these groups are mixed already in a considerable degree," while in his 1935 inaugural address, Governor Clyde Tingley spoke of the state as a "land of a fusing of the cultures of peoples." But without visual iconography to reflect the actual, complex history of cultural mixing and intermarriage, stereotypes of distinct ethnic groups have predominated down to the present.[28]

Following World War II, during that era of greater assimilation to mainstream American norms associated with the Eisenhower years, interest in regionalism lessened across the country, and few innovations occurred in New Mexico's visual iconography, tourist arts, and attractions. Images of Indians wrapped in white and striped blankets standing in front of Taos Pueblo and of María Martínez at work on her pottery continued as mainstays of tourism promotion. Martínez appeared on the July 1955 cover of *New Mexico Magazine* working intently on a pot, for instance, observed by Anglo tourists—the wife in a fiesta dress with ricrac substituting for a squash-blossom necklace and her husband confined, even on vacation, in a business suit.

Attempts to link contemporary Hispanics to Spanish culture—for instance, to flamenco dancers wearing mantillas or fringed shawls—continued to strain plausibility and to have less appeal for tourists than Indian subjects. During the Santa Fe and Taos fiestas, however, conquistador reenactments and the selection of a fiesta queen intensified into major expressions of contemporary Hispanic identity.

Following the period of simplified women's clothing before and during World War II, fashion reverted to a romantic, nineteenth-century-inspired style championed by French designer Christian Dior. In Santa Fe and Taos, fiesta dresses with voluminous skirts developed into a fixture of regional clothing. If a businessman, professional, or politician in a suit and tie represents a norm of modern authority and utility, then traditional Indian and

Figure 1.9. July 1955 cover of *New Mexico Magazine*.

Spanish costumes and the romantic women's clothing produced in New Mexico cast these groups as various forms of the exotic other. As with the adoption of native crafts for home decorating, romantic clothing styles tend to feminize the image of the Southwest.[29]

The Chicano movement of the late 1960s and early 1970s mounted the most significant challenge to the ideology and visual iconography of triculturalism. In contrast to the earlier emphasis on pure Spanish ancestry, Chicanos argued for a realistic acknowledgment of Native and Spanish cultural mixing and intermarriage. One visual icon for this mixing—this *mestizaje*—was a three-part, Janus-like head. The Aztec pyramids, circular calendars, and plumed serpents in Chicano murals embraced Mexican origins, while clenched-fist power salutes, work clothes, and hard hats cast Chicanos as politically organized laborers. If high-profile Chicano activism and the contemporaneous American Indian Movement played out by the late 1970s, politically inclined artists and academics have continued to challenge ethnic and gender stereotypes. In a parallel vein, this and other essays in this volume reflect the sort of demythologizing found today in academic culture studies.

But tourists come to New Mexico to escape the pressures of the modern world, and they have continued to prefer nonrepresentational crafts such as Pueblo pottery and Navajo blankets, howling coyotes and Kokopeli statues, landscape paintings, and art with socially conservative content—witness the recent renascence of Hispanic religious art. Simultaneously over the last two decades, many Native Americans and Hispanics have chosen to cast their personal identities in terms of a romantic ideology of tradition and authenticity.

In this spirit, state and local cultural institutions and tourism promotion agencies continue to propagate tricultural iconography with only minor inflections. The logo for Southern Methodist University's Fort Burgwin Research Center near Taos, for instance, shows the profiles of an Indian, a conquistador, and Kit Carson. Similarly, a 1987 poster commemorating the seventy-fifth anniversary of statehood portrays the three cultures with portraits of three men in 1912. An Indian wearing a squash-blossom necklace, head bandanna, and blanket over his shoulder fulfills a long-standing stereotype. Rather than working clothes, the Hispano is dressed in the suit coat, stiff collar, and tie of a professional or businessman, while the Anglo appears dressed for a dude ranch in a casual, open collar and Tom Mix–style cowboy hat. (Cowboy clothing, art, furniture, and poetry have flourished across the western United States in recent decades as signifiers of contemporary Anglo ethnic identity.)

The cover of the *Official 1998 Santa Fe Visitors Guide* similarly characterizes the three cultures through the historic costumes of an Indian girl with painted face and feather fan, a Latina in an embroidered blouse holding a bowl of red and green chilies, and a mountain man in fringed buckskins holding the rope bridle of a chestnut stallion. This carefully assembled image follows long-established patterns of tricultural iconography by coding social hierarchy in terms of age, gender, and ethnicity. In a sense this is an update of those images of Elle of Ganado with her "daughters," but now with the Anglo photographer stepping from behind the camera to pose in historical costume. If this interpretation strikes you as far-fetched, imagine how disconcerting it would be to our stereotypes if the roles were reversed, say, with a Pueblo woman in the background and a young Latino man beside an Anglo boy in the foreground.

Glenna Goodacre's 1990 piece *Sidewalk Society* also recapitulates long-established ethnic/sexual personas to create a diagram of contemporary triculturalism. Lacking skin pigment as a distinguishing feature, Goodacre adeptly deploys facial features and clothing to convey race and social class. In Goodacre's idyllic world, Indian single mothers wear their traditional costumes for the benefit of tourists while teaching their daughters to perform the same role. Hispanics inhabit the working class and assume a posture of deference to Anglo authority, while Anglos are permitted a variety of modern roles: not only the customary businessman, but also the new professional woman, the carefree adolescent consumer, and the family on vacation (implicitly staying at the nearby Hyatt Regency).

Iconic distillations such as the UNM murals, tourism brochures, and *Sidewalk Society* have helped make the regional socioeconomic hierarchy seem natural and inevitable. This assertion may be difficult to prove scientifically; it is like proving that violence in the mass media helps perpetuate violence in our society. But it seems to me that encoding social differences in terms of ethnicity, gender, clothing, arts, and technology has affected the educational and occupational opportunities available to different groups throughout the twentieth century and has thereby helped reproduce prevailing social hierarchies. Although the details of ethnic and gender personas vary from region to region—each with its own history and social mix—the patterns I have outlined for the Southwest recur elsewhere in public art, celebrations, tourist images, and details of the everyday as mundane as the local color trailers that begin nightly newscasts.

Judging by the interviews Goodacre gave when her work was installed, I think any racism was unconscious and unintended. She simply works with popular mythic types without having delved deeply into their origins and unspoken implications. Public criticism of the piece focused on the stereotypical Hispanic laborer and Anglo developer and on the lack of an African-American figure. As far as I have been able to determine, no one challenged the casting

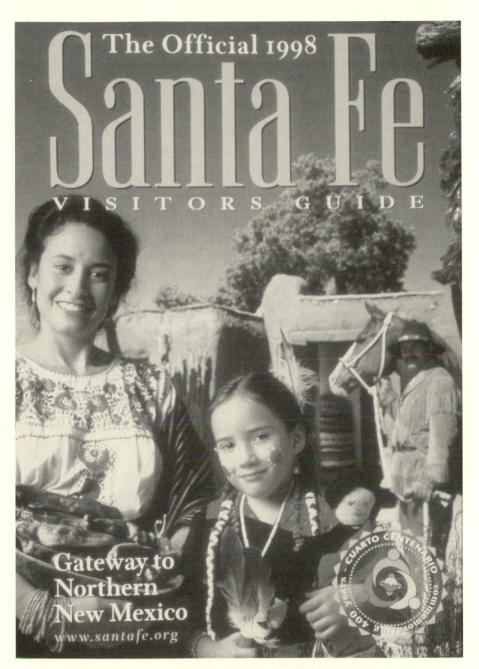

Figure 1.10. Cover of *The Official 1998 Santa Fe Visitors Guide*, City of Santa Fe Visitors and Convention Bureau.

of Indian women in their now traditional role as tourist attraction, let alone the Anglo developer dressed for success.[30]

Embarrassed by the controversy, city administrators have sought to recontextualize the piece, first, by placing an already existing statue of Lebanese-American businessman George Maloof on an opposite corner and then, in 1997, by commissioning a memorial to Dennis Chavez, U.S. senator from 1933 to 1964. The leading national Hispanic politician of his generation, Chavez sits beside a Hispanic woman constituent. He wears the uniform of modern authority—a suit and tie—and at his side sits his hat, one similar to that worn by his friend and fellow New Deal Democrat Lyndon Johnson. With the addition of these two works, Albuquerque's sidewalk society begins to transcend tourist stereotypes and to project a more complex and inclusive vision of society. But if I had my way, I'd add a few more figures, perhaps beginning with a statue of Julián Martínez dressed as he was at the Pajarito Plateau excavations—a young man in a working man's overalls, simple felt hat, and kerchief, with heavy silver rings in his ears and a paintbrush in his hand.

Acknowledgments

Thanks to David Weber, Jane Elder, and Virginia Scharff and the other authors in this volume for their suggestions and to Anne Boynton for research assistance. The conception of this essay was informed by Sylvia Rodriguez, "Art, Tourism, and Race Relations in Taos: Toward a Sociology of the Art Colony," *Journal of Anthropological Research* 45 (spring 1989); Camille Paglia, *Sexual Personae: Art and Decadence from Nefertiti to Emily Dickinson* (New Haven: Yale University Press, 1990); and discussions with Rodriguez over the years, including those about her essay-in-progress while I was drafting this: "Tourism, Whiteness and the Vanishing Anglo," in *Seeing and Being Seen: Tourism in the American West*, ed. David M. Wrobel and Patrick T. Long (Lawrence, Kans.: University of Kansas Press, 2001), 194–210. To a certain extent the essay is a coda to my book *The Myth of Santa Fe: Creating a Modern Regional Tradition* (Albuquerque: University of New Mexico Press, 1997).

Notes

1. John Villani, "Sidewalk Society," *Albuquerque Magazine*, January 1991, 6, 10; John Villani, "Glenna Goodacre," *Southwest Art*, September 1991, 62–68; Sally Eauclaire, "Glenna Goodacre, Sculptor," *The Santa Fean Magazine*, March 1992, 24–28.
2. *Daily New Mexican*, February 6, November 16, and November 18, 1874; October 18, 1875; September 28, 1876. Former acting New Mexico governor W. F. M. Arny wears the centennial blanket over his shoulder in the photo in *Handbook of the North American*

Indian, vol. 10, *Southwest*, ed. Alfonso Ortiz (Washington, D.C.: Smithsonian Institution, 1983), 518.

3. L. Bradford Prince, *Historical Sketches of New Mexico, from the Earliest Records to the American Occupation* (New York: Leggat Brothers, 1883).

4. Wayne Mauzy, "The Tertio Millennial Exposition," *El Palacio* 37 (December 1934): 185–201.

5. Diana F. Pardue and Kathleen L. Howard, "Making Art, Making Money: The Fred Harvey Company and the Indian Artisan," in *The Great Southwest of the Fred Harvey Company and the Santa Fe Railroad*, eds. Marta Weigle and Barbara A. Babcock (Phoenix: Heard Museum, 1996), 67–68; Robert W. Rydell, *All the World's a Fair: Visions of Empire at American International Expositions* (Chicago: University of Chicago Press, 1984).

6. Andrew K. Gregg, *New Mexico in the Nineteenth Century; A Pictorial History* (Albuquerque: University of New Mexico Press, 1968); E. Boyd, *Popular Arts of Spanish New Mexico* (Santa Fe: Museum of New Mexico Press, 1974), 288–90; Edwin L. Wade, "The Ethnic Art Market in the American Southwest, 1880–1980," in *Objects and Others: Essays on Museums and Material Culture*, ed. George W. Stocking, Jr. (Madison: University of Wisconsin Press, 1986); Christopher Wilson, "The Santa Fe, New Mexico, Plaza" (master's thesis, University of New Mexico, 1981), fns. 8–10, 151–52; Jonathan Batkin, *Pottery of the Pueblos of New Mexico, 1700-1940* (Colorado Springs: Colorado Springs Fine Arts Center, 1986), 28–29; Jonathan Batkin, "Tourism Is Overrated: Pueblo Pottery and the Early Curio Trade, 1880–1910, in *Unpacking Culture: Art and Commodity in Colonial and Postcolonial Worlds*, eds. Ruth B. Phillips and Christopher B. Steiner (Berkeley: University of California Press, 1999).

7. J. J. Brody, *Between Traditions: Navajo Weaving Toward the End of the Nineteenth Century* (Iowa City: University of Iowa Museum of Art, 1976), sec. 1.

8. Ibid., sec. 3.

9. Ibid., sec. 2 and notes.

10. "Renowned Navajo Weaver Passes to Happy Hunting Ground," *Santa Fe* [Railway] *Magazine* 17 (February 1924): 42–43; Kathleen L. Howard, "Weaving a Legend: Elle of Ganado Promotes the Indian Southwest," *New Mexico Historical Review* 74 (April 1999): 127–54; T. C. McLuhan, *Dream Tracks: The Railroad and the American Indian, 1890–1930* (New York: Harry N. Abrams, 1985); Kathleen L. Howard and Diana F. Pardue, *Inventing the Southwest: The Fred Harvey Company and Native American Art* (Flagstaff, Ariz.: Northland Publishing, 1996).

11. Chris Wilson, *The Myth of Santa Fe: Creating a Modern Regional Tradition* (Albuquerque: University of New Mexico Press, 1997), 127, 195–205.

12. The evolution of tourist crafts is determined by the market: artisans make what sells. But direct written documentation of cultural workers and tourism promoters instructing native artisans on appearance is relatively rare. See, for instance, Weigle and Babcock, *The Great Southwest*, 42. But changes in Indian clothing in response to the tourism market are documented in the photographs of Tewa Pueblo Indians at the Photo Archives, Museum of New Mexico, Santa Fe (MNM), which include not only staged tourist images, but also relatively unguarded scenes in the villages, the more mundane work at the Pajarito excavations, and images of the Martínezes while they lived at the museum. In addition to the MNM photo files for "Persons Known," "San Ildefonso," "Santa Clara," "Santa Fe Fiesta," "Frijoles," "Otowi," and "Puyé," see Gregg, *New Mexico in the Nineteenth Century*; Ortiz, *Handbook of the North American Indian*, vol. 10, *Southwest*; Susan Peterson, *The Living Tradition of María Martínez* (Tokyo: Kodansha International, 1977); and Richard L. Spivey,

María (Flagstaff, Ariz.: Northland Press, 1979), for additional useful images of the Martínezes and other Pueblo Indians.

13. Batkin, *Pottery of the Pueblos;* Wilson, *Myth of Santa Fe,* especially 117–24, 195. Although he wore a large tie with horizontal stripes with his outfit at the 1920 fiesta, it disappears from subsequent photos. In later years, when Naranjo put in his big silver earrings and braided fur strips in his hair, his neighbors at Santa Clara knew he was expecting visitors from Santa Fe.

14. Batkin, *Pottery of the Pueblos,* 31–32; Peterson, *Living Tradition,* 78, 89–90; Spivey, *María,* 15, 18, 22, 60.

15. Peterson, *Living Tradition,* 91–92; Spivey, *María,* 11; Kenneth M. Chapman, *The Pottery of San Ildefonso Pueblo* (Albuquerque: University of New Mexico Press, 1970), v, 34–35. Why did black-on-black pottery become popular with tourists so quickly? The beauty and quality of the Martínezes' work certainly contributed to its popularity, and novelty is an important factor in a consumer culture. Likewise, a recognizable style associated with a particular village (and with María and her narrative of redemption through handcrafts) permitted tourist "connoisseurship." But did the subconscious response to World War I and the 1918 influenza pandemic, which killed Crescencio Martínez and other Tewa artists of Julián and María's generation, also contribute to Julián's return to work on black-on-black glazes in 1918 or 1919 and the quick marketing success of the new style?

16. Most women reserved their traditional dark dresses for ceremonial occasions, but María sometimes wore hers for tourist photo sessions.

17. While Julián was still alive, he and María were sometimes portrayed in tourist publications together as the very image of a wholesome, industrious Indian couple, although just as often, she was shown alone at her work. The excellent literature on creation of the tourist image of Pueblo women, in particular of María Martínez, includes Barbara Babcock, "'A New Mexico Rebecca': Imaging Pueblo Women," *Journal of the Southwest* 32 (1990): 400–437; Barbara Babcock, "Mud Women and White Men: A Meditation on Pueblo Potteries and the Politics of Representation," in *Discovered Country: Tourism and Survival in the American West,* ed. Scott Norris (Albuquerque: Stone Ladder Press, 1994), 180–95; Barbara Babcock, "Marketing María: The Tribal Artist in the Age of Mechanical Reproduction," in *Looking High and Low: Art and Cultural Identity,* eds. Brenda Jo Bright and Liza Bakewell (Tucson: University of Arizona Press, 1995), 124–50; Leah Dilworth, "Discovering Indians in Fred Harvey's Southwest," in Weigle and Babcock, 159–67; Dilworth, *Imagining Indians in the Southwest: Persistent Visions of a Primitive Past* (Washington, D.C.: Smithsonian Institution Press, 1996).

18. Anne Hollander, *Sex and Suits: The Evolution of Modern Dress* (New York: Alfred A. Knopf, 1994); Joan L. Severa, *Dressed for the Photographer: Ordinary Americans and Fashion, 1840–1900* (Kent, Ohio: Kent State University Press, 1995); "Persons Known" and "Fiesta" files, MNM.

19. On painting and pottery prices, letter, William Wisude (sp?) to J. D. Rockefeller, Jr., 20 February 1925, "Western Trips, 1924, Misc." file, Rockefeller Family Collection, Rockefeller Archives Center (RAC), Tarrytown, N.Y.; "Western Trip 1926, Articles Purchased" file, RAC. See also Howard and Pardue, *Inventing the Southwest,* 40, 42, 45.

20. Hollander, *Sex and Suits,* 122–38, 142–50.

21. Howard and Pardue, *Inventing the Southwest,* 121–28; "A 'Delight Maker,'" *Sunset Magazine* 54 (January 1925): 38 [profile of Erna Fergusson]; "Women Guides, de Luxe," *The Christian Science Monitor,* 25 January 1927; D. H. Thomas, *The Southwestern Indian Detours: The Story of the Fred Harvey/Santa Fe Railway Experiment in Detourism* (Phoenix: Hunter Publishing, 1978), 46, 75, 80–81. I have been unable to find documentation to

either confirm or disprove the rumor that when Fergusson left Indian Detours in 1928, it was in part because of a dispute over the couriers' uniforms.

22. For a sampling of the late-nineteenth- and early-twentieth-century clothing of Spanish Americans see the "Persons Known" and "Fiesta" files, MNM, and the New Mexico files of the Bureau of Agricultural Economics, Still Photography Division, National Archives, Washington, D.C. In addition, the invaluable documentary photographs taken in the 1930s and early 1940s by the Farm Security Administration–Office of War Information are available at the Library of Congress in a microfiche version and, many of them, on the Library of Congress's World Wide Web site.

23. Wilson, *Myth of Santa Fe*, 192–228; "Persons Known" and "Santa Fe Fiesta" files, photo archives, MNM. One Fred Harvey Company, Indian Detours brochure from about 1930, for instance, includes a photograph of a touring car stopped in front of the Cordova church with a señorita in a mantilla with a large, open lace fan, leaning on the passenger's window.

24. Marta Weigle, *New Mexicans in Cameo and Camera: New Deal Documentation of Twentieth-Century Lives* (Albuquerque: University of New Mexico Press, 1985); Suzanne Forrest, *The Preservation of the Village: New Mexico's Hispanics and the New Deal* (Albuquerque: University of New Mexico Press, 1989).

25. Weigle, *New Mexicans*; Forrest, *Preservation of the Village*; Charles L. Briggs, *The Wood Carvers of Córdova, New Mexico: Social Dimensions of an Artistic "Revival"* (Knoxville: University of Tennessee Press, 1980); Peter Bermingham, *The New Deal in the Southwest, Arizona and New Mexico* (Tucson: University of Arizona Museum of Art, ca. 1980).

26. Bermingham, *New Deal in the Southwest*; "Library Murals by Adams," *Daily Lobo* [UNM student newspaper], 8 February 1939; Felipe Gonzales and Terry Gugloitta, "The Three Peoples of New Mexico: Art in Controversy," brochure, March 1990, in "Library Murals" vertical file, Center for Southwest Research, Zimmerman Library, University of New Mexico, Albuquerque (UNM-VF); Dean A. Porter et al., *Taos Artists and Their Patrons, 1989–1950* (Notre Dame, Ind.: Snite Museum, 1999), 363. An excerpt from James Zimmerman's funding proposal to the Carnegie Corporation is posted on the wall below the final panel.

27. Rodriguez and Gugloitta, "Three Peoples"; "Zimmerman Library Mural Damaged During Holiday," *Daily Lobo*, 30 November 1970; letters to the editor, *Daily Lobo*, 23 October, 5 November, 1, 3, 4, 7 December 1970, and 22 March 1993; articles, *Daily Lobo*, 3 March 1993, 6 and 12 October 1994; "Assessing Damage," *Campus News* [UNM faculty/staff newspaper], 7 February 1974; "Hey! Why Are They Demonstrating?" handbill, October 1994, UNM-VF.

28. Joaquin Ortega, "New Mexico's Opportunity" (Albuquerque: University of New Mexico Press, printed for the author, 1942), 2, 8; Thomas J. Mabry, *Inaugural Address and Legislative Message of Governor Thomas J. Mabry of the State of New Mexico* (Santa Fe: State of New Mexico, 1949), unpaginated, second-to-last page; Joaquin Ortega, "The Intangible Resources of New Mexico," *Papers of the School of American Research* (Santa Fe, N.Mex.: Archeological Institute of America, 1945), 6–7; Clyde Tingley, *Inaugural Address and Legislative Message of Governor Clyde Tingley of the State of New Mexico* (Santa Fe: State of New Mexico, 1935), unpaginated, last page.

29. Hollander, *Sex and Suits*, 166–67; Mildred T. Crews, "Taos Fashions," *New Mexico Magazine* (NMM), August 1961, 12–15; "Fiesta Dresses of the Fifties," NMM, July 1976, 22–25; Linda Shockley, "Fiesta: Always in Fashion," NMM, September 1991, 78–87.

30. Villani, "Sidewalk Society"; Villani, "Glenna Goodacre"; Eauclaire, "Glenna Goodacre"; Robert Rodriguez, "Civic Plaza Sculpture Can't Escape Controversy," *Albuquerque Journal*, 2 May 1991, D-2.

IN SEARCH OF HISTORY AND ROMANCE
ON EL CAMINO REAL ⟶

PHOEBE S. KROPP

In "The Spell," a fiction serial appearing in *Sunset Magazine* in 1911, a dapper young man escorts a visiting beauty on a driving tour of the California coast, trying to woo her with the enchanting sights of the old Franciscan missions. The front illustration depicts the fashionable pair sitting by a fountain, just alit from their gleaming automobile. The caption sets the scene: "They left the motor purring before the shrine of Santa Barbara. Nick had saved the Mission until the last, for he had his heart set on showing it to her at sunset, an hour that gives back to the cloister all the vanished splendor of the past." The California missions furnished an evocative backdrop for this sentimental tale, almost necessary catalysts for California romance. A travel feature accompanied the story, suggesting readers follow the characters' route along California's mission road. El Camino Real, it proclaimed, was "the Royal Road of the motor tourist," the automobile, the vehicle to a romantic past.[1]

Tourists agreed and set out for El Camino Real in droves. In the nineteen-teens and twenties, California missions became highly popular tourist attractions and the road between them became a destination unto itself. El Camino Real linked the state's twenty-odd Spanish missions, running northward from San Diego through Los Angeles and Santa Barbara, up the coastal valleys to Monterey, San Francisco, and finally Sonoma. Developed over the first few decades of the twentieth century as both a tourist byway and a state highway, El Camino Real also linked modern California to its Spanish past. The road's boosters promoted it as a pathway to the past, where travelers could revisit

PAINTED BY J. A. CAHILL

They left the motor purring before the shrine of Santa Barbara. Nick had saved the Mission until the last, for he had set his heart on showing it to her at sunset, an hour that gives back to the cloister all the vanished splendor of the past.

(*Illustrating "The Spell," page 421*)

Figure 2.1. In this scene from the "The Spell," a 1911 *Sunset Magazine* serial story, a young couple has just descended from their automobile to pause at Santa Barbara Mission at sunset. Their faces suggest the possibility of transcendence and romance while driving El Camino Real. A related travel feature in the same issue suggested that readers repeat exactly this moment on their own mission tours.

Courtesy *Sunset Magazine*.

California's supposed golden age, that most romantic era when Franciscan friars governed harmonious colonies of peaceful Indians. Automobile tourists in particular responded to this appeal and began to drive the road even before it had received the attention of engineers. In their newfangled contraptions, they traveled El Camino Real with great zest and wrote copiously about it. A motor tour of El Camino Real promised a unique experience, full of picturesque ruins, ghostly echoes, and romantic adventure.

Missions, however, were not ready-made repositories of historic meaning. In the late nineteenth century, white Californians judged them unimportant remnants of a primitive era, and travelers rarely included them on California itineraries. Early-twentieth-century tourists, however, undertook a re-imagination of El Camino Real. Missions accumulated new meanings as these tourists and their guides gradually fastened an attractive and usable past onto the adobe structures; this memory in turn sponsored a local reworking of regional identity along Spanish lines. As tourists glued their souvenirs and photographs into albums, they also glued meaning onto the missions.[2] The mission myth they applied not only glorified the romantic ruins, distancing California's "primitive" past, but also eulogized a vanishing race and the missionaries themselves, ordering regional history by racial and national succession. Praise for American conquest and the automobile permitted a celebration of progress amidst the nostalgia. Traveling El Camino Real allowed tourists to make sense of the missions, defining Spanish California in a way that explained American California. The Camino Real myth thus made missions more than popular tourist attractions. The tourist search for history and romance transformed them into enduring symbols of and for California.

"The Autoist's Royal Road"

El Camino Real began to appear on the tourist map due to the efforts of a group of southern Californians who advertised its romantic possibilities and lobbied the state to build it. The plan was to turn the legendary route into a unified state highway, paved for efficiency and publicized for recreation. Led by Harrie Forbes, a wealthy newcomer to Los Angeles and a former mission tourist herself, this campaign attracted a wide range of support in the region. By the inauguration of the statewide Camino Real Association in 1904, the roster of supporters included historical societies, chambers of commerce, automobile clubs, women's clubs, tourist businesses, and local governments. After determining the route, the association began in 1906 to mark the road with emblematic Mission Bell Guideposts—a replica mission bell hung from a tall standard, curved at the top, to which was fastened a sign listing directions and distances to the nearest missions, north and south. These guideposts were good publicity, calling attention to the Camino Real project. Designed and manufactured by Forbes, these bells also came in miniature form for purchase as souvenirs.[3] They can still be found on the shelves of mission gift shops and are avidly traded on eBay.

To persuade the state government to undertake construction, Camino Real leaders made common cause with the Good Roads movement. These Progressive road boosters promoted state responsibility for improved transportation as a part of their desire to modernize and order the national infrastructure in various arenas. Better highways, they argued, made for a better economy.[4] Camino Real advocates borrowed their logic, offering the new King's Highway as a profitable combination of good works, good business, and good times. Eventually this formula convinced the state government to make the route a major component of its first state highway system. With construction begun in 1919, this state effort turned a mostly dirt, frequently narrow, often steep El Camino Real into a paved, predictable, and smooth boulevard for automobiles spanning six hundred miles of coastal California.

Over the course of the Camino Real campaign, California became a mecca for automobile tourists, a veritable "motorist's paradise" according to one travel writer. The state led the nation in cars per capita, a number that swelled with the ranks of wealthy wintertime tourists who brought their autos with them. Camino Real boosters boldly proffered their creation as the best in tourist experience—the "autoist's royal road . . . destined to become the most popular automobile tour on this whole continent."[5] Thus by the later teens, tourists commented on the multitude of cars on El Camino Real. A 1915 guidebook mentioned that "a constantly increasing stream of motorists flows by the rude portals of these California Cathedrals." Typical was the note on the back of a Santa Barbara mission postcard—"We have lizzied California so much."[6] Tourists particularly enjoyed posing for photographs in front of missions with their cars. They made a deliberate point of documenting the presence of their automobiles at the missions, whether or not the travelers themselves appeared in the car or in the photograph at all. This image appeared in guidebooks, magazines, albums, and travel diaries. Twice in the 1920s the scene graced the cover of *Touring Topics*, a southern California travel magazine. Tourists could even buy postcards that replicated the experience for them, offering views of anonymous automobiles in front of various missions.[7] Promoters geared the mission road to the automobile, and tourists responded, making the Camino Real tour definitively a motorized experience.

Even while the road was under physical construction, tourists and

Californians alike took to El Camino Real in their automobiles and began to build its memory. Writings on El Camino Real during this period had many authors, though they were overwhelmingly middle- to upper-class whites who owned automobiles. Some were promoters of the campaign itself, whose journeys served to advertise their efforts. Others came from the tourist industry, producing guidebooks and postcards for sale or penning articles for travel magazines. Still others were local historians, writing descriptive pamphlets about a portion of the road or an individual mission. But many were simply tourists who wrote a formal diary of their trip, perhaps for publication, or assembled an album of photographed memories. Nearly all of the writers were engaged with tourism in some way, taking the mission road with an eye to tourist experience.[8] Despite the fact that Camino Real tourists generally traveled on an individual basis (as opposed to guided tours), their accounts echoed one another, repeating key themes, interpretations, images, and prose. If tourists and writers could conceivably depart from this consensus, few did.[9]

Camino Real writers shared a common focus on narrating the automobile tour, and they confronted a common dilemma in their desires to find romance in the mission past. The Spanish mission era seemed both alarmingly near and disconcertingly incongruous. Visiting the missions, one guidebook author observed, was "almost like visiting a foreign land, and why should it not seem so? California was, less than 75 years ago, a foreign land to us, just as Mexico is to-day."[10] Particularly in southern California, the Spanish/Mexican era was not long passed, as Anglos claimed the upper hand in demographics and culture only in the latter parts of the nineteenth century.[11] In early guidebooks and diaries, the recentness of the mission era was a subject of some nervousness.

Unnerving also was the swiftness with which Anglo-Americans transformed the urban and social landscape, which prompted many tourists and residents to see California's recent past at disturbing variance from its otherwise thoroughly modern society. Guidebook author James Steele confessed his discomfort in an 1892 commentary on the missions.

> The crumbling towers of these ancient temples keep one all the time wondering if this be any lawful portion of the great American inheritance and perhaps one sometimes wishes them entirely out of the way. Daily the incongruity between the then and the now becomes more striking and daily the crumbling walls remind more strongly of a modern usurpation of what was meant for other uses. So long as they shall stand there is a feeling that this is not entirely a Saxon country. Flowers and eternal summer are not the natural surroundings of the race.[12]

Figure 2.2. This picture from the pages of a *Sunset Magazine* travel feature in 1913 graphically displays the incongruity and awkwardness of some mission/automobile imagery. The dissonance is heightened by the artificiality of the hand coloring and the fact that the car and its passengers are literally pasted into the archway.

Courtesy *Sunset Magazine.*

For Steele, missions were of dubious value for modern life, evidence of an incomplete conquest. Tourist photography echoed this ambiguity. For all the repetition, motorcars and missions often created disjunctive images. That tourists and Californians came to see the automobile as the perfect visual complement to ruined adobe represented the end of an interpretive process. At the turn of the century, both missions and automobiles might have seemed out of place. By driving and imagining El Camino Real over the next four decades, tourists worked out an interpretation that fit the two together in a normative history and made both appear normal features of the California landscape.

Romance, Ruins, and the Golden Age

Narrators of El Camino Real began after the turn of the century to view the anomalous position of the missions in a more positive vein, seeing them as representations of a lost romantic life. Mission days appeared in their tales as brave ones, full of adventure and religious devotion, a time when courageous padres, pious Indians, dashing caballeros, and sultry señoritas cavorted in a picturesque landscape. The Santa Fe Railway helped to create the frame for this picture, billing the greater Southwest as an enchanted and romantic land. In California, missions offered the most tangible mise-en-scène for tourists to enact this romantic history. One guidebook gushed that just the name El Camino Real "summons visions of a vanished age, an idyllic epoch, a time of Missions, and siestas and languorous existence in a land of golden plenty, which by the incomparable gifts of nature barely escaped being Paradise itself."[13] For all the florid language and hyperbole, the repetition of such sentiments established El Camino Real as a conduit to romantic experience.

Many tourists explained their motives for taking a Camino Real tour in exactly these terms. One travel diarist began his memoir by recalling his initial anticipation: "We feel that we shall find in the crumbling, vine-covered ruins a glamour of romance and an historic significance that would make our journey worth while even if it did not take us through some of the loveliest and most impressive scenery in the world." Another hoped that on his journey from "mission to mission" he might "slowly, leisurely, becom[e] acquainted with the beautiful legends and history connected therewith . . . for in their history lay the charm and romance which appeals to one so."[14] At first glance, this purple prose suggests liberal embroidering by tourist promoters on the make. A few Camino Real tourists did detect exaggeration and found fault with their guidebooks' promises when views and visits fell short of the astoundingly picturesque.[15] Yet however disappointed some may have been in the delivery of mission romance, their sincere expectations suggest how readily they adopted the tone of romanticism.

Camino Real writers affiliated the missions with a resurgent cultural taste for romanticism in the period. From the popularity of Joan of Arc biographies to Gothic Revival architecture, a fascination with "romantic historicism" took hold among elite Americans in the late nineteenth and early twentieth centuries. This romance depended upon historic associations, as writers found in the modern era few opportunities for the kind of heroism or drama of yore.[16] Labeling something romantic, in this sense, necessarily placed it the past, a time both distant and indistinct. An advertisement for a Camino Real tour on the Southern Pacific Railroad immersed the mission past in an ethereal fog: "Over it all and through it all is an aroma of romance and an atmosphere of historic association that blends and envelops like a fine ether the materialistic sense of modern life."[17] When Camino Real tourists invested the missions with a romance they found wanting in their own time, they began to put distance between themselves and the Spanish past.

Built into the rhetoric of romanticism was the assumption that such romance was fundamentally irretrievable. One Camino Real tourist recalled that "the old Mission buildings with their quaint architecture speak very tenderly of the past, the broken past which will never be revived."[18] The more anachronistic the missions appeared, the more elusive, remote, and thus more precious their romance. Whether traveling in 1903 or 1933, tourists claimed to discover mission romance just before it disappeared for good. Indeed, the missions receded further backward into a hazy, bygone era at approximately the same rate as they appeared more frequently in the present as tourist attractions and California landmarks.

For mission tourists and writers, a leading indicator of the missions' "broken past" was that many of them were literally broken, in ruins. The rhetorical meditation on mission ruins called forth writers' most sentimental impulses. The author of a 1914 guide prepared her readers for a visit to Mission San Antonio de Padua, a structure in nearly complete ruin. Instead of bemoaning its appearance, she remarked, "Its very ruins are piles which speak of mystic beauty."[19] The discourse on ruins in promotional articles, guidebooks, and tourist diaries deposited significant meaning in the missions, both adding to their romantic allure and pushing them farther back into the past.

Guidebook and feature writers suggested that the most profound mission experiences could be had at those in ruins. "Pathetic though lovely," the ruined buildings evoked for them the "sad sublimities of departed glories" and possessed "all the melancholy beauty of moss-grown decay." One author beseeched his readers to visit San Juan Capistrano: "I beg of you to visit this ancient ruin, as you will be repaid by an impressive view, particularly on a moonlight night, when the imagination clothes the ruined Mission with all the beauty and magnificence of its former days."[20] These commentators even suggested that the missions offered opportunities for experiences beyond everyday romance. As an early guidebook prompted, "Visit them, if possible, after the moon has risen. . . . From the hollow corridors you will hear the voices of the hooded padres at prayer. Listen, and you will hear the gathered Indians, chanting as of old the Ave Maria, look and you will behold gardens of tropical beauty, sweeping orchards, and majestic buildings."[21]

The mystical, even ghostly aspects of the mission ruins captivated observers of the time. Keen observer Charles Francis Saunders tried in 1915 to identify what so intrigued people about the ruins by remarking that "one hardly expects to meet ghosts in California. We are too new, and also, I think, there is too much sun. But if ghosts there be in this hustling century and this most modern of States, then certainly the Missions are the places where one might expect to see . . . them." In early-twentieth-century southern California, the missions offered the most remote representation of the region's past. The fact of ruins provided critical evidence for, as one scholar has termed it, the "dramatic discontinuity" between romantic origins and modern times. Missions had a "touch of human antiquity," something the newborn towns and cities of California lacked.[22] That the missions might be so distant made them less troubling on the modern landscape—remnants of days dead and gone rather than awkward interlopers in the present time.

So popular were ruins, many tourists harbored a keen skepticism toward locals' attempts to restore missions to a more pristine state. At San Luis Obispo in particular, where shingles had replaced the tile roof and white clapboards covered the adobe walls, tourists judged the rebuilding distasteful. Traveler Hi Sibley remarked that "there is something incongruous about curtains in the windows . . . wicker chairs and chaise-lounges in the patio." The restoration, not the mission, now seemed regionally inappropriate, turned as one guidebook claimed into an "ugly New England meeting house" with "prosaic shingles."[23] Camino Real writers wrestled with the problem of restoration itself. Thomas Murphy pondered, "While it is desirable that any mission be restored rather than fall into complete ruin, it certainly is to be regretted when the work is done so injudiciously as at San Luis Obispo." Restoration entailed loss of the ruin. San Luis Obispo was a "disappointment to the tourist" because its "crumbling walls" had been "sheathed in boards."[24] With modern accouterments and sturdy walls, the missions seemed not like missions at all. Not only had travelers come to expect the ruins, they had come to see the missions as quintessentially in a state of ruin.

To prove the worth of these ruins, Camino Real writers reached far back in time and geography, beyond the Southwest or the eastern United States. They likened the missions to European cathedrals and medieval ruins, comparing them favorably to England's abbeys and Romanesque basilicas. One travel writer found that "the legacy of romance which lingers in broken arches, piles of adobes, and quaint Spanish names . . . goes a long way to supply the deficiency of our country in that element which makes European travel so interesting." Particularly during World War I, when travel to Europe was impossible, this allusion to Old World sites was all the more relevant.[25]

With their suggestion of great age, ruins hinted at a grand and romantic regional past. A travel writer submitted in 1912 that the missions' "deplorable state of disrepair . . . emphasizes the old age of the wonderful structures and lends an added charm to their inspection." Diarist David Steele observed a few years later that the missions were "among the few monuments of a country that has nothing very old."[26] While the buildings themselves were often

Figure 2.3. This hand-tinted image of Mission San Fernando in the Los Angeles area was one of many postcards that posed empty automobiles in front of empty missions, a vivid illustration of "dramatic discontinuity." The arrangement represented El Camino Real in shorthand, which tourists might reuse to reflect their own experience of the mission motor tour.

Postcard from author's collection.

less than a hundred years old at the time these tourists visited them, visitors often described them in terms of antiquity. Constructed between 1769 and 1823, missions became in their diaries medieval or ancient; as one traveler put it, "In the eerie moonlight these have the appearance of an ancient Grecian pile." One writer reached back even farther: "Though it is the youngest part of the youngest among the great nations, its monuments and relics reach back beyond man's vision into the prehistoric past."[27] In this way, Camino Real commentators distanced the regional past in as explicit a manner as possible.

The Automobile Club of Southern California stitched together the various strands of the romantic attachment to mission ruins in 1915:

> More splendid in their melting glory than the Cathedrals of the Old World, California's dust-brown missions call the motorist to the trails of yesterday over the highways of today. Wearily waiting for the inevitable end, when their tired walls have at last melted to the dust from which they sprang, when rain and wind have called earth's own back again, these ruins sleep majestically on the rounded breasts of their native hills.[28]

More than anything else, the ruins naturalized the end of the Spanish era in California, providing an organic but definitive break in regional history. One travel diarist invoked religious life-cycle metaphor when she wrote, "La Purisima's work is done. Earth to earth, ashes to ashes, dust to dust!"[29] The demise of the missions was, in these interpretations, inevitable, a natural rather than a historical process of change. Emphasis on the missions' ruined state reminded one that their days were over, their only occupants ghosts—perhaps many more than their visitors might have supposed.

Indians, Padres, and the Fall

Camino Real writers linked the ruined missions to the "vanishing race" of California Indians who had once peopled them. When tourists visited California missions, they rarely saw Indians. They viewed either empty, roofless structures overgrown with grass or operating churches that catered largely to Spanish speakers. As one guidebook writer reminded his readers, "Not a vestige of an Indian remains." Either way, as tourists would expect to see them, Indians were not present. Their absence prompted an oft-repeated assumption that their people had largely vanished from the earth; any living Indians appeared as mere relics of a dying culture. One guidebook made this relationship clear: "Where oxcarts creaked, where padres walked, twentieth century fliers are hurtling, still the dust is the same, the walls are there, and still, under the shadow of the self-same cross, the children of the missions, the Indians, are waiting for the end."[30] As mission visitors assumed the adobe missions would soon crumble back into the earth, propelled by inescapable forces of nature, they believed this erosion and disappearance to be the fate of their Indian dwellers as well.

Native population numbers appeared to confirm the Anglo presumption of inevitability about their extinction. The Indian population in California bottomed out in 1900 at around 15,000, a precipitous decline from an estimated 150,000 in 1845.[31] Visual evidence appeared to corroborate the assumption that this rate of decline would only accelerate. The most popular tourist images of Indians took as their subjects the oldest-looking people available. Typical of many photographs that displayed elderly Indians was one titled "Mission Indian women—woman on right 130 years old, daughter on left, 100 years."[32] Captions frequently related Indians directly to the crumbling adobe settings that surrounded them. In an image titled "Ancient Belles of San Luis Rey," three aged women appear seated in the grass in front of the ruined colonnade. The text on the reverse suggests that these women "helped build the mission" ninety-five years before.[33] If the missions were eroding away to nothingness, would not these women soon disappear as well? Represented only by the oldest people one might imagine, a logical assumption by viewers was that as a group Indians would soon die out—and die of natural causes.

The concept of the vanishing race buttressed the assumed natural explanation for the missions' demise with a social Darwinist logic, validating national and racial succession in California. Though the trope of the vanishing race was neither new nor unique to California, Camino Real tourist narratives braided it into the state's American origin myths. Indians, a sympathetic *Overland Monthly* writer decreed in 1901, were "rapidly passing away under the march of civilization, and will in the near future be so totally obliterated and lost as to be but a memory of the past."[34] The march of civilization appeared unstoppable, a force of progress that gradually emptied the landscape of its native inhabitants and logically led (white) Americans to possess the land.

The verdict remained the same even among those tourists who voiced disappointment with the Indians' disappearance or hinted that Americans shouldered some of the blame—the vanishing was inevitable. Auto tourist Thomas Murphy reckoned with the situation in his book *On Sunset Highways*: because of "the American conquest . . . the once happy and industrious natives were driven back to the hills and their final extinction seems to be at hand." Despite some regret, most absolved Americans from any fatal role. Another writer reasoned, as did many, that the California Indians, whom he termed "a race without laws or rules, following the common animal habits of savage life," were becoming extinct because of those inherent faults, in this "decadent condition perhaps for centuries." They were, he suggested, "already a dying race."[35] This writer laid the responsibility for extinction at the feet of the Indians themselves.

White Californians' remembrance of the Indians, however full of nostalgia, rarely failed to characterize them as degraded. If picturesque within the confines of the mission system, natives appeared in these narratives to be fundamentally an inferior race, perhaps the lowest race in a North American hierarchy. As Camino Real writer Trowbridge Hall passed judgment on the race, "Altogether it was a lazy, filthy people, 'more beastly than the beasts.'" Guidebook author Nolan Davis agreed: "It has to be accepted as incontrovertible fact that these Indians were the most stupid, brutish, filthy, lazy and improvident of the aborigines of America." This habitual portrayal of California Indians as the lowest of the low appeared to legitimize their extinction, seemingly assured by the turn of the twentieth century, as an inferior race giving way to one more evolved.[36] Mission nostalgia softened the blow by making the disappearance somehow picturesque, an irreversible demographic slide that even well-meaning Americans could do nothing to halt.

Tourists' great esteem for the Franciscan agenda to Christianize and civilize the indigenous people sprang from this low assessment of Indians' worth. The lower their estimation of the Indians, the loftier was their praise for the padres and their difficult tasks. An 1897 author judged the Franciscans' efforts "Herculean," given the "intellectual and moral caliber of the natives—lazy, dull, cowardly, covetous, and weak of will." Indians here appeared in great need of these missionary enterprises. Like many of her fellow tourists, Mary Crehore Bedell applauded the padres in 1924 for ministering to these Indians: "It was very impressive to me to see the enormous amount of good work the early Mission Fathers did in this wild country, which was in quite a state of savagery when they built these Missions." When she looked at a mission, she wrote, it reminded her of the "high-minded attempt of some great men to raise the Indian out of his ignorance and superstition." Even Nolan Davis, on the same page that he labeled California Indians the "most stupid" of all American natives, complimented the Franciscans for trying to "turn them into self-respecting, moral, law-abiding citizens."[37] By 1927, the Los Angeles Chamber of Commerce was repeating nearly the same logic and language as tourists. In a speech at the annual banquet, the chamber president decreed that

> the Digger Indian, said to be lowest type of aborigine on the American continent . . . in his crude way eked out a bare existence until up from Old Mexico came the Spaniards and with them the padres. These sainted men took that Digger Indian and out of him made a tiller of the soil, an artisan, a producer. The Missions, each in their ruins, remain as tributes to the zeal and devotion of the padres. . . . Next came a race of stalwarts, . . . those who became the pioneers of American civilization in the West.[38]

The padres and their "good works" became the heroic protagonists of the opening chapters in Camino Real writers' story of California's progress.

Tourists consistently related their Camino Real drives to the journeys of these beloved padres. Eleanor Gates subtitled her serial travel diary in *Sunset Magazine* "A Gasoline Pilgrimage in the Footsteps of the Padres." In his preamble, Thomas Murphy also invoked the metaphor of pilgrimage: "Like many a pious pilgrim of old, we set out on the King's Highway. . . . We shall follow in the footsteps of the brown-robed brothers of St. Francis." Junípero Serra, first leader of the California missionaries, sat at the apex of this hero worship. Travel diarist Letitia Stockett confessed that over the course of her tour, Serra had "become a real and living person, traveling down El Camino Real beside us." Local boosters again took up the refrain; a leader in the Native Daughters of California, Eliza Keith, remarked about the padres that "they were the makers of Christian communities in the midst of heathendom. They were the first. . . . They sowed the ground." The Franciscan missionaries never failed to earn high marks from Camino Real tourists for bringing civilization and Christianity to California.[39] Yet the insistence that they were "first" contained an assumption that there would be others to succeed them.

From this high point, Camino Real writers turned to explanations for the fall of the mission system. In comprehending the loss of the golden age, they saved their special wrath for Mexico and its policy of secularization. Part of the postindependence plan to divest the church of its wide temporal and political power, this policy intended to downgrade the California missions to simple parishes. Put into effect in the 1830s, it turned over the padres' valuable lands to private enterprises and released the Indians from mission control. In the words of Camino Real writers, this was calumny. They called it "the dread order of secularization," "a disastrous scheme," and a "polite term for political

Mission Santa Barbara- California 125

Figure 2.4. Padres at the Mission Santa Barbara fountain were popular subjects for postcard views like this one, sent in 1912. While praise for the Franciscans' good works and picturesque appearance abounded in diaries, this correspondent simply wrote: "Have been all through the mission to-day."

Postcard from author's collection.

robbery." They blamed the removal of Franciscan power for the natives' subsequent decline. The end of forced labor and conversion did not mean freedom in this rendering; it spelled vagrancy, neglect, starvation, and death. Many attributed the secularization plan as base Mexican moneygrubbing, a "desire to pay her debts with other people's property." This alleged greed thus "sounded the death knell to this dream of patriarchal government."[40] Unwilling to find fault with the padres' efforts, secularization and the Mexican people became the scapegoats for both the apparent Indian extinction and the perceived underdevelopment of California on the eve of American annexation. The mission era became a romantic interlude in a longer ladder of progress, as the vanishing race made room for Anglo civilization.

Americans, Automobiles, and a Reconquest

The Mexican secularization episode provided the necessary catalyst for the American conquest of California. Camino Real writings began to upstream the narrative, incorporating the mission era as merely a precursor to the higher destiny of California as an American state. The missions became "outposts of *our* first civilization" and "the earliest relic of the beginning of civilization on *our* great Pacific Coast." One Camino Real booster proclaimed that the "glorious achievements" of the "good friars, who planted the Christian religion and best traditions of Spain among the savages," formed the "foundation for *our* present Western civilization."[41] Californians began to honor Junípero Serra—"our first citizen"—and his colleagues as the state's founding fathers. A monument in Riverside depicted "the beginning of Civilization in California" with Junípero Serra ministering to the Indians and honored him as "Apostle, Legislator, Builder" of that civilization. In 1913, state leaders declared November 24 as Serra Day, a state holiday.[42] Such acts and memorials did more than recognize the Spanish missionaries as the first Europeans to settle in California; they prefigured American California in the founding of Spanish California.

Among all the accolades for the padres, Camino Real accounts led up to American annexation as the culmination of California history. Writers often issued reminders to appreciate *American* heroes—gold miners, overland pioneers, and city builders. As one travel diarist put it, "The true empire builders out here were the men who made the empire habitable. These were they who linked it up by iron rails and tied it with telegraph lines to other older seats of human habitation."[43] If less romantic than the silver-spurred conquistadors, Americans still succeeded them, as one supporter intriguingly noted, "following Spain around both oceans, gradually picking up the pieces of the old

Spanish Empire." Commending American ambition for properly developing California's abundance, one guidebook writer found it "remarkable that the padres and conquistadors of an earlier age should have overlooked the opportunity that a later, energetic race has so successfully developed." Americans, in this view, appeared better suited to direct the region to its highest ends and more deserving of its spoils.[44] By showing the Spanish missions as inevitably giving way to American enterprise, Camino Real history not only explained the presence of Anglo-Americans in California, but explained it as the end result of a long march toward civilization. The assembled narrative allowed missions to serve as romantic reminders of the past while sustaining the American possession of the present.

American flags were convenient reminders along El Camino Real of the nation's conquest and modern control of California. Not only did they fly in front of many a mission, but rhetorical and visual allusions also strengthened the connection. One photographic montage posed road boosters and a Mission Bell Guidepost draped in the Stars and Stripes.[45] But making the missions into markers of patriotism required more than the red, white, and blue. Guidebooks and postcards informed tourists that American settlers raised the "California Republic" Bear Flag at Sonoma and that John C. Frémont quartered his soldiers at Mission San Fernando Rey "on their way to Los Angeles to fight the Californians . . . to complete the American conquest of California."[46] The missions, therefore, became not simply reminders of California's romantic past, but sites that commemorated its conquest. The Automobile Club of Southern California claimed the missions quite explicitly for the nation: "Now, these missions are not the relic of any creed. They are the property of the people of the United States in a finer sense than that given by deed or title. Like the battlefield of Gettysburg, like Plymouth Rock, Bunker Hill and the Liberty Bell, they belong to the soil of the Nation— they are the nation's wards."[47] In that group of national landmarks, the Spanish missions might appear the likeliest candidates for a game of "which one of these things doesn't belong." In the interpretations Camino Real writers worked out, the missions could spark just as telling a remembrance of national achievements as the other, more familiar monuments of patriotism.

Tourists came to see the missions as part of American history as they wrote themselves into the story. With constant reference to their own journeys, their presence on the landscape, and in particular their automobiles, tourists themselves became the link between mission past and modern America. As Eleanor Gates recalled, "As we spun along, I could not help but think how the brave old padres had to plod over this same way. . . . They would have marveled at us!"[48] Camino Real writers measured progress in terms of their own tours.

Automobiles provided the most ready example of the superiority of modern life, for drivers believed their vehicles represented the pinnacle of progress. As road builder Anthon Westgard told them in his memoirs, "The wheel is the emblem of human progress. The supreme evolution of the wheel is the automobile." Automobilists on El Camino Real admired their own machines, the "marvelous speed of our new powers," the "power and swiftness . . . [of] the blast of our motor engines." Writers even began to cloak the automobile in the romantic language typically reserved for the missions themselves: "The satiny highway gleams under the light from auto-lamps where the modern pilgrim speeds, even at night, over the historic day-path of the Padres."[49] Coupled with nostalgia for the past and glory in conquest, the praise for a motor-driven progress cemented the celebration of the missions in a consistently hierarchical view of history that put tourists themselves at the wheel.

Yet praise for modernity was not the whole story, particularly as the road itself sometimes made the element of speed entirely theoretical. Rough conditions often slowed automobile progress to a crawl. Even in the 1920s, El

Figure 2.5. This postcard sketches the imaginative landscape of El Camino Real as the "Road of Romance." Included on the back is not only a map of the road and its missions, but also a list of "Outstanding Hotels," provided by the Central California Coast Highway Hotel Association.

Postcard from author's collection.

Camino Real in places remained without bridges, pavement, or maintenance, an imaginary road marked only by Mission Bell Guideposts. Drivers had to work hard to keep their cars on the road. Not only did they have to deal with mechanical breakdowns and up to 30-percent grades, but they often had to ford streams, dislodge tree stumps, and have their vehicles towed out of the mud by horse teams. Motorists in fact gave up many modern comforts on such trips. Touring on winding dirt roads, open to the sun and dust, "with meager springs and little padding . . . was an arduous, bumpy, drafty ordeal," historian Warren Belasco reminds.[50] Compared to the luxurious Pullman coach, these were rustic conditions.

Automobile tourists turned these apparent drawbacks into advantages. They argued that in the very struggle to navigate less-tamed territory, the automobile offered more intimate and individual touring experiences than was possible from a train. *Sunset Magazine* recommended a western automobile vacation for the man "who thrills in an elemental contact with the reality of nature." Murphy and his party thought El Camino Real's San Marcos pass difficult but found themselves "more than repaid for our trouble by the magnificence of the scenery and the glorious far-reaching panoramas that greeted us during the ascent." Perhaps they felt the landscape a bit more glorious for the effort.[51]

Moreover, automobile tourists applauded the individual skill and ingenuity these roads demanded, documenting their difficulties in great detail. Diaries included extensive commentary and photography of their machines on muddy roads, stuck on large boulders, or negotiating hairpin curves. The proof of adversity evidenced a pride in overcoming it. Eleanor Gates both complained and rejoiced in recounting her passage over the same San Marcos pass between Mission San Fernando and San Buenaventura.

> The motor guidebooks speak of it as a "pass" and no doubt as a pass for aeroplanes it would answer very nicely; but for automobiles it is not a success, being full of twisting grades that are described as 21% but seem at least 45%. . . . Our cars were distinctly put out at the gyrations they were compelled to perform over the first half of that climb. Their blood fairly boiled in their pipe-veins, . . . but they made it valiantly.[52]

Though few argued to leave roads in such poor conditions, conquering these wretched roads was an achievement drivers recalled with satisfaction. By 1933, when Irwin Delp began his Camino Real tour, the road was more consistently graded; undeterred, he deliberately chose "the old trails . . . , sometimes in preference to good roads. Bare passability was all that was required." Automobilist bravado would surely impress fellow travelers and readers, and their travelogues reveled in rough going.[53]

As active participants on gasoline pilgrimages, Camino Real tourists inserted themselves into the narrative. Theirs would be a kind of romantic adventure, too, a conquest of its own. Auto tourists imagined themselves traveling in the footsteps not only of the padres, but also of their own fore-fathers, pioneers of the westward expansion, blazing an auto trail through the wilderness. Many early automobilists adopted this role of road pioneer, describing their trips in terms of reclaiming their own land and rediscovering their own history.[54] An early automobile advocate promoted "the rediscovery of America by the automobile." Imagine, he asked, "how much more thoroughly Columbus could have discovered America had the good Queen been able to pawn an extra jewel to place an automobile . . . at his command!" In their automobiles, modern, city-bound Americans might lay claim to their own country by playing Columbus, discovering it "as they never have discovered . . . [it] before."[55] From the driver's seat, auto tourists on El Camino Real discovered California's mission past, claiming the land and the history for themselves, in a sense, reenacting the conquest.

Conclusion

If a carload of automobile tourists followed El Camino Real to its northern terminus in San Francisco, they would come to a Mission Bell Guidepost standing in Portsmouth Square. At the 1909 dedication ceremony for this bell, a speaker called attention to the significance of this placement. While El Camino Real reminded one of the padres, the "original pioneers of California, . . . Portsmouth Square awakens memories of the later pioneers, those hardy goldseekers who set an example by their fortitude and courage that inspires the Native Son and Daughter of California to sing their praises and revere their sacred memories." For it was in Portsmouth Square that Americans "hauled down the Mexican flag, and amid the cheers of the assembled people, raised the Stars and Stripes." The placement of the Mission Bell in this square, in his words, linked the "loyalty and affection for those brave and devoted pioneer fathers, with faith in our city, State and Nation."[56] Camino Real writers were engaged in the production of a public memory about the nation, one that celebrated its many conquests and where the division of past and present cleaved on national and racial lines.

The larger narratives of conquest thus linked tourist and padre, California and America, mission and motorcar in a romantic regional history. While tourists wrote themselves into a national myth, they also helped to write the missions into California memory. Producing El Camino Real for a tourist market, white Californians began to employ the Spanish past to develop the region, both physically and imaginatively. The missions, and the romantic myths they inspired, began to appear across the urban and cultural landscape, from domestic architecture to fourth-grade classrooms. In booster publications and as the backdrop for many Hollywood films, mission imagery abounded in telling the story of California's promise and progress.[57]

Camino Real tourists of the early twentieth century bequeathed to California a lasting interpretation of its mission past, though El Camino Real itself is no longer the tourist destination it once was. In fact, portions of Highway 101, the successor to the original state road, could rarely be mistaken for any romantic byway to the past, more often resembling a highway to some certain commuter hell. Nonetheless, it is striking that Californians are still trying to mark it with Mission Bell Guideposts. The California

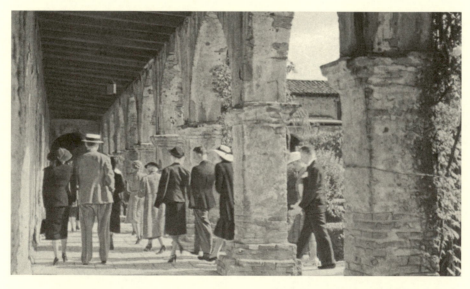

Figure 2.6. The caption on the reverse of this 1939 Union Oil Company postcard claims that the missions "give California a unique and interesting background" and "mark an important era in the development of the West." The missions had become famous enough for the caption to boast that "they attract visitors from all over the globe" and to entice still more tourists with its slogan: "See the West with 76 Gasoline."

Postcard from author's collection.

Federation of Women's Clubs, a booster of the original project, recently undertook a campaign to re-bell the road in honor of the state's sesquicentennial celebration of admission to the Union. Publicity reports reflect the enduring reverence for the missionaries. A March 1999 article in *The San Diego Union-Tribune* opened, "As every fourth-grader knows, El Camino Real is the footpath Father Junípero Serra trod." Moreover, the author lamented that "the graceful, dark-green monument—an 11-foot shepherd's crook and bells symbolizing the hard going to an on-foot quest from the tip of Baja to Sonoma—had all but disappeared from the coastal roadscape." One report of the project to replace the bells alluded to the national tourist significance of the road. "Restoring the landmarks that travelers across this country cherish makes perfect sense." So accepted are these bells of El Camino Real that these accounts even imply that there were some "original bells" existing prior to Harrie Forbes's project. "From 1904 to 1914," another article claimed, "the Federation set up *replacements* the length of the state where the paths of Father Junípero Serra and later Juan Bautista de Anza crisscrossed Spanish California."[58] The myth of El Camino Real and its mission bells has become ingrained to such a degree that Californians are now trying to restore the earlier tourist invention as a genuine marker of regional history.

In traveling El Camino Real, tourists put together a powerful myth. It celebrated a romantic past and its colorful inhabitants at the same time that it applauded the progress following their fall. What made this myth so compelling was not that it located the missions in an appropriate place in the past, but that it allowed tourists—modern white Americans—to locate themselves in the mission landscape. Photographing their automobiles in front of ruined missions, tourists might visualize their place in the timeline, that is, at its pinnacle. The tourist myth allowed white Californians to reconquer their past, assembling a history that would be commemorated in holidays, taught in standard curricula, symbolized in regional styles. Californians incorporated the memory of a romantic golden age, the celebration of past conquests, and the logic of racial succession into contemporary agendas and local identities. As El Camino Real paved the way for California tourists, nostalgia for a romantic past helped to drive the development of modern California in many of its aspects—both its inescapable red tile roofs and its persistent racial divides.

Notes

1. C. N. Williamson and A. N. Williamson, "The Spell," parts XIV–XVI, *Sunset* 26, no. 4 (April 1911): 424–36; J. A. Cahill, ["They left the motor purring . . ."], [drawing], *Sunset* 26, no. 4 (April 1911): 362; Lloyd Osbourne, "Motoring Through California," *Sunset* 26, no. 4 (April 1911): 364. El Camino Real served as a central plot vehicle or setting for

several fiction pieces of the era, including Annie L. Adair, "Mission Bells, a Love Tale of California: Romance and Reality in Serial Form," *Grizzly Bear* 7, no. 6 (October 1910): 1, 4; Madeline Deaderick Willard, *The King's Highway: A Romance of the Franciscan Order in Alta California* (Los Angeles: Grafton Publishing Co., 1913); and Jarrett T. Richards, *Romance on El Camino Real: Reminiscences and Romances Where the Footsteps of the Padres Fall* (St. Louis: B. Herder, 1914).

2. I borrow the idea of "gluing" memory from Shahid Amin, *Event, Metaphor, Memory: Chauri Chaura 1922–1992* (Berkeley: University of California Press, 1992), 10–11. Scholarly work on public memory has yet to focus carefully on the contributions of tourists to local remembrance, although tourism scholars have demonstrated the importance of tourists to changing local identity. For a helpful discussion of the debates on construction of public memory, see David Glassberg, "Public History and the Study of Memory," *The Public Historian* 18, no. 2 (spring 1996): 7–23. For a review of tourism's impact on local identity see Hal Rothman, *Devil's Bargains: Tourism in the Twentieth-Century American West* (Lawrence: University Press of Kansas, 1998).

3. For a more detailed history of the local booster campaign for El Camino Real, see Phoebe S. Kropp, "'All Our Yesterdays': The Spanish Fantasy Past and the Politics of Public Memory in Southern California, 1884–1939" (Ph.D. diss., University of California, San Diego, 1999), chap. 1; Mrs. A. S. C. [Harrie] Forbes, *California Missions and Landmarks: El Camino Real* (3d ed., Los Angeles: n.p., 1915); and Max R. Kurillo, "Marking the Past: A History of the Road Called El Camino Real, El Camino Real Association and the Bells," *The Ventura County Historical Society Quarterly* 37, nos. 3–4 (spring/summer 1992): 1–65.

4. Hal Barron in *Mixed Harvest: The Second Great Transformation in the Rural North, 1870–1930* (Chapel Hill: University of North Carolina Press, 1997), chap. 1, gives Good Roads a brief but perceptive treatment. For discussion of Progressive desires for order, see Robert Wiebe, *The Search for Order, 1877–1920* (New York: Hill and Wang, 1967), 174–76, 195, 223; and Daniel T. Rogers, "In Search of Progressivism," *Reviews in American History* 10, no. 4 (1982): 113–32, among others.

5. Walter V. Woehlke, "San Diego, the City of Dreams Come True," *Sunset* 26, no. 2 (February 1911): 139; Osbourne, "Motoring Through California," 363. For the history of southern California's great affinity for the automobile, see James J. Flink, *The Automobile Age* (Cambridge, Mass.: MIT Press, 1993); and Richard Longstreth, *City Center to Regional Mall: Architecture, the Automobile, and Retailing in Los Angeles, 1920–1950* (Cambridge, Mass.: MIT Press, 1997).

6. J. B. Scofield, ed., *The Land of Living Color; A Pictorial Journey from the Storied Southwest through the Gardens and Missions and Scenic Splendor of the Pacific Coast Country to the Eternal Snows of Alaska* (San Francisco: Sunset Publishing House, 1915), 22; [Alice] to [Mother], New York, 3 September 1920, on postcard: *Santa Barbara Mission, Cal.*, Carte De Luxe, 1920.

7. Examples of this image are nearly ubiquitous in the mission imagery of the period. See Eleanor Gates, "Motoring Among the Missions," *Sunset* 28, no. 3 (March 1912): 307; Eleanor Gates, "Motoring Among the Missions—Second Chapter of an Auto Journey," *Sunset* 28, no. 4 (April 1912): 439; Henry F. McNair, "Following the Spanish Padres by Motor," *Travel* 30, no. 3 (January 1918): 12; Touring Information Bureau of America, *TIB Automobile Route Book, Coast-to-Coast* (Kansas City, Mo.: The Bureau, 1915), 257; Charles Hamilton Owens, "The Bell Tower, Pala Mission, San Diego County, California," *Touring Topics* 15, no. 2 (February 1923): cover; [drawing], *Touring Topics* 17, no. 8 (August 1925): cover; "California Missions: Souvenir Folder," [postcards] ca. 1915, Warshaw Collection of Business Americana, Archives Center, National Museum of American

History, Smithsonian Institution; "Mission San Fernando, Californi[a]," [postcard], no. 5316 (San Francisco: Pacific Novelty Co., ca. 1910); Effie Price Gladding, *Across the Continent by the Lincoln Highway* (New York: Brentano's, 1915), 32; *California: Winter's Summer Garden* (Chicago: Chicago, Milwaukee & St. Paul Railway, ca. 1910), cover.

8. My analysis cannot include *all* of the possible tourist narratives or interpretations; not all travelers wrote diaries and fewer still published them. Yet early automobile tourists were particularly prolific in writing about their experiences, and there were a variety of publication outlets for their narratives. The commonality among these early automobile enthusiasts was partially due to the high cost of operation, which initially limited auto tourists to the elite. In the later teens, the Model T and World War I in Europe increased the pool of automobile tourists. In the 1920s, improved roads and facilities made the automobile vacation a middle-class possibility. By this time, however, the Camino Real experience had already been well developed by the garrulous upper-class automobilists that preceded them. Carey S. Bliss, *Autos Across America: A Bibliography of Transcontinental Automobile Travel: 1903–1940* (Los Angeles: Dawson's Book Shop, 1972); Anne Farrar Hyde, "From Stagecoach to Packard Twin-Six: Yosemite and the Changing Face of Tourism, 1880–1930," *California History* 69, no. 2 (summer 1990): 160; Flink, *Automobile Age*, 37–38, 169.

9. As Marguerite Shaffer has demonstrated, tourists were active interpreters who tried to place their individual experiences into words, through diaries, and into tangible reminders, like albums and mementos. Their attempts to individualize their experiences represented, on the one hand, a rejection of what was becoming a standardized narrative. On the other hand, the homogeneous appearance of their individual memories demonstrated the inescapability of the nascent tourist industry. Once early tourists and promoters began to establish missions' "official" meanings, the guidebooks, souvenirs, and other touring materials produced all began to reflect that story and sell it to a wider audience. See Marguerite Shaffer, "Playing American: The Southwestern Scrapbooks of Mildred E. Baker," this volume.

10. Charles F. Carter, *Some By-Ways of California* (San Francisco: Whitaker and Ray-Wiggin Co., 1902), 187.

11. For discussion of the changing demographics and social milieu in southern California, see Robert M. Fogelson, *The Fragmented Metropolis: Los Angeles, 1850–1930* (Berkeley: University of California Press, 1993; Berkeley and Los Angeles: University of California Press, 1967); Lisbeth Haas, *Conquests and Historical Identities in California, 1769–1936* (Berkeley: University of California Press, 1995); Leonard Pitt, *The Decline of the Californios: A Social History of the Spanish-speaking Californians, 1846–1890* (Berkeley and Los Angeles: University of California Press, 1966).

12. James Steele, *Old Californian Days* (Chicago: Morrill, Higgins and Co., 1892), 11–12.

13. *The Sightseer* (Los Angeles: Pacific Tours), 1, no. 1 (January 1907). For the development of the Southwest as a tourist destination full of romance and exotic peoples, see Chris Wilson, *The Myth of Santa Fe: Creating a Modern Regional Tradition* (Albuquerque: University of New Mexico Press, 1997); Barbara Babcock and Marta Weigle, eds., *The Great Southwest of the Fred Harvey Company and the Santa Fe Railway* (Tucson: University of Arizona Press and the Heard Museum, 1996); and Erika Bsumek, "Making Indian-Made: The Production, Consumption, and Legal Construction of Navajo Identity, 1880–1930" (Ph.D. diss., Rutgers University, 1999).

14. Thomas D. Murphy, *On Sunset Highways: A Book of Motor Rambles in California* (Boston: The Page Company, 1915), 159; Thomas J. O'Shaughnessy, *Rambles on Overland Trails* (Chicago: privately printed, 1915), 123–24.

15. For evidence of such disappointment, see, for example, Trowbridge Hall, *Californian Trails: Intimate Guide to the Old Missions* (New York: Macmillan Company, 1920), 61; W. C. Scott, *Westward, Ho! A Story of an Auto Trip to the Pacific Country* (n.p.: privately printed, 1921), 21. Interestingly, most of the evidence of disappointment that I found was in later narratives such as these.

16. T. J. Jackson Lears, *No Place of Grace: Antimodernism and the Transformation of American Culture, 1890–1920* (Chicago: University of Chicago Press, 1981), 103–7; Wilson, *Myth of Santa Fe*, 5–6, 110–13.

17. [Southern Pacific], "El Camino Real," [advertisement], *Sunset* 1, no. 6 (October 1898): 88.

18. O'Shaughnessy, *Rambles*, 60.

19. Maria Antonia Field, *Chimes of Mission Bells: An Historical Sketch of California and Her Missions* (San Francisco: Philopolis Press, 1914), 16.

20. John S. McGroarty, "At the Sign of the Poinsettia," *Sunset* 29, no. 6 (December 1912): 623; Vernon J. Selfridge, *The Miracle Missions* (Los Angeles: Grafton Publishing Co., 1915); Aimee Tourgee, "Mission Ruins," *Out West* 21, no. 6 (December 1904): 533.

21. Laura Bride Powers, *The Missions of California: Their Establishment, Progress and Decay* (San Francisco: Doxey Press, 1897), 9.

22. Charles Francis Saunders and J. Smeaton Chase, *The California Padres and Their Missions* (Boston: Houghton Mifflin Co., 1915), 213; John Brinckerhoff Jackson, *The Necessity for Ruins and Other Topics* (Amherst: University of Massachusetts Press, 1980), 102; Murphy, *On Sunset Highways*, 160.

23. Hi Sibley, "Byways of El Camino Real," *Westways* 26, no. 9 (September 1934): 37; Saunders and Chase, *The California Padres*, 230. Other restorations that tourists criticized included San Buenaventura and San Luis Rey and a "fake reconstruction" near Mission San Antonio de Padua.

24. Murphy, *On Sunset Highways*, 232; Charles Francis Saunders, *A Little Book of California Missions* (New York: Robert M. McBride and Co., 1925), 35.

25. Irwin W. Delp, *The Santa Fe Trail to California* (Boston: Christopher Publishing House, 1933), 157–58. For a discussion of World War I's effect on tourism, see Anne Farrar Hyde, *An American Vision: Far Western Landscape and National Culture, 1820–1920* (New York: New York University Press, 1990), 296; John A. Jakle, *The Tourist: Travel in Twentieth Century North America* (Lincoln: University of Nebraska Press, 1985), 225–26.

26. A. L. Westgard, "The Path of the Mission Fathers, California's Scenic Coast Route," *American Motorist* 4, no. 3 (March 1912): 203; David M. Steele, *Going Abroad Overland: Studies of Places and Peoples in the Far West* (New York: G. P. Putnam's Sons, 1917), 49.

27. Sibley, "Byways," 37; Scofield, *Land of Living Color*, 9.

28. Automobile Club of Southern California [ACSC], *California's Mission Tour* (Los Angeles: The Club, 1915), 3.

29. Gates, "Second Chapter," 445.

30. Selfridge, *The Miracle Missions*, n.p. ACSC, *California's Mission Tour*, 4.

31. After 1900, the native population began to climb slowly, reaching twenty thousand during the 1950s and expanding more rapidly since. James J. Rawls, *Indians of California: The Changing Image* (Norman: University of Oklahoma Press, 1984), 171, 214.

32. C. C. Pierce, "Mission Indian women," 1890, Photograph #3307, C. C. Pierce Collection, Henry E. Huntington Library (hereafter cited as Pierce Collection); [Taber Co.], "The Oldest Indians of San Diego Co.," in "California and the West, 1900–1910," Album 49, Huntington Library. While Pierce and other photographers did capture images of community activity at various missions, the views of Indians reproduced most often in tourist

guides overwhelmingly drew from the series of the elderly. My understanding of these images owes much to Jennifer Watts's interpretation of the photography of "old Indians" in the region and their relationship to the constructions of nature. Jennifer Watts, "Nature's Workshop: Photography and the Creation of Semi-Tropic Southern California, 1880–1930" (paper presented at the Southern California Environment and History Conference II, September 1997, Northridge, Calif.).

33. C. C. Pierce, "Ancient Belles of San Luis Rey," 1893, Photograph #2870, Pierce Collection. Placing Indians amidst ruins increased the appearance that Indians were "living relics," as Leah Dilworth has noted, "simultaneously appearing from the past and disappearing from the present." It is interesting to note that these images are in great contrast to the photography of Pueblo Indians, which most often showcased women, young girls, and children. Leah Dilworth, *Imagining Indians in the Southwest: Persistent Visions of a Primitive Past* (Washington, D.C.: Smithsonian Institution Press, 1996), 3, 80; Barbara Babcock, "'A New Mexican Rebecca': Imaging Pueblo Women," *Journal of the Southwest* 32 (winter 1990): 400–437; Chris Wilson, "Ethnic/Sexual Personas in Tricultural New Mexico," this volume.

34. Alfred V. LaMotte, "The California Indian," *Overland Monthly*, 2d. ser., 37, no. 4 (April 1901): 831.

35. Murphy, *On Sunset Highways*, 165; Nolan Davis, *The Old Missions of California: The Story behind the Peaceful Conquest of the State* (Oakland: Claremont Press, 1926), 70–71.

36. Hall, *Californian Trails*, 8; Davis, *The Old Missions*, 70. As James Rawls has argued, this rhetoric of degradation helped to rationalize Indian extinction, whether or not it was viewed as regrettable or desirable, as an inevitable process. Rawls, *Indians of California*, 200–201; Dilworth, *Imagining Indians*, 3, 80.

37. Powers, *The Missions of California*, 104–5; Mary Crehore Bedell, *Modern Gypsies: The Story of a Twelve Thousand Mile Motor Camping Trip Encircling the United States* (New York: Brentano's, 1924), 124; Davis, *The Old Missions*, 70.

38. D. F. McGarry, president, Los Angeles Chamber of Commerce, [speech given at annual banquet], in *The Members' Annual* (Los Angeles: Board of Directors, 1927), 214–15.

39. Gates, "Motoring Among the Missions," 703; Murphy, *On Sunset Highways*, 159–61; Letitia Stockett, *America: First, Fast & Furious* (Baltimore: Norman-Remington Co., 1930), 200; Eliza D. Keith, quoted in "Native Daughters and Native Sons Erect Bell Posts," *Grizzly Bear* 6, no. 2 (December 1909): 9. For a discussion of tourist use of the language of pilgrimage in narrating their tours, see John F. Sears, *Sacred Places: American Tourist Attractions in the Nineteenth Century* (New York: Oxford University Press, 1989), 5–6. For a discussion of the religious issues involved in this largely Protestant worship of a Catholic missionary project, see Roberto Lint Sagarena, "Inheriting the Land: Defining Place in Southern California from the Mexican American War to the *Plan Espiritual de Aztlán*" (Ph.D. diss., Princeton University, 2000); and Kropp, "All Our Yesterdays," 137–45.

40. Charles Augustus Keeler, *Southern California* (Los Angeles: n.p., 1899), 89–90, 132; Mrs. A. S. C. Forbes, *California Missions and Landmarks and How to Get There* (Los Angeles: Official Guide, 1903), 95–96; H. E. Booth, [speech], quoted in Lillian Ferguson, "El Camino Real Plans Pledge Prompt Action," *San Francisco Examiner*, 26 April 1904; Landmarks Club, *The Landmarks Club: What It Has Done, What It Has to Do* (Los Angeles: Out West Co., 1903), 9; Hall, *Californian Trails*, 12.

41. Emphasis added, Davis, *The Old Missions*, 9; Murphy, *On Sunset Highways*, 118; Alfred Roncovieri, [speech], quoted in "Native Daughters," 8.

42. Bishop Thomas Conaty, quoted in Selfridge, *The Miracle Missions*, n.p. "Father Serra

Memorial Tablet at Riverside, Gift of Frank Miller," Photograph #3983, Pierce Collection; "Father Junípero Serra Monument, Golden Gate Park, San Francisco," Photograph #3993, Pierce Collection; "Mission Capistrano and Father Serra Monument," Photograph #3988, Pierce Collection; "Native Daughters," 8.

43. Steele, *Going Abroad*, 192.
44. Harriet Russell Strong, "Europeans on the Pacific," TS, [ca. 1920], Harriet Russell Strong Papers, Huntington Library; Davis, *The Old Missions*, 12–13; Ernest McGaffey, "The Path of the Padres," *Touring Topics* 15, no. 4 (April 1923): 20, 29.
45. [Photograph], in Anna F. Lacy, "Dedicate Mission Bell as Sequel to Celebration," *Grizzly Bear* 7, no. 6 (October 1910): 7.
46. Steele, *Going Abroad*, 192; Edward H. Mitchell, pub., *Missions of California: Historic Monuments of California's Early Civilization* (San Francisco: n.p., ca. 1908); Saunders and Chase, *The California Padres*, 112.
47. ACSC, *California's Mission Tour*, 8.
48. Gates, "Second Chapter," 438.
49. A. L. Westgard, *Tales of a Pathfinder* (New York: A. L. Westgard, 1920), 8; McGroarty, "At the Sign," 624; Eleanor Gates, "Motoring Among the Missions: Concluding Chapter of a Gasoline Pilgrimage in the Footsteps of the Padres," *Sunset* 28, no. 6 (June 1912): 708; Scofield, *Land of Living Color*, 22.
50. Warren J. Belasco, *Americans on the Road: From Autocamp to Motel, 1910–1945* (Cambridge, Mass.: MIT Press, 1979), 30–31.
51. "Main Roads Traveled in the Sunset Country," *Sunset* 39, no. 7 (July 1917): 82; Murphy, *On Sunset Highways*, 196.
52. Gates, "Second Chapter," 438.
53. Delp, *The Santa Fe Trail*, 8. A prime example of a travel diary that provided a running commentary on the difficulty of the road was Thomas Murphy's. Like others, it exhibited a braggadocio in conquering the steep and dangerous passes, which perhaps was the point. They warned off eastern drivers who did not know "what real driving is." Murphy, *On Sunset Highways*, passim, but especially 184–240. For a discussion of automobile diaries' focus on difficulties, see Belasco, *Americans on the Road*, 35; and Bliss, *Autos Across America*.
54. Victor Eubank, "Log of an Auto Prairie Schooner," *Sunset* 28, no. 2 (February 1912): 191; Bliss, *Autos Across America*, xiii–xiv. This kind of transference, imagining themselves pioneers, was common to automobile tourists, who often followed other pioneer trails like those of the covered wagons, the Donner Party, or the forty-niners. See Marguerite Shaffer, "See America First: Tourism and National Identity, 1905–1930" (Ph.D. diss., Harvard University, 1994), 230.
55. G. B. Betts, "The Rediscovery of America by the Automobile," *Outing: Sport, Adventure, Travel, Fiction* 42 (May 1903): 167, 175.
56. Roncovieri, in "Native Daughters," 8. Glen Gendzel ("Pioneers and Padres: Competing Mythologies in Northern and Southern California, 1850–1930," *Western Historical Quarterly* 32 [spring 2001]: 55–79) has detected a contradictory impulse in northern California, especially in San Francisco, that disparaged the padres in order to highlight the memory of gold rush pioneers. Driven by regional rivalry, this battle of memories clearly influenced remembrance of the Spanish past. Indeed, southern Californians exhibited a more determined pursuit of romance in the missions than their northern counterparts, and they were clearly the leaders in the Camino Real booster campaign. Nonetheless, San Francisco hosted its share of celebrations for the padres and the mission past and repeated many familiar tourist refrains.

57. For an analysis of the "Spanish fantasy past" as a wide-ranging regional public memory and cultural phenomenon, see Kropp, "All Our Yesterdays."

58. Logan Jenkins, "Donated Bells Rope in Ringing Endorsement," *San Diego Union-Tribune*, 15 March 1999; Barbara Brill, "Ivey Ranch Students Help Restore Fading Historic El Camino Real Bell Marker," *North County Times* [San Diego], 13 October 2000; Betty Barnacle, "Campbell Unveils Mission Bell Replica: Stretching History Off El Camino Real," *San Jose Mercury News*, 12 July 1998, emphasis added.

ANGLO ARTISTS AND THE CREATION OF PUEBLO WORLDS ⟶

RINA SWENTZELL

I am an Indian person from Santa Clara Pueblo in northern New Mexico. However, when I was in the tenth grade, my family moved to Taos, which is about an hour north of Santa Clara. We did not move into Taos Pueblo, but rather lived on the boundary between the pueblo and the town of Taos. During the 1950s, when I lived there, the legacy of the early society of Taos artists was very real. The artists of the 1950s were still mostly painting in the romantic style of the early 1900s Taos colony. The works in the galleries were of archetypical and idealized Indians—mostly Indian men. The artists still gathered in the dark lobby of the Don Fernando Hotel on the plaza. We Indians seldom went in there, and if we did, it was for very short times. We were not comfortable. We felt that we did not belong even though the paintings hanging on the walls were of us.

The paintings, however, were interesting to us because we would look to see who we could recognize. They were distant images of relatives or people connected to a particular family within the Pueblo. We would move away, not always sure how to feel or react because we could not be comfortable in those strange places, yet it was the paintings of us or pots made by us that really made those places what they were. They set the tone for those places. The pots, drums, and paintings made them special—different—and, moreover, gave them a feeling of well-being and status. Those items, paintings, pots, etc., obviously reminded the white people of why they had moved to this place of romance, "this haven of happy, peaceful Indians."

We Indians (and I would guess everybody else) knew that the people in the paintings were not the simple Indians who were portrayed. Outside the Don Fernando Hotel was a parking lot that served a grocery store, and this was where the drunks—drunk Indian men—gathered. They'd sit against the wall of the hotel until they passed out, strewn in the dirt alongside the hotel wall. Even in the early 1900s, when Anglo-American artists began painting the Taos Indians, alcoholism and cultural depression were already problems. So why were we being presented only as happy and noble people? The paintings, it seems, were really about what those Anglos needed to see for themselves. Their paintings were efforts to fill a need inside themselves. They wanted assurance that the technological and consumeristic world that was growing around them had not yet pervaded every corner of the globe.

Eanger Irving Couse, for instance, who in 1912 became the first president of the Taos Society of Artists, had been intrigued with Indians even when he lived in the East. Born in 1866, he belonged nonetheless to the tradition of Emerson and Thoreau, who also yearned for unspoiled nature and untouched natives. The Indians back East, however, already lived very disjunctive and disrupted lives and were a disappointment to lovers of nature and Indians. E. I. Couse, and other artists with his sensibilities, found the Pueblo communities to be more cohesive. There was still some semblance of what the Pueblo people's lives might have been like in the not too distant past. Particularly at Taos, the Pueblo community was architecturally intact and gave the feeling of a place where daily life was lived in a different rhythm than the Anglo artists had experienced elsewhere. Dances in the plazas and ceremonies in the kivas were still common practices. The men still draped themselves in blankets, and the women wore wide-legged moccasin boots and mantas, or cloth-draped dresses tied at the waist with a woven belt. Travel was by foot or wagon. Hunting, gathering, and farming were the primary means of providing food and items for trade.

The greatest attraction that the Pueblo Indians of that time held for the Anglo artists was their belief system, which stressed the connectedness of humans to the natural world. Pueblo people believed that they were given birth by the mother, the earth, who was impregnated by the sky. The entire cosmos is bounded by the far mountains and enclosed by the sky. The people lived in this bounded world knowing that they were dependent on the trees, rocks, and other animals for their survival. The sun was greeted and talked to every day, and at Taos footraces were run to give energy to the sun when it was at its lowest point in the sky. Interaction of humans with the sun and with all other beings was accepted. At Taos Pueblo there is still a quiet season during the wintertime when the people take off their shoes and do not drive cars or make loud noises because the mother, the earth, is resting. As they ask for consideration from the earth and the sky, the parents of all life, they also must give consideration. Nature is an organic being with people only one part. There is no superhuman god. All other creatures, rocks, animals, and plants are considered by humans to be brothers and sisters.

Those early artists who gathered in Taos were, I believe, sincerely searching for an alternative lifestyle that would give promise and hope for their own lives within American culture and society. E. I. Couse "charmingly and poetically presented the American Indian at peace in his habitat." He wanted so much to see peace and human oneness with the natural world. He was biased toward painting Pueblo men in peaceful and thoughtful poses, and I think not only because men would pose with fewer clothes than the women would, but also because he knew that in Anglo culture, aggressive and socially disruptive activities are generally initiated by men. If he could find peaceful, loving, gentle men in the world, there was hope for where he saw modern life going.

How did his seemingly innocent motivations to paint Indians influence the lives and the world of the Indians themselves? During those years that I was a teenager, I worked at a tourist gift shop in downtown Taos. I visited galleries during my breaks and lunch hours because it was all very intriguing—the paintings, artifacts, as well as the people who ran the galleries. (And it was really very different than Santa Clara Pueblo and Española, the closest town to Santa Clara. Española was and is not a place that the Anglo painters or romantics took a liking to. Española is a typical Chicano town—poor and without the upper-class Anglo tastes in clothes and buildings.) Taos was different. The wealthy Anglos really did set the tone for the place. As we looked at those images of who we were supposed to be—and really, no one living in Taos or Taos Pueblo could escape seeing these renderings from the late 1800s to the 1950s of images of Indians because they were everywhere in Taos—we felt idealized, yet unworthy of that adoration. There was always the feeling that we were not good enough or could not measure up to how we were represented. As people saw us, their questions and interactions with us suggested that we were what those images presented. And what was presented, underneath it all, were values, attitudes, and relationships.

Art does communicate all those things: values, attitudes, and models for relationships. We talk about colors having value—and they do. Colors and the curve of a line do set a mood, a tone for what to feel and a way to know what is more important. In Couse's work, we have soft muted colors representing warm, romantic feelings. They are feelings of a good, faraway place that we all began to claim for ourselves. But for Indians, it sets the standards for what one is supposed to be like. Granted that what Couse was proposing for the Indian was not bad in terms of who we once were—or still might work toward being. It does manipulate conformity to another's ideas of our behavior, actions, and even dress. It does what Rousseau felt about himself having to accept other men's definitions of one's self. Rousseau said it leads to inauthenticity. But Rousseau, writing in the mid-1700s, saw no way out of it and saw no hope for authenticity in the world he lived in. He longed to stop time at the moment when "he was drunk in the charms of nature."

Members of the Taos Society of Artists, so well exemplified by E. I. Couse, were of that vein. In their enthusiasm over the discovery of a cultural group that possessed characteristics they were looking for, they wanted to prolong, revive, and protect it. In their eagerness to do so, they forgot they were dealing with people and not objects. Or perhaps they were really acting as products of a worldview in which objects are the end rather than a by-product of striving for some greater end. In any case, they could not truly relate to the values they sensed as valuable in the other group and, consequently, imposed the values that they were themselves trying to escape. It is like the Heisenberg principle in modern quantum science that says whatever is observed is changed by the act of observation—and by the observer.

And then there is the issue of what happened to those renderings—those paintings. They, of course, were sold for a lot of money—a whole lot of money especially to us, Indians, who had so little. We could not afford those representations of ourselves. They went to people out there in the other world—into that other world that had economic means that we, Indians, were already yearning for. As these artists themselves struggled to enter the commercial art world through advertising with the Fred Harvey system, commercialization of art was the model to be emulated by Indians and non-Indians alike. Remember that during those years, around the 1920s, romantic Indian organizations were forming, such as the New Mexico Association on Indian Affairs, later known as the Southwest Association on Indian Affairs, which runs the very popular Indian Market in Santa Fe. Their goal was to work for fair prices, to establish markets, and to collect artifacts. As a result of all that was happening for their benefit, Indians very soon found, as had the Taos artists, that the economic reasons were very compelling for the creation of art. Functional and ceremonial art is almost nonexistent today in the Pueblo communities. Undeniably, modern Indian art has a strong veneer of money and fame.

Paintings by artists such as Couse were done in a representational manner that also influenced how art was to be approached but, more importantly, how reality was to be known and defined. Indian people, traditionally, expressed themselves in symbolic and metaphorical ways. Designs, which represented clouds, mountains, the sun, the earth, snakes, lightning, were all symbols pointing to forces larger than the individual. They pointed to connecting energies in the world. The lightning moves from the sky to the earth, from the male to the female, connecting them. The content of petroglyphs and designs on pots encouraged people to remember nonphysical forces, energies, in the world. Their gaze was not to stop at the physical form. Reality was in the movement of the clouds, the water, and the wind; human creations were a way of realigning with the formless. The act of creation was to use the form as a way to see beyond the form itself. Art was not done for art's sake. It was a means to experience the power beyond the actual creation.

In the realistic paintings of Couse's era, we have a focus on the very real human individuals doing very real things in very specific places. Moreover, the focus on the skin tone and texture of the individuals sends the message that this physical human world is of primary utmost importance. It is almost as if these artists wanted to make what they found so attractive about the Indians as real for themselves as possible.

Again, in traditional Pueblo thought we have many realities, many realms of existence, simultaneously. This realm in which we live is only one of four realms that we acknowledge, and we have the capability to move between those realms. Additionally, the human realm is only one level of reality and therefore is not where primary meaningfulness lies. As we work within our very mundane lives we are always conscious of the movement that can take us into the clouds and into the worlds under the lake.

For Pueblo people, explicitness of form and subject matter also limits the possibility of interpretations. These artists were very explicit about what they wanted to communicate. We Pueblo people are uneasy with one interpretation of anything, maybe because we are part of an oral tradition where the written or even spoken word does not limit our communication. In an oral tradition, interpretation of song, story, or design by one person does not become standardized. Even songs and stories are given the respect of being alive because they change. For instance, the borrowing of songs, stories, and myths between Pueblo communities is a common event. In the Tewa communities, which is where I come from because the Santa Clara people speak Tewa, we often "borrowed" songs from the Hopis in Arizona. Such songs are recognizable by the Hopi people, but everyone understands that when a Tewa group sings the song, it will become Tewa because it moves with the rhythms of the Tewa people.

And so also with the Taos artists? Or whoever else takes on the work of painting another group of people—or writing about them? They paint or write with the ideas that have been formed in their head, with the sensibilities in their fingers and with the rhythms of their soul. In the case of E. I. Couse, it is no wonder that people talked about "Couse's Indians."

And so we are. As the Hopi songs transform in Tewa voices, so have we Indians been transformed by Couse's paintings. It is part of the movement of life—we Indians find ourselves valuing realism over spiritualism, individualism over community and connectedness, explicitness over subtle interpretations—creating for money, running after recognition and fame, and wanting to possess objects, things, paintings for ourselves. We want to be like the rest of the world and collect our own works now because that represents well-being.

But of course, who we are as Indians can't all be laid at the feet of Couse and his contemporaries. However, they are undeniably part of that western world that is so alluring. So alluring that the options we Indians once offered in terms of alternative lifeways, ways of thinking, and understandings of the world have been transforming into something closer to what we know as western ways and thinking. On the other hand, we Indians and non-Indians are all continuously creating our own worlds, given all the influences and thoughts and values we choose to take in. Pueblo thought tells us that this is exactly what should be happening. Yet one always wonders. What if that person didn't impose those images, values, and thoughts? What kind of world might we have created for ourselves through today? What possibilities have been closed?

There has been much tension in the Taos community through the years because of the alignments between the Anglo artists and the Indians. And usually, these alignments have been initiated by the Anglos. The Hispanics in the area have felt left out because they were not seen or regarded as special as the Indians by the Anglos. But really, in the end, who are the more fortunate people? Those who can move and grow more with their own rhythm or those who do not know their own rhythm anymore because of overpowering outside impositions and expectations?

PLAYING AMERICAN
THE SOUTHWESTERN SCRAPBOOKS
OF MILDRED E. BAKER

MARGUERITE S. SHAFFER

In the fall of 1998, *Martha Stewart Living,* the mouthpiece of contemporary do-it-yourself highbrow culture and consumption in America, ran a how-to article on scrapbooks. Illustrated in standard Martha Stewart style with nine pages of sumptuous photographs depicting an assortment of elaborate scrapbooking techniques, the article explains that "we are all driven to document our lives—on paper, in photographs—to give permanence to what is fleeting." And as the delicate watercolors, the photomontages, the wax rubbings, and the carefully folded accordion pages in the photographs reveal, scrapbooks offer an ideal form for artistic design and display of personal mementos and one-of-a-kind experiences. "A trip down memory lane can be a creative excursion. Even the most traditional theme can be made personal and unique," the writer explains. "Think of it as your novel. The scope can be small or large, focused or loose, a chronological narrative or a visual montage." Although the article details a variety of scrapbook subjects, the travel scrapbook takes center stage. Noting that many early travel scrapbooks consisted of pressed flowers "from various ports," similarly, the modern-day scrapbook allows one to gather tangible memories and impressions of a trip. The writer suggests that a daily diary and "a small kit—of scissors, magic markers, rubber cement, and a portable water color set"—could help one capture unique experiences and novel sights and transform the tourist experience into a priceless personal memento. As the article concludes, "Whether future generations treasure yours as a collectors' item or not, the true value between the covers is personal."[1] Tapping into an array of cultural messages and meanings concerning travel, collecting, status, and individual expression, the article reflects the long-standing contradictions of tourism as a consumer experience.

Generally speaking, the tourist has been a much-maligned cultural figure.[2] Even the word *tourism* as it originated in the nineteenth century had negative connotations, suggesting that the tourist was a passive spectator engaged in an empty ritual of commodity exchange.[3] Although we have all been tourists at one time or another, I suspect we have all shunned the tourist hordes scurrying from one spectacle to the next with their guidebooks in hand, posed for the camera, exuding a superficial yet insatiable curiosity. We take precaution to choose the right clothing so we will not look like tourists; we behave discreetly so as not to act like tourists; we strive to get off the beaten path to escape the tourists. We seek to be in the world of tourism but not of it. This ambivalence speaks to the inherent contradictions of the tourist experience. Born of modern consumer capitalism, tourism offers a paradoxical promise: a self-fulfilling, one-of-a-kind experience as a mass-produced phenomenon. The tourist is constantly caught between individual desire and marketed spectacle. These contradictions are especially apparent in the Southwest, where the tourist industry has re-imagined the region as a land of enchantment replete with picturesque Indians, sublime desert scenery, and frontier history and where tourists have traveled for decades in search of authentic experience, therapeutic escape, and "real" life. Are all these tourists simply dupes, hypnotized by the tourist spectacle? Or are tourists able to transcend the marketed tour? An exploration of the tourist experience suggests that the answer is more complicated than either/or. Just as scholars have shown that the southwestern tourist industry is the product of multifarious negotiations between corporate interests, local communities, and outside promoters, so the tourist experience is also a complex exchange among these same market forces combined with larger cultural expectations and individual desires.[4] By looking more closely at the narratives of one tourist who traveled repeatedly to the Southwest, I seek to dissect this complex exchange as it was played out in the tourist landscape.

Assessing the value of one of her trips to the Southwest in commercial terms, Mildred E. Baker pinpointed the conflicting forces of mass consumption and personal meaning inherent in the tourist experience. "We had not in these two months added to our material possessions," she wrote; "we had merely by supreme effort come to know the most violent river as few can ever know it. While memory lasts, I have a priceless possession in the recollection of these glorious, thrilling, dangerous days on 'rough water.'"[5] Between 1931 and 1942, Baker, a private secretary in a Buffalo, New York, investment firm, made five trips to the Southwest. In the ensuing ten years she visited many of the central tourist attractions of the region: Rainbow Bridge, the Grand Canyon, Kayenta, Betatakin, Inscription House Ruins, Monument Valley, Santa Fe, Taos, Carlsbad Caverns, and El Paso. She took pack trips, bought Indian rugs, pottery, and jewelry, and rafted down the Colorado and Green Rivers. She amassed an array of inimitable experiences—"priceless" memories. To capture these experiences, to memorialize her journeys, she created elaborate leather-bound volumes with hand-colored, illuminated title pages and typescript narratives illustrated with captioned snapshots, cutouts from tourist brochures, postcards, and purchased photographs for each trip. She also included transcriptions of poems, newspaper clippings, and lists of the plants and birds she observed. These scrapbooks convey the essence of her tourist experience. They reveal not only the tourist landscape, but also the cultural ideals and expectations that shaped her romantic image of the Southwest. Although these scrapbooks are from just a single tourist, they shed light on the dynamic cultural interplay that defined the tourist experience in the context of modern consumer society.

Historians of consumer culture have shown that in the years surrounding the turn of the century, business leaders, advocates of the leisure industry, advertisers, social theorists, and the like helped to create what one scholar has called a "culture of abundance."[6] The development and experience of tourism was integrally connected to this modern corporate culture. It depended on the newly expanded commercial nexus of consumption, leisure, social fluidity, salaried workers, and the expansion of the print media and transportation net-

Figure 4.1. Opening pages of Mildred E. Baker's travel scrapbook "Navajo Mountain" (1931). Photographic Collections.

(This item is reproduced by permission of the Huntington Library, San Marino, California.)

works. As a consumer experience, tourism occupied a strange middle ground between consumption, leisure, and mass media.[7] Like consumption, it was dependent on interactive exchange. However, like leisure activities and mass media, it was centered on the creation and dissemination of spectacle and illusion. The tourist was simultaneously a consumer and a viewer. In crossing all these boundaries, tourism manifested the unique possibilities of the emerging consumer culture: the possibility of intense personal experience, an escape to liminal space where the self could be temporarily re-imagined or refashioned, an opportunity for physical and mental reinvigoration, a glimpse of the "good life." However, the experience of tourism offered no tangible product. In other words, the possibilities of tourism as a consumer experience also defined its limitations. It offered the potential of a personalized, one-of-a-kind experience, but at the same time it offered no proof of purchase—no visible meaning in a world defined by consumer goods. It promised both the exchange of interactive consumption along with the wonders of spectacle, but the exchange was intangible. Theoretically, it had no discernible meaning in the context of consumer consciousness.

The production of souvenirs, postcards, and scenery albums and the creation of tourist mementos suggest that the tourist industry and tourists themselves were conscious of the dilemma of tourism as a consumer experience. Tourists understood that in order to make sense of the experience in the context of this emerging consumer consciousness, they needed to somehow objectify their experience. Many tourists kept detailed diaries or created meticulous scrapbooks memorializing their journeys; others settled for ready-made souvenirs and postcards.[8] These personal mementos reveal more than just the various routes followed or the "sights" visited. They show the consciously constructed visual, verbal, and physical narrative of the actual and imaginative journey. Meticulously compiled photo albums and scrapbooks suggest that tourists made their journeys into stories, highlighting the sites and events that were most "memorable" and locating themselves in the tourist landscape. These compilations provide a view into the give-and-take between marketed tourist experiences and individual tourist fantasies and the connection between the two.

Mildred Baker produced five elaborate scrapbooks documenting her trips to the Southwest. The first, "Navajo Mountain," details a five-day pack trip to Rainbow Bridge and an "Indian Detour" to Santa Fe and Taos taken in August 1931. Under the guidance of Jack Wilson, proprietor of Rainbow Lodge, Baker and her friend, Florence Huck, rode along the Rainbow Trail from Cliff Canyon through Redbud Pass to Bridge Canyon, where they camped in a natural amphitheater at the base of the bridge. After viewing the bridge, where they entered their names in the registry book, listing themselves as the 1,488th and 1,489th "white people who have ever visited the Bridge," they continued on to the summit of Navajo Mountain and then back to the Rainbow Lodge.[9] From there they commenced the second part of their journey, traveling by train from Flagstaff to Santa Fe, where they stayed at La Fonda Hotel. After seeing the Palace of the Governors and the art museum, they took an Indian Detour to Frijoles Canyon, Ildefonso Pueblo, and the Puyé Cliff Dwellings. They spent the night in Taos, visiting the Pueblo de Taos the next morning, and then returned to Santa Fe to begin their trip home.

Four years later Baker traveled back to the Southwest. After "scanning the literature of the Santa Fe Railroad on Dude Ranches in New Mexico and Arizona," she and her companion, Florence Huck, decided on the Double S Ranch in Cliff, New Mexico, because it "appeared not too 'dudified.'"[10] Her scrapbook, "A Glimpse of the Old West," recounts the experiences of dude ranching, prefaced by tales of Geronimo and Billy the Kid. The pair spent their days riding, hiking, and "botanizing," returning to the ranch house to socialize in the evenings.[11] After a two-week stay at the ranch, Baker and Huck left for El Paso. From there they took a day trip to Carlsbad Caverns and then returned to El Paso for the journey back to Buffalo.

Baker took her next trip to the Southwest in the summer of 1938. As presented in her scrapbook "Peace of Rainbow and Canyon," the three-week tour began with a stop at the Grand Canyon. She and her two companions this time, Florence Huck and Katherine Crisp, rode from the rim at Hilltop down Cataract or Havasu Canyon on the Topocobya Trail. There they stayed with Indian agents, the Shafer family, learning about the Supai Indians, exploring the canyon, and hiking to Mooney Falls. Then they rode back out of the canyon to Bright Angel Lodge and headed, once again, to Rainbow Lodge. The trio repeated the five-day pack trip to Rainbow Bridge that Baker and Huck had done in 1931. Baker continually compared this trip to the earlier trip, exclaiming, "Twice to have seen that glory! Surely I have had a wonderful life to have been given that privilege."[12] After returning to the lodge to get cleaned up and reorganized, the party took a second pack trip to Betatakin, Keet Seel and Inscription House ruins, and Shonto. On their return, they spent one last night at the lodge and then began the trip home.

Mildred Baker's fourth journey to the Southwest marked a departure from her earlier experiences. During her pack trip to Rainbow Lodge in 1938, their party had met up with the Nevill Expedition, which was attempting to navigate the Green and Colorado rivers to Boulder Dam. Baker initiated a correspondence with Norm Nevill, and in 1940 she was invited to join another Nevill raft trip in an attempt to be the first expedition to carry two women

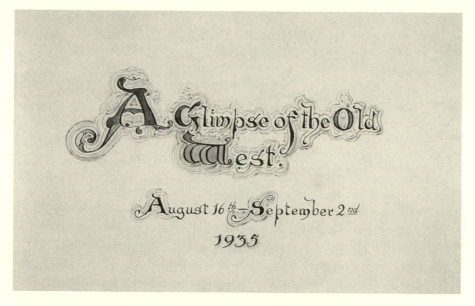

Figure 4.2. Title page from Mildred E. Baker's second travel scrapbook, "A Glimpse of the Old West" (1935). Photographic Collections.

(This item is reproduced by permission of the Huntington Library, San Marino, California.)

down the Colorado and Green rivers. Her scrapbook "Rough Water: Down the Colorado and Green Rivers" provides a chronicle of the trip. This time Baker traveled alone and met up with the rest of the crew, including Norm Nevill and his wife, Doris, "D. W. Deason, assayer of Salt Lake City, John S. Southworth, Mining Engineer of Glendale, California, Dr. Hugh C. Culter of the Missouri Botanical Gardens of St. Louis, Del Reid, Boatman, Woodcarver and prospector of Mexican Hat, Utah, Charles W. Larabee, Official Photographer of Kansas City, Missouri," and herself. Barry Goldwater, future senator of Arizona, and Anne Rosner, a schoolteacher from Chicago, also joined the party.[13] The group rafted 1,163 miles along the Green and Colorado rivers from Green River, Wyoming, to Boulder Dam, stopping to see Rainbow Bridge along the way.[14]

This trip proved more difficult than her earlier forays into the southwestern tourist landscape. As a member of the crew, Baker was no longer simply a guest; rather, she was expected to bear her burden of the work both in camp and on the river. Like her earlier narratives, her scrapbook documents the various campsites and landmarks of the journey, reflecting on her interactions with the wonders of the natural landscape. As a representative of the Buffalo Science Museum, Baker was charged with collecting "specimens." She dutifully listed the birds and plants she sighted. She also commented on the spectacular scenery of the canyons as seen from the river. However, this scrapbook, unlike the others, also contains hints of contention and complaint. Gendered comments about dish duty, headaches, and grandstanding are sprinkled through the narrative.

After her ordeal with the Nevill Expedition, Baker chose to return two years later to a more familiar and less strenuous tourist destination. She took her final documented trip in the summer of 1942 to Rainbow Lodge. Traveling with Florence Huck, Katherine Crisp, and a third companion, Mildred Netsch, Baker and her group were met in Flagstaff by Jack Wilson. On the way to Rainbow Lodge they stopped to inspect various Indian ruins as well as the Painted Desert, the Petrified Forest, and Kayenta. They stayed for a night in Monument Valley to see the sights and take photographs, admiring a Navajo summer hogan and the views of the Rainbow Plateau. Once at Rainbow Lodge the group took a series of pack trips to various destinations: Rainbow Bridge, the summit of Navajo Mountain, some little-known cliff dwellings, and Navajo Canyon. Her scrapbook of the trip, "Turquoise Skies and Copper Canyons," includes a short narrative and lists of the birds, animal life, grasses, trees, shrubs, and miscellaneous plants identified. It is the least polished of her five scrapbooks. She admitted in the final pages that she did not keep good notes of the journey and had to rely on those of Katherine Crisp, suggesting that some of the novelty and wonder of the Southwest had begun to fade for her.[15]

Mildred Baker never explained why she made these scrapbooks or how she used them. Yet a quotation from Sophocles inscribed in one of her western albums provides a clue: "Yea, it becomes a man to cherish memory, where he had delight."[16] Clearly the albums were meant to serve as personal mementos, touchstones for her journeys, that she might return to again and again to refresh her memory. Added clippings, notations, and obituaries suggest that over the years she did return to them. When Otis Marston, a noted river runner and amateur historian of the Colorado River, asked if she kept a diary of her trip, her response revealed its personal value. She wrote, "I did keep a diary of the trip, but am frank to say I should hate to trust it to the mails, for it is the only copy I have and contains photographs as well as written matter. Moreover I have gone to considerable expense to have it hand-bound."[17] In 1974, she wrote to Marston again about her diaries, explaining that a curator from the Huntington Library "came down here and I gave him my Colorado River diary . . . to take for safe-keeping. Also gave him my handbound books, and I have

... willed all of my collection to the library."[18] Four decades after her original journeys, the scrapbooks themselves had become the "priceless possessions" needing "safe-keeping." The reified memories of her tourist experiences had become irreplaceable objects, works of art, to be preserved or passed on to another generation.

Together these five scrapbooks provide a unique and compelling set of sources that reveal the complex and dynamic interplay between Baker's southwestern fantasies and the tourist landscape of the Southwest. As scholars have shown, the Southwest was marketed as a land of enchantment replete with sublime scenery, domesticated Indians, and frontier romance. Following the lead of Fred Harvey and the Santa Fe Railroad, tourist promoters in the Southwest constructed a tourist landscape that revolved around notions of the primitive.[19] The Harvey–Santa Fe partnership "fostered a remarkably coherent—and persistent—version of the Southwest as a region inhabited by peaceful, pastoral people, 'living ruins' from the childhood of civilization."[20] Other tourist promoters added to this primitive imagery, touting the region as the last western frontier, where tourists could rejuvenate themselves by embracing the simple life in an unspoiled wilderness.[21] The tourist's Southwest embodied an authentic, natural, preindustrial culture set in a dramatic desert landscape, offering an ideal escape from workaday urban-industrial routine. As Mildred Baker's scrapbooks show, tourists clearly bought into the marketed ideal of the Southwest. However, Baker's scrapbooks also suggest a more complicated give-and-take between individual fantasy and marketed allure.

Although Baker's scrapbooks give no clear explanation of her fascination with the Southwest and the historical record remains fairly silent about Baker's life, oblique references throughout her narratives and contextual material do begin to illuminate her interests. Born in Buffalo, New York, sometime around 1900, Baker came from an "average" middle-class family. She lived with her mother for her early adult life, not marrying until she was in her mid-forties (after her documented travels to the Southwest).[22] Although she left an estate of $1.5 million to various nature organizations after her death in 1987, she was not a part of the Buffalo elite.[23] Like other single women of her generation, Baker gained some financial independence as a white-collar worker, making somewhere in the realm of $1,500 to $3,500 a year.[24] Her ability to afford these repeated trips to the Southwest during the Depression years (one of which is known to have cost at least $600) suggests an established level of financial security.[25] As a private secretary for Peter C. Cornell, a prominent physician and civic leader, she probably occupied the more professional side of female office work. She worked in this

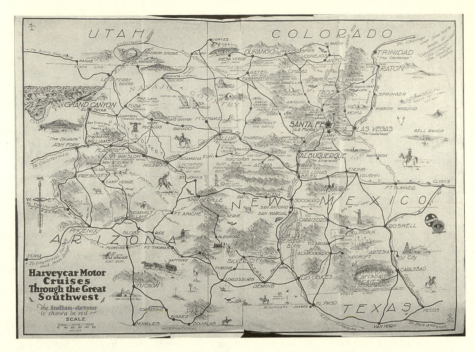

Figure 4.3.   Fred Harvey "Indian Detour" map of the Southwest pasted in Mildred E. Baker's travel scrapbook "Navajo Mountain" (1931).

(This item is reproduced by permission of the Huntington Library, San Marino, California.)

capacity until she married Philip Rosa, a commercial artist, and moved to southern California in 1949. She would marry two more times but have no children. In all, this scant family and occupational history sheds little light on her southwestern journeys.

Rather, it is her avocational interests and pursuits that reveal the context and influence for her tourist experiences. Baker was an active participant in Ernest Thompson Seton's woodcraft movement and an avid birder. Seton, a cofounder of the Boy Scouts of America, had split from the scouts in 1915 to create his own outdoor organization, which came to be known as the Woodcraft League of America.[26] Baker pursued these interests at a noted nature retreat outside of Buffalo known as Sunset Hill. This twenty-one-acre farm, which served as a meeting place for the Ojenta tribe of the Woodcraft League of America, was the summer home of recognized bookbinder John F. Grabau. Grabau had served as an assistant foreman and later shop manager at Elbert Hubbard's Roycroft Press in East Aurora, New York, a nearby sub-urb of Buffalo.[27] Hubbard had been influential in popularizing and promoting the Arts and Crafts movement in the United States.[28] Following Hubbard's example, Grabau had opened his own bookbinding studio in Buffalo in 1905, making hand-tooled books for such distinguished patrons as Theodore Roosevelt, Ernest Thompson Seton, George Wharton James, and Henry Van Dyke. Inspired and aided by his associates Charles Neumann, a local histo-rian who specialized in Native American tribes, and William Alexander, cura-tor of adult education at the Buffalo Museum of Science, and a protégé of Anna Botsford Comstock, the promoter of the Nature Study movement, Grabau completely reshaped the farm into a sanctuary for wildlife and nature appreciation.[29] Drawing from the ideas of the Arts and Crafts movement, the Nature Study movement, and the Woodcraft League of America, Grabau, who in addition to his Roycroft training was also chief of the Ojenta Tribe of the Woodcraft League, designed and built a bungalow using the materials gathered from the farm and then added the Poet's Glen, studio space, and an official Woodcraft Council Ring. He also enhanced the natural environment by planting wildflowers and over eight hundred trees on the property to trans-form the old potato farm into an ideal nature retreat. There Baker partici-pated in Woodcraft League activities: botanizing, bird watching, bookbinding, hiking, camping, reciting poetry, and "playing Indian."[30] It was at Sunset Hill that Baker would have come in contact with the ideas and writings of Ernest Thompson Seton and George Wharton James, both avid advocates for the Southwest and its unique combination of Native American culture and pris-tine wilderness. References from Baker's papers suggest that she had met both men.[31] At Sunset Hill, she associated with a community of like-minded indi-viduals who shared and reinforced her romantic conceptualization of nature and Native Americans. Simultaneously the southwestern mystique and Native American crafts were gaining widespread popularity as tourist mate-rials, popular literature, department stores, and mass circulation magazines marketed the Southwest to an eastern audience.[32]

As a number of historians have explained, the arts and crafts revival and the related enthusiasm for nature study and the woodcraft movement, all in some ways connected with tourism, emerged in the early decades of the twen-tieth century as an ambiguous antimodernist response to the increasing frag-mentation and rationalization of modern urban-industrial living.[33] Just as Teddy Roosevelt advocated for rural living and the strenuous life, upper- and middle-class Americans sought "authentic" experience, "real" life, and self-fulfillment through handcraftsmanship, romantic nature, and the noble sav-age. These forays into an idealized premodern past served as a palliative for

The Ojenta Council Ring
Sunset Hill.

Figure 4.4. Snapshot of the Ojenta Council Ring at Sunset Hill. From Mildred E. Baker's "Birthday" scrapbook (1929). Photographic Collections.

(This item is reproduced by permission of the Huntington Library, San Marino, California.)

the ills of urban-industrial society. As one historian has explained, "Nature study often displayed this primitivist cast, emphasizing holistic experience over the fragmentation of the city and insisting that to feel nature one had to journey back in time to a simpler life, grasp the experience, and then return, richer but unable to articulate what this pseudomystical encounter had been all about."[34] Bored by the bureaucratic, rationalized routines of urban-industrial life, nature enthusiasts, tourists, and the like strove to assuage their longing for the genuine, the handmade, and the real by embracing what they believed was the simple life or escaping temporarily to a seemingly more authentic primitive past.[35] In other words, tourists, "through their own displacement, are looking for that which they feel their own society has lost—nature, purity, wisdom, childhood, originality, freedom."[36]

Baker's "back-to-nature" experiences and activities at Sunset Hill provided a cultural context for her trips to the Southwest, but her narratives also suggest that she followed a long-established tradition of Victorian women travelers who journeyed to exotic places in search of adventure, education, and cultural authority.[37] Like her nineteenth-century predecessors, Baker kept detailed diaries of her travels, she documented the places she visited, and she read widely about her destinations. Her excursions functioned in some measure as extended educational experiences where she could pursue her interests in nature study, botany, ornithology, western history, and Native American culture.

Baker's travel narratives are also steeped in the literature of romanticism, western fiction, and popular ethnography. Clearly literature, as much as experience, provided the substance for her fantasies of the Southwest. Her narratives are sprinkled with quotations and references to Zane Grey's western adventures and Henry Van Dyke's western poetry, among references to other western booster literature. Commenting on the beauty of Surprise Valley during her first pack trip to Rainbow Bridge, she notes, "Sheer cliffs shut in the vale to the east and west, while on the north between the cliffs, one gazes

Figure 4.5. Snapshot of Mildred E. Baker and her friends "playing Indian" at the Sunset Hill Ojenta Council Ring. From Mildred E. Baker's "Birthday" scrapbook (1929). Photographic Collections.

(This item is reproduced by permission of the Huntington Library, San Marino, California.)

over immense boulders down the valley . . . to the red rocks of the Colorado and the looming mass of Wild Horse Mesa. No wonder Zane Grey made this the home of Lassiter and Jane in his 'Riders of the Purple Sage' and 'the Rainbow Trail.'"[38] This literary West was the antithesis of the mundane urban-industrial, overly civilized East. It was a West of untouched wilderness, picturesque Indians, and frontier justice; a romantic frontier populated by cowboys and Indians, frontiersmen and outlaws. This mythological western frontier provided a wide array of stories and predictable settings for tourists to appropriate. Scholars of tourism have argued that many tourists "choose to visit a place in order to rediscover in themselves an identity which they cannot find in their everyday lives."[39] And for a single female office worker like Baker, who might have had some financial independence and perhaps nominal prestige in her job but little social status or power in the male-dominated society of Buffalo, New York, the imaginary geography of the tourist Southwest offered an ideal setting in which to temporarily escape the humdrum of daily existence and find self-fulfillment in acting out the ideal of the strenuous life.

Baker's scrapbooks intermingle promotional literature with personal travelogue, connecting literary allusion with real-life experience in a collage of visual and verbal imagery. Snapshots and postcards, maps and brochures are all mixed together to illustrate the chronicle of her journeys. At times, the line between the promotional and the personal becomes blurred as Baker narrates her experiences. For example, the concluding remarks about her first trip to the Southwest assumed the tone of a tourist brochure. She wrote, "This Navajo Empire through which we just passed is the last domain in the United States where Wilderness and Wildness reign supreme. It is a semi-arid grazing area larger than the States of Massachusetts and Connecticut combined, with a total population of 35,000 pastoral, nomadic Indians, plus a handful of white men—traders and members of the Indian Service. It is a region unspoiled by civilization, where the only wholly self-supporting tribe of Indians in the United States live a happy and industrious life."[40] Snapshots and illustrations also mimicked the promotional material. Illustrating her ride through Red Bud Pass, she juxtaposed a snapshot of the group on the trail with a promotional image. The snapshot is captioned, "Through Red Bud Pass from Cliff Canyon. A very narrow defile, part of which had been blasted out to permit pack animals to pass through." The caption on the tourist image is almost identical: "Climbing down the trail in Redbud Pass. It took four days to blast a way with dynamite, black powder, and T.N.T through one of the three vertical rock ledges."[41] On one level, Baker's scrapbooks read, at times, like booster literature, suggesting that she bought into the marketed tourist image of the Southwest, yet this promotional material is constantly subsumed by the larger collage.

Baker did more than simply copy the visual and verbal imagery used by tourist promoters. She borrowed established strategies of plot used by tourist promoters and popular western fiction to narrate her own journey. Her narratives played on themes of adventure, discovery, and escape and invoked the well-established tourist tropes of exploration, conquest, and romance. Just as historical narratives work as "extended metaphors" that do not simply reproduce events as they actually happened, but rather tell stories that reveal how "to think about events" and that "charge our thought about the events with different emotional valences," so Baker's touring narratives do not simply chronicle her journeys, but rather provide a cultural framework that allows her experiences to be both personally and culturally meaningful.[42] In narrating and illustrating her travels, in translating her experiences into book form, and in arranging and binding these visual and verbal memories into a coherent product with a beginning and an end, a buildup and a climax, Baker was consciously and unconsciously borrowing, responding to, imitating, and adding to a wide array of cultural texts and stories that intersected in the southwestern tourist landscape.[43]

Prefacing the description of her fourth trip to Rainbow Bridge, Baker wrote, "This pack-trip is the key to the wilderness. It is a lesson in self-reliance, in the rare companionship of faint trails and campfires. It is royal sport for anyone with red blood, good health and even a speaking acquaintance with horsemanship. And it brings glorious memories that will abide forever as a hedge against the troubles of civilization."[44] In celebrating wilderness, adventure, and individualism, Baker represented herself as a modern-day pioneer— a rugged individualist braving the challenges and uncertainties of the western frontier. An implicit commentary on gender identity underlies this personal celebration of the wilderness experience. In drawing attention to her vigor and independence, Baker embraced the masculine imagery of the strenuous life and positioned herself as a "new woman" perfectly comfortable and capable in a man's world, albeit the personal and extraordinary world of the tourist landscape. Numerous references throughout her scrapbooks reinforced this imagery. Not only did she draw attention to the dangerous trails "where one mis-step is the end of all misery," but she also characterized her various pack trips as forays into uncharted territory.[45] Also in describing ruins or landforms seen on various rides, she repeatedly remarked that she and her party were "probably the first white people to enter much of the territory covered."[46] Or, as she noted about a ride to Navajo Mountain, "Ours was the first party encircling the Mountain this year, one party had gone through last year, and Mr.

Wilson, our guide had been over the route once four years ago."[47] Despite the fact that she was participating in a tourist experience available to a wide cross section of upper- and middle-class Americans, she used the gendered language and metaphor of discovery to suggest that she was confronting uncharted terrain, mapping new ground.

Similarly, she recounted her interaction with Indians as a kind of "Columbian encounter"—a confrontation between the civilized and the primitive.[48] Describing one of her excursions from Rainbow Lodge, she noted, "K. C. and I, with Violet and Marguerite, went with Bill to Red Shirt's hogan. We stopped enroute to visit a lively young Indian squaw who was outside her hogan making a blanket. We took several pictures. She had a very sweet face and was greatly pleased with the cigarette Marguerite handed her."[49] She then noted that the party went on to purchase rugs and jewelry at the Navajo Mountain Trading Post. As one scholar has explained, encounters between tourists and Indians resulted in unequal exchanges in which Indian reactions were "characterized as uncomprehending, simplemindedly literal, and childlike," while tourists reaped large material benefits.[50]

The mythology of the frontier and references to the Wild West enhanced these metaphors of discovery and exploration. Providing a context for her trip to the Double S Ranch, she wrote, "This whole region is a storied land of romance—and romance that is not so very old at that." She went on to recount the legends of Geronimo and his infamous cattle raids and of Billy the Kid and his murderous escapades, noting, "It was a wild and turbulent country and still is wild and unsettled. A gun is still regarded like a shirt or hat as an ordinary detail of costume."[51] One snapshot of the ranch trip labeled "Me and my bluejeans and tie" drew attention to her "western" attire, suggesting that she was self-consciously aware of playing cowboy.[52] Comments linking the scenery to "movie scenes of western country" also imply that Baker imagined her experience in the context of popular western adventure films.[53]

As part of these metaphors of exploration and discovery, Baker also linked her experience to salvage anthropology and popular ethnography of the Southwest, suggesting that in viewing and photographing Indians and Indian ruins and in consuming Indian crafts, she was in some way engaged in a form of scientific or scholarly pursuit.[54] During her trip to the Grand Canyon she quoted from George Wharton James's *In and Around the Grand Canyon* and then noted of her own experience: "In going and coming on this trip we passed a hewa or hogan of an old Indian woman who claims to be 107 years old. She still makes baskets too, and while she looks old, she certainly does not seem as ancient as that. The young women too are making

Me and my blue jeans and tie. Helen Younger at left.

Figure 4.6. Snapshot of Mildred E. Baker in front of the corral at the Double S Ranch in Cliff, New Mexico. From Mildred E. Baker's scrapbook "A Glimpse of the Old West" (1935).

(This item is reproduced by permission of the Huntington Library, San Marino, California.)

baskets again and I bought a small tray made of willow and cat's claw made by Mecca Uquella."[55] Similarly, describing the drive from Kayenta to Monument Valley, she recounted, "We packed our camera equipment, for of all places where you want plenty of film, this is one of the best. In the afternoon we came to a Navajo's summer hogan where we had a photographer's paradise of picture-taking of the older women weaving, spinning and carding wool, grinding corn etc."[56] Snapshots and tourist images pasted in her scrapbooks served to illustrate her observations. Informative captions such as "Looking into the home of an ancient cliff dweller" or "Ladder leading to the ruins of communal dwellings at top of Puyé Cliff" explained the significance of her snapshots.[57] These images were juxtaposed with tourist images with labels such as "In a 'modern' pueblo where one may catch archeology alive."[58] As a kind of personal reaffirmation, Baker scripted her consumption of Indians through the tourist spectacle as part of the scholarly and scientific process of discovery and observation in which she was engaged.

Baker also embraced this scientific perspective in describing the landscape and wildlife of the Southwest. In effect, she positioned herself as an amateur practitioner of geology, ornithology, and botany. Her association with William P. Alexander, the curator of adult education at the Buffalo Museum of Science, and her charge to do "fieldwork" for the museum legitimized the tone of scientific observation. Each of her scrapbooks is appended with a list of the birds, plants, and animals she encountered on her trips. She also sprinkled her narratives with observations of animal behavior and geologic formations and with botanical notes. For example, on her raft trip down the Colorado and Green rivers, describing the passage from Chokecherry Draw to Flaming Gorge, which she identified as "the gateway to the canyons," she noted, "The color is, as one would assume, red but not more so than any of the other canyons and there is some displacement of strata running up about six or seven hundred feet. Above there were Douglass Fir, Western Yellow Pine and Juniper, while along the water's edge there were willows and alder thickets."[59] Or commenting on the wildlife, she wrote, "Again bird life was abundant. A red-tail hawk was being molested by two swallows, evidently having come too close to their nests for their comfort. The cliff swallows nests were plastered all along the cliffs. Many robins were singing happily, while in the stream ahead of us I saw my first western grebe."[60] The narrative goes on to comment on sightings of Canada geese, rabbits, and great blue herons. Similarly, her scrapbook from the Double S Ranch trip included remnants of flowers and grasses, with such labels as "piece of Gamma Grass" or "Specimen of Red Gum" pressed between the pages, revealing her penchant for "botanizing."[61] Baker assumed the role of amateur naturalist and in the process translated her experiences, which resulted from a commercial exchange, into educational terms. Through this language and imagery of scientific and scholarly observation, Baker transformed the tourist experience from a purchased tour into an educational experience—a middlebrow consumer experience into a highbrow cultural experience.

At the same time that Baker characterized her experiences in terms of science and exploration, she also scripted her tourist journeys as romantic wilderness adventures, celebrating her trips as solitary encounters with untouched nature. "To few people is given the privilege of life in the wilds in these days of supercivilization," Baker wrote in the opening sentences describing her first trip to Rainbow Bridge.[62] Sublime nature not only offered an antidote to the ills of urban-industrial culture, but also a sense of therapeutic escape. The presence of nature at times overwhelmed Baker. Viewing the Grand Canyon from the Colorado River, she wrote, "This is the beginning of the Grand Canyon, and to say that I was thrilled because I was down in the Canyon is putting it mildly. Words are utterly useless in trying to describe how I felt. . . . Surely in all the wide world there is no more glorious sight than these canyon walls. I wanted to cry because of the beauty of it all—a land 'whose beauty takes the breath like pain.'"[63] Similarly, she depicted a night in camp along the Colorado River: "I had the feeling of a protecting sky closely enfolding me, with the whole world below and the stars within arm's reach. These glorious nights, although we did not sleep well, were worth the whole trip, the glow of moonlight on the canyon walls, the glittering stars, the mysterious wilderness were incomparably beautiful."[64] Encounters with Indians were also described in romantic terms. Commenting on the Indians at Pueblo de Taos, she wrote, "The youths of this tribe seem to be more handsome than any Indians we had seen before. The dark slender maidens have an Italian sort of beauty and the young men have fine features and trim, athletic physiques, while the costumes are most picturesque."[65] Using the language of the sublime, Baker also glorified the experience of viewing the dramatic natural landscapes of the Southwest in terms of spiritual renewal. "'We thank the Lord, for such spots of peace as this, where the soul finds strength and healing,'" she wrote after viewing the Rainbow Bridge by moonlight.[66] From the vantage point of the solitary observer, Romantic nature offered intense, emotional, authentic experiences in contrast to the artificiality of modern existence.

However, Baker's scrapbooks were not simply seamless webs of prescribed tourist prose and imagery. Hints of contradiction and complaint suggest a more complicated interplay between the marketed tourist landscape and her personal appropriation of the tourist experience. Specifically, her characterizations of Indians and the wilderness experience reveal contention in the narratives. Although Baker's scrapbooks convey a fascination with the tourist Indians, the depictions of her encounters with real Indians exhibit a certain uneasiness. Navajo Indians served as assistants and guides on many of her Rainbow Lodge pack trips. Baker named and photographed them in her scrapbooks as part of the larger southwestern tourist experience. However, she often expressed dissatisfaction with or distrust toward her Indian guides. On a pack trip to Navajo Canyon she noted that at one point the two guides had to leave the party to find another guide, because they were uncertain about the trails. Baker grew concerned about water and safety. "We really did not relish being left alone here with so many Navajos wandering freely around, but there seemed no help for it," she wrote.[67] To photograph and interact with domesticated tourist Indians who were usually women was one thing; to depend on Navajo men as guides and equals was quite another. Baker's unease with Navajos "wandering freely" exposed the charade of the tourist fantasy. Only captive or domesticated Indians were safe. Picturesque and exotic tourist Indians who willingly collaborated in the staged authenticity of the southwestern tourist experience were acceptable and appealing because they were, in effect, willing prisoners of the tourist spectacle.[68] As objects on display, they became aestheticized consumer products.[69] The real Navajo—the "interior Indians, those within American social boundaries"—on the other hand, represented capricious ethnic Others who threatened the predictability of the tourist spectacle and challenged the tourist's control of the tourist experience.[70]

The dissonance in Baker's narratives between her enchantment with the tourist Indians and her uncertainty about the intelligence and reliability of the Navajo guides, as well as her concern about the Navajos "wandering freely," revealed Baker's underlying fantasy of the Southwest. She was not embracing the Southwest on its own terms, but rather imposing her own expectations and anxieties onto the tourist experience. Those expectations and anxieties in the context of the tourist landscape and experience helped to define the Southwest as a region. Indians were acceptable as long as they conformed to conceptualizations of Indianness that extended from playing Indian and popular literary Indians. When Indians challenged the predictability and familiarity of her tourist narrative, they became disturbing. Yet the southwestern tourist experience in some ways depended on this tension between tourist Indians and real Indians. Real Indians added an unpredictable sense of drama to the tourist experience. The threat of real Indians made the staged authenticity of the tourist experience seem all the more real.

Baker's appreciation of the southwestern tourist landscape also depended on very specific ideas about how to understand and experience nature. She understood the dramatic landscapes and the flora and fauna of the Southwest in both reverential and educational terms. The wilderness experience was meant to inspire the soul and uplift the mind. Any deviation from this romantic view spoiled the allure of nature. The many tours and pack trips she took while visiting the Southwest supported this perspective. The rustic accommodations of Rainbow Lodge combined with the full-service pack trips allowed tourists like Baker to rough it in style. For example, on one of her pack trips to Rainbow Bridge she noted that the party camped at a permanent camp in the natural amphitheater near the bridge. There the guides "brought out our cots with real mattresses and spread our bed rolls on them under the stars."[71] With all of their needs cared for, tourists were free to focus solely on the wonders of nature. Like the tourist Indians, nature was domesticated through the production of the tourist spectacle, and this wilderness tourist fantasy depended on the comforts of full service.

Most of Baker's experiences on her southwestern travels resulted in romantic encounters with the southwestern landscape. However, at times,

Very old Navajo at Red Lake Trading Post. Note shirt-tail hanging out.

Figure 4.7. Breaking from the more stereotypical and pervasive images of Native American guides and tourist attractions, this snapshot presents a more disparaging view of the Native Americans Baker encountered in her travels of the Southwest. From Mildred E. Baker's scrapbook "Peace of Rainbow and Canyon" (1938).

(This item is reproduced by permission of the Huntington Library, San Marino, California.)

nature or guides did not cooperate, and this spoiled her wilderness adventure. Baker's narrative of her raft trip down the Colorado and Green rivers with the Nevill Expedition revealed these fissures in her wilderness fantasies. Not only was this the most physically challenging of her tourist excursions to the Southwest, it was also the farthest removed from the standardized southwestern tourist experience of the period. As a member of the crew, Baker was not afforded the luxuries of roughing it in style. Rather, she was expected to do her share of the work of maintaining the boats and setting up camp. She explained later that she had agreed to help with the cooking in exchange for an allowance to discount the cost of the trip but that she never received it.[72] Although she tried to narrate her experiences using the standard tourist tropes of adventure, discovery, and romance, veiled complaints and quarrels fractured these formulaic narratives. Issues of gender and class constantly intruded on her tourist fantasy. For example, extolling the possibilities for bird watching, she noted, "What a chance for an ornithological expedition down these rivers! The willow thickets along the shores were alive with birds, which would fly ahead as we approached." However, she lamented, "And as I was in the last boat, I never did get a good look at them."[73] She also complained of bad headaches that were exacerbated by rocks and rapids. As one entry recounted, "We hit many rapids today, some two-liners, which did not help a bad headache that was bothering me. We hit rocks continually, and in one of the rapids when we whammed up against a rock, a most violent pain shot through my head, the first direct re-action."[74] Recollecting the trip, she commented, "It turned out I worked my way down the canyons. I'd work like mad. . . . The men did nothing to help in cooking the whole trip. . . . Sometimes I was so dead tired from constant work at night—our camps were no pleasure."[75] Wet clothes and gear, dish duty, and competition among the men in the party resulted in dissatisfaction.

She grew particularly cross with Norm Nevill, the leader of the expedition. Not only did she dislike his grandstanding, but she also felt that he viewed the trip as a mere publicity stunt rather than as a scientific expedition or wilderness adventure. His lack of reverence for the wilderness experience particularly galled her. At one point she noted in her diary that Norm was "incapable of slowing down to enjoy the scenery."[76] Describing a hike from the river to Rainbow Bridge, she revealed her displeasure. "We went at a rapid pace without stopping except for a pause at a spring," she commented irritably, "all the time Norm either singing at the top of his not-too-good voice, or spouting inane chatter, when I so wanted to enjoy the peace and quiet of that to me—well-nigh holy spot."[77] Norm's irreverence disturbed the sanctity of the nature experience, as did his lack of chivalry. He failed to assist her with the torn sole of her shoe and only lent a helping hand on a difficult part of the trail after she had to ask. She even intimated that Norm put her, Anne, and his wife, Doris, in danger when climbing up the bridge. She recounted,

> Norm decided we should not use the rope, which we had brought along, despite the fact that Hugh had previously advised me not to attempt it without the rope. There is an iron ring fastened above to secure the rope, but Norm thought we would make a better record if we did not use the rope. He made Doris, who had a bum leg at the time, climb down and up without the rope, but Anne and I refused point-blank to risk a broken leg in the wilderness for any whim of Norm's, so when it finally dawned on him that we meant it, he held the rope for Anne and myself.[78]

She later commented that "Norm was really unbearable."[79] Clearly, Norm did not measure up to her previous guides, who were quick to assist at any sign of difficulty or discomfort. Norm wanted to conquer nature; Baker wanted to revere it. Baker wanted Natty Bumpo, but instead she got a crass river runner. Consequently, Norm's bravado spoiled Baker's enchanted view of Rainbow Bridge. Once at the bridge the party met up with the Wilsons from Rainbow Lodge and Baker admitted, "Had it not been for being considered a quitter, our whole crowd agreed that right then and there they would have gone back to the lodge with them."[80] The Wilsons provided a welcome foil to Norm's disrespectful bluster.

These moments of complaint and contention reveal that Baker's understanding and appreciation of the tourist's Southwest depended on a culturally and individually prescribed interpretation of the nature experience. Baker embraced what one scholar has called the romantic form of the tourist gaze "in which the emphasis is upon solitude, privacy and a personal, semi-spiritual relationship with the object of the gaze."[81] From this perspective the tourist could contemplate the self in spiritual terms; she could imagine her life in creative ways, far removed from the seemingly inauthentic humdrum of the modern world. Although Baker's narratives used the established tourist tropes of discovery and adventure to celebrate the frontier West, she rejected any notion of conquest or triumph in connection with the nature experience. Any challenge to the romantic view of nature as sanctuary or laboratory seemed blasphemous in her view. Norm's behavior disturbed Baker because it sullied her ideal of pristine nature with issues of class, commercialism, and sexism. Baker implicitly and explicitly criticized Norm for his lack of education, his crassness, his selfishness, his arrogance, and his propensity for self-promotion. From her perspective, Norm did not understand his place in nature. She insinuated that Norm was not a gentleman because he did not approach nature with the proper respect and reverence. Consequently, he shattered the illusion of Baker's tourist fantasy. But Baker's criticisms also reveal the underlying assumptions and limitations of her romantic view of nature. She embraced an elitist and exclusionary view of nature, a view that served to mask and even obfuscate the social and commercial realities that underlay the tourist experience.

Baker's touring narratives reveal that individual tourists were not just pawns of "corporate dominion," market manipulation, capitalist hegemony, and hedonistic consumption.[82] Rather, tourism represented a cultural dialectic in which tourists invested the marketed experience with their own culturally defined dreams and memories.[83] The allure of the tourist experience resulted from a dynamic interplay between individual desires, associated meanings derived from cultural texts and images, and marketed fantasy. Tourists, in buying, embracing, one might even say, collaborating with the staged authenticity of tourism, shared in the production of the tourist experience. They engaged in controlled or bounded fantasies, setting their quest for authentic experience and a larger sense of individual meaning and identity within a scripted landscape shaped and defined by cultural texts and commercial aims.

Tourists such as Baker were drawn to the tourist experience because of its predictable, yet still intriguing, narratives. The scripted tourist landscapes offered comprehendible stories in which the individual (the tourist) could participate in an ongoing drama. Tourist sites act as stage sets. Through the mechanisms of tourism, places are transformed into scenery and spectacle. As spectator, voyeur, actor, and consumer, the tourist stands at the center, empowered by the all-encompassing tourist gaze not only to possess the tourist landscape, but also to weave a totalizing narrative. Predictable tourist narratives gave tourists the opportunity to temporarily re-imagine themselves in creative ways and thus transcend the confines of their everyday social identities. In this way tourism provided a welcome contrast to the sense of anonymity, powerlessness, inauthenticity, and fragmentation that characterized the monotony and the routine of modern existence.

As Baker's scrapbooks reveal, the Southwest, with its formulaic stories of western adventure, picturesque Indians, and scientific discovery, provided a particularly alluring dreamscape for tourists who sought a temporary respite from urban-industrial society. In narrating the tourist experience as a process of discovering uncharted territory, observing exotic cultures, and communing with nature, Baker tried to revive and act out the American ideal of rugged individualism on the western frontier. She left behind her home and job, with all the associated social and cultural expectations, for a world of fantasy where she could re-imagine herself as a heroic figure. Western drama transformed tourism from an experience of passive consumption into an encounter of active agency. Dramatic desert and canyon landscapes combined with the remnants of preindustrial Indian cultures offered an ideal stage set for tourists to refashion themselves by playing cowboy or Indian, ethnographer or pioneer. In the southwestern tourist landscape Baker was no longer a mere secretary from Buffalo, New York; she became a western adventurer—a cohort of Zane Grey's Lassiter and Jane, a companion of George Wharton James, a follower of John Wesley Powell. But more importantly, she became the narrator, in control of her own story.

The Indian in me coming out at last.

Betatakin

Figure 4.8. Tourists such as Mildred E. Baker used the southwestern tourist experience to re-imagine themselves and play "American." Snapshot from Mildred E. Baker's scrapbook "Peace of Rainbow and Canyon" (1938). Photographic Collections.

(This item is reproduced by permission of the Huntington Library, San Marino, California.)

As the article on scrapbooks in *Martha Stewart Living* reveals, Mildred Baker's scrapbooks are not just historical aberrations. Tourists today are still very much engaged in making tourist mementos. Now the process is both easier and more complex. Hallmark stores and the Exposures catalog sell an array of scrapbooking supplies ranging from leather-bound photo albums and blank books, which can be stamped with gilded titles of the purchaser's choice, to old-fashioned photo corners, archival glue, and acid-free paper to ensure that one's memories will last a lifetime. "Martha Stewart," Martha Stewart's web page, offers a Folding Memories Book, Heirloom Photo Albums, and a Travel Watercolor Set so that you can paint your own post-cards.[84] These businesses have capitalized on the fact that tourists still want to personalize and memorialize their individual journeys. And I think new technologies will only up the ante. The MTV generation will not be content with surround sound and the participant feel of IMAX. Rather, they will want to star in, direct, and produce their own tourist movies with video cams and digital cameras. Tourism was and still is about the possibilities of consumption, and ultimately, the paradoxical promise remains the same: individual, one-of-a-kind, self-fulfilling experiences as a mass-produced phenomenon.

Acknowledgments

In addition to the participants at the Southern Methodist University seminar at the Fort Burgwin Campus, Taos, New Mexico, September 24–26, 1999—William L. Bryant, Jr., Leah Dilworth, Jane Elder, Susan Guyette, Sylvia Rodriguez, Hal Rothman, David Weber, David White, and Chris Wilson—I am indebted to William Deverell, Phoebe Kropp, Martin Ridge, and Jennifer Watts for reading and commenting on this essay.

Notes

1. Coco Meyers, "Scrapbooks," *Martha Stewart Living*, September 1998, 236–45. Quotations from pages 237 and 242.
2. Scholars have contributed to this negative characterization of the tourist. In particular Daniel Boorstin has described tourism as a "pseudo-event": a "diluted, contrived, prefabricated" experience. See Daniel J. Boorstin, "From Traveler to Tourist: The Lost Art of Travel," in *The Image: A Guide to Pseudo Events in America* (New York: Atheneum, 1980), 79.
3. The *Oxford English Dictionary* notes in its definition of *tourism* that the word is "usually depreciatory." *Oxford English Dictionary*, vol. 11 (Oxford: Clarendon Press, 1933), 190.
4. On southwestern tourism see Barbara A. Babcock, "'A New Mexican Rebecca': Imaging Pueblo Women," *Journal of the Southwest* 32 (1990): 400–437; Barbara A. Babcock,

"Bearers of Value, Vessels of Desire: The Reproduction of the Reproduction of Pueblo Culture," *Museum Anthropology* 17 (October 1993): 43–57; Leah Dilworth, *Imagining Indians in the Southwest: Persistent Visions of a Primitive Past* (Washington, D.C.: Smithsonian Institution Press, 1996); Scott Norris, ed., *Discovered Country: Tourism and Survival in the American West* (Albuquerque, N.Mex.: Stone Ladder Press, 1994); Sylvia Rodriguez, "The Tourist Gaze, Gentrification, and the Commodification of Subjectivity in Taos," in *Essays on the Changing Images of the Southwest*, eds. Richard Francaviglia and David Narrett (College Station, Tex.: Texas A&M Press, 1994), 105–26; "Art, Tourism, and Race Relations in Taos: Toward a Sociology of the Art Colony," *Journal of Anthropological Research* 45 (spring 1989): 77–99; Marta Weigle, "Finding the 'True America': Ethnic Tourism in New Mexico During the New Deal," *Folklife Annual 88–89* (1989): 58–73; Marta Weigle, "From Desert to Disney World: The Santa Fe Railway and the Fred Harvey Company Display the Indian Southwest," *Journal of Anthropological Research* 45 (1989): 115–37; Marta Weigle, "Southwest Lures: Innocents Detoured, Incensed Determined," *Journal of the Southwest* 32 (1990): 499–540; Marta Weigle, "Exposition and Mediation: Mary Colter, Erna Fergusson, and the Santa Fe/Harvey Popularization of the Native Southwest, 1902–1940," *Frontiers: A Journal of Women Studies* 12 (summer 1991): 117–50; Marta Weigle and Barbara Babcock, eds., *The Great Southwest of the Fred Harvey Company and the Santa Fe Railway* (Phoenix: Heard Museum, 1996); and Chris Wilson, *The Myth of Santa Fe: Creating a Modern Regional Tradition* (Albuquerque: University of New Mexico Press, 1997).

5. Mildred E. Baker, "Rough Water," *American Forests* 50 (November 1944): 573; Mildred Baker, Letters—Comment, 1948–1949, Otis Marston Manuscripts, Huntington Library, San Marino, Calif. Hereafter cited as Marston Mss.

6. Warren I. Susman, *Culture as History: The Transformation of American Society in the Twentieth Century* (New York: Pantheon Books, 1984), xx. For the historiography of consumer culture studies see Jean-Christophe Agnew, "Coming Up for Air: Consumer Culture in Historical Perspective," in *Consumption and the World of Goods*, eds. John Brewer and Roy Porter (New York: Routledge, 1993); and *Acknowledging Consumption: A Review of New Studies*, ed. Daniel Miller (New York: Routledge, 1995).

7. For a discussion of tourism as consumption see Hal K. Rothman, *Devil's Bargains: Tourism in the Twentieth-Century West* (Lawrence: University Press of Kansas, 1998), 10–28.

8. Little scholarly work has been done on tourist mementos. On souvenirs see Joe Benson and Rob Silverman, "Tourist Photographs as Souvenirs," *Prospects* 11 (1987): 261–72. On family photograph albums see Richard Chalfen, *Turning Leaves: The Photographic Collections of Two Japanese American Families* (Albuquerque: University of New Mexico Press, 1991).

9. Mildred E. Baker, "Navajo Mountain," 18, Mildred E. Baker Collection, Album 237, Photographic Collections, Huntington Library. Hereafter cited as Baker Scrapbooks.

10. Mildred E. Baker, "Glimpses of the Old West," 1, Baker Scrapbooks.

11. Ibid., n.p.

12. Mildred E. Baker, "Peace of Rainbow and Canyon," 13, Baker Scrapbooks.

13. Mildred E. Baker, "Rough Water: Down the Colorado and Green Rivers," 2, Baker Scrapbooks.

14. For an overview of the Nevill Expedition see David Lavender, *River Runners of the Grand Canyon* (Grand Canyon, Ariz.: Grand Canyon Natural History Association, 1985), 96–105; and Roy Webb, *Call of the Colorado* (Moscow, Idaho: University of Idaho Press, 1994), 106–7, 133.

15. Mildred E. Baker, "Turquoise Skies and Copper Canyons," Baker Scrapbooks.

16. Mildred E. Baker, "Wilderness Wanderings in Jasper and Mt. Robinson Parks, July 3rd to 23rd, 1936," 6, Baker Scrapbooks.

17. Mildred E. Baker to Otis Marston, 8 January 1948. Mildred Baker, Letters—Comments, 1948–1949, Marston Mss.

18. Mildred Baker McVey to Otis Marston, 26 February 1974. Mildred Baker McVey, 1950–1974, Marston Mss.

19. For example, see Weigle and Babcock, eds., *The Great Southwest of the Fred Harvey Company and the Santa Fe Railway*.

20. Dilworth, *Imagining Indians in the Southwest*, 78–79.

21. For example, see Rothman, *Devil's Bargains*, 113–42.

22. Phone interview, Richard Rosche, Pasadena, Calif., 5 January 2000; and phone interview, Winston Brockner, Pasadena, Calif., 7 January 2000.

23. Joseph DiDomenico, "The Mildred Baker McVey Inheritance," *The Prothonotary* 58 (February 1992): 20. Facsimile supplied by Lisa Seivert, Buffalo Museum of Science Library, Buffalo, N.Y.

24. On white-collar office work for women see Nancy F. Cott, *The Grounding of Modern Feminism* (New Haven: Yale University Press, 1987), 131–33. For clerical salary estimates during the 1920s and 1930s see *Historical Statistics of the United States: Colonial Times to 1970, Part I* (Washington, D.C.: Government Printing Office, 1975), 321; and Scott Derks, ed., *The Value of a Dollar: Prices and Incomes in the United States, 1860–1989* (Detroit: Gale Research Inc., 1994), 232–33, 260–61.

25. Baker told Otis Marston that she paid $600 to participate in the Nevill Expedition (Mildred Baker Journal, 1940, Marston Mss.).

26. For a history of Ernest Thompson Seton and the Woodcraft League of America see H. Allen Anderson, *The Chief: Ernest Thompson Seton and the Changing West* (College Station, Tex.: Texas A&M University Press, 1986). See also Philip J. Deloria, *Playing Indian* (New Haven: Yale University Press, 1998), 97–127.

27. "John F. Grabau Dies at 70; Famed for Leather Artistry," *Buffalo Evening News*, 21 June 1948. Facsimile supplied by Lisa Seivert, Buffalo Museum of Science Library, Buffalo, N.Y.

28. For a history of Elbert Hubbard and his influence on the Arts and Crafts movement in the United States see T. J. Jackson Lears, *No Place of Grace: Antimodernism and the Transformation of American Culture, 1880–1920* (New York: Pantheon, 1981), 68–75; Robert Koch, "Elbert Hubbard's Roycrofters as Artist-Craftsmen," *Winterthur Portfolio* 3 (1967): 67–82; Marie Via and Marjorie Searl, eds., *Head, Heart and Hand: Elbert Hubbard and the Roycrofters* (Rochester, N.Y.: University of Rochester Press, 1994).

29. "William P. Alexander Dies; 20 Years at Museum of Science," facsimile supplied by Lisa Seivert, Buffalo Museum of Science Library, Buffalo, N.Y.; and "C. A. Neumann Dies; Historian on Indian Tribes," facsimile supplied by Lisa Seivert, Buffalo Museum of Science Library, Buffalo, N.Y.

30. For information on Sunset Hill see clipping "Nature Lover's Paradise All but Forgotten," 19 September 1962; Book Binding and Photos of Sunset Hill; "Remembrance Book of Sunset Hill"; "Anthology of Sunset Hill"; and clipping "Woodcraft Chief Makes Wild Life Sanctuary of Farm," in untitled Birthday book to Mildred E. Baker, 23 December 1929; all in Baker Scrapbooks.

31. "Remembrance Book of Sunset Hill" includes a clipping showing Mildred Baker and her friends Florence Huck, Katherine Crisp, and J. Berbard Bogel "of the Ojenta book-binding class" giving Ernest Thompson Seton a hand-bound book. Also Baker gave a number of inscribed books to the Huntington Library, including *The Gospel of the Red Man*, by Ernest Thompson Seton, and almost all of George Wharton James's publications.

32. Erika Bsumek, "Making 'Indian Made': The Production, Consumption, and Legal Construction of Navajo Identity, 1890–1930" (Ph.D. diss., Rutgers University, 1999).

33. Lears, *No Place of Grace*, 68–75.

34. Deloria, *Playing Indian*, 102.

35. For a history of the simple life see David E. Shi, *The Simple Life: Plain Living and High Thinking in American Culture* (New York: Oxford, 1985).

36. Marie-Françoise Lanfant, "International Tourism, Internationalization and the Challenge to Identity," in *International Tourism: Identity and Change*, eds. Marie-Françoise Lanfant, John B. Allcock, and Edward M. Bruner (London: Sage, 1995), 35.

37. Maria H. Frawley, *A Wider Range: Travel Writing by Women in Victorian England* (London: Associated University Press, 1994).

38. Baker, "Navajo Mountain," 35; Baker Scrapbooks.

39. Marie Françoise Lanfant et al., "Introduction," in *International Tourism*, 9.

40. Baker, "Navajo Mountain," 46, Baker Scrapbooks.

41. Ibid., 16.

42. Hayden White, "The Historical Text as Literary Artifact," in *The Writing of History: Literary Form and Historical Understanding*, eds. Robert H. Canary and Henry Kozicki (Madison: University of Wisconsin Press, 1978), 52, 53.

43. For a discussion of the ways in which individual narratives are shaped by surrounding cultural texts, see Jay Clayton and Eric Rothstein, eds., *Influence and Intertextuality in Literary History* (Madison: University of Wisconsin Press, 1991).

44. Baker, "Turquoise Skies and Copper Canyons," 1, Baker Scrapbooks.

45. Baker, "Navajo Mountain," 34, Baker Scrapbooks.

46. Baker, "Turquoise Skies and Copper Canyons," 29, Baker Scrapbooks.

47. Baker, "Navajo Mountain," 26, Baker Scrapbooks.

48. For a discussion of the tourist experience as "Columbian encounter," see Dilworth, *Imagining Indians in the Southwest*, 77–124.

49. Baker, "Peace of Rainbow and Canyon," 18, Baker Scrapbooks.

50. Dilworth, *Imagining Indians in the Southwest*, 119–20.

51. Baker, "A Glimpse of the Old West," 4, 5, Baker Scrapbooks.

52. Ibid., n.p.

53. Ibid., 13.

54. For a discussion of the tourist experience as an extension of salvage anthropology and popular ethnography see Weigle and Babcock, eds., *The Great Southwest of the Fred Harvey Company and the Santa Fe Railway*, 1–8.

55. Baker, "Peace of Rainbow and Canyon," 9, Baker Scrapbooks.

56. Baker, "Turquoise Skies and Copper Canyons," 12–13, Baker Scrapbooks.

57. Baker, "Navajo Mountain," 57, 67, Baker Scrapbooks.

58. Ibid., 66.

59. Baker, "Rough Water," 12, Baker Scrapbooks.

60. Ibid., 10.

61. Baker, "A Glimpse of the Old West," n.p., Baker Scrapbooks.

62. Baker, "Navajo Mountain," 5, Baker Scrapbooks.

63. Baker, "Rough Water," 82, Baker Scrapbooks.

64. Ibid., 28–29.

65. Baker, "Navajo Mountain," 11, Baker Scrapbooks.

66. Baker, "Peace of Rainbow and Canyon," 13, Baker Scrapbooks.

67. Baker, "Turquoise Skies and Copper Canyons," 32, Baker Scrapbooks.

68. For a discussion of staged authenticity see Dean MacCannell, *The Tourist: A New Theory of the Leisure Class* (New York: Schocken Books, 1989), 91–107.

69. As Leah Dilworth argues, "In the touristic encounter with Indians, the tourist is always the receiver of information; the Indian is always the object of the gaze, a commodity to be consumed visually." (See Dilworth, "Discovering Indians in Fred Harvey's Southwest," in *The Great Southwest of the Fred Harvey Company*, eds. Weigle and Babcock, 163.)

70. Deloria, *Playing Indian*, 103.

71. Baker, "Peace of Rainbow and Canyon," 13, Baker Scrapbooks.

72. Mildred E. Baker Journal, 1940, Notes, Marston Mss.

73. Baker, "Rough Water," 23, Baker Scrapbooks.

74. Ibid., 32.

75. Notes, Otis Marston interview with Mildred E. Baker, 15 April 1948; Letters—Comments, 1948–49; both in Marston Mss.

76. Baker, "Rough Water," 28, Baker Scrapbooks.

77. Ibid., 67.

78. Ibid., 68.

79. Notes, Otis Marston interview with Mildred E. Baker, 15 April 1948; Letters—Comments, 1948–1949; both in Marston Mss.

80. Baker, "Rough Water," 73, Baker Scrapbooks.

81. John Urry, *Consuming Places* (New York: Routledge, 1995), 137.

82. For a discussion of the idea of corporate dominion see Marta Weigle and Kathleen L. Howard, "'To Experience the Real Grand Canyon': Santa Fe/Harvey Panopticism, 1901–1935," in *The Great Southwest of the Fred Harvey Company*, eds. Weigle and Babcock, 23.

83. Defining a theory of modern consumption, Colin Campbell argues that "many cultural products offered for sale in modern societies are in fact consumed because they serve as aids to the construction of day dreams." He goes on to note, "Fragments of stories or images taken from books or films are often used as the foundation stories for these continually extended dream edifices." See Colin Campbell, *The Romantic Ethic and the Spirit of Modern Consumption* (Oxford: Basil Blackwell, 1987), 92–93.

84. See http://www.marthabymail.com.

"HANDMADE BY AN AMERICAN INDIAN"

SOUVENIRS AND THE CULTURAL ECONOMY

OF SOUTHWESTERN TOURISM

LEAH DILWORTH

No-one is interested in other people's souvenirs.
—Susan Pearce, *Museums, Objects, and Collections*

At the risk of proving Susan Pearce right, I'm going to begin by writing about two souvenirs that belong to me.

The first is a souvenir of my childhood. It is a kachina purchased for me by my parents at a trading post in Tuba City, Arizona, while we were on a family vacation to the Grand Canyon when I was about ten years old. I had a collection of dolls at home that friends and relatives had given to me. The dolls were mainly from "foreign" lands, where these adults had traveled. At some point in the mounting excitement as we prepared for the vacation, my parents told me that they would like to buy me a kachina "doll" to add to my collection. I had no idea what a kachina was or who the Hopis were, but it sounded neat, and it thrilled me that my parents seemed to place so much importance on it. I remember Tuba City as a great disappointment, basically a dusty crossroads. The trading post, though, was interesting, full of all sorts of exotic items. Behind a counter were shelves filled with kachinas, which I thought were strange looking and not very appealing. After talking to the white saleslady, my parents selected two for me to choose from. Measuring about a foot tall each, they had human bodies but odd, robotlike heads. I had no idea how to choose; these were alien objects, completely beyond my ken. One was new looking and was holding a bow and arrow and cost $20; the other held a rattle and what looked like a deer antler and seemed a bit faded. It cost $18. As

I stood between my parents, unable to decide, the saleslady offered some information: the faded one had been used by a Hopi family. This seemed meaningful to my parents, and I could feel the balance tip in favor of the "used" kachina. Relieved, I said I would take that one. Back home, the kachina quickly became my prized possession. It was too tall to fit on the shelf with the other dolls, so I put it on a shelf by itself. There it seemed to reign over all my

Figure 5.1. Hopi kachina doll.

Author's "collection."

other childish possessions. I decided that the kachina would be the one thing out of all my belongings I would save if our house were burning down.[1]

The other souvenir I want to discuss was given to me by a coworker at my part-time proofreading job while I was in graduate school. He knew I was interested in southwestern Indian things, and when he came across this object at a garage sale in Philadelphia, he bought it for a dollar. The object is, I suppose, another souvenir doll, representing a miniature Navajo weaver seated before a loom. The weaver is wearing a purple velvet blouse and a beaded necklace. She sits on a piece of real sheepskin, and beside her is a swaddled baby doll. There is a half-completed weaving on the loom. On the bottom of the base of this object is a bright orange sticker that reads "HAND MADE BY AN AMERICAN INDIAN."

As souvenirs of the Southwest, these objects reveal, first, some of the major themes of tourism in the region and, second, how souvenirs function, how they carry or make meaning. I want to examine the meanings these two objects suggest and then look at the wider significance of the production and consumption of Indian-crafted objects in the "cultural economy of tourism." "Handmade by an American Indian" is the standard trope for authenticity in this economy, and I'd like to spend some time unpacking it, looking first at the significance of the "handmade" and then at how Indian and tourist identities are constructed within the markets for Indian arts and crafts.

Susan Stewart defines souvenirs as "traces of authentic experience."[2] This definition includes not only objects made for purchase by tourists but also any objects that serve as reminders or evidence of an authentic experience. My kachina is such a "trace" of our family's trip to a place redolent of authenticity: in the touristic Southwest the desert landscape represents a kind of raw yet sublime nature; the natives are "primitives" untouched by modernity. That trip took us out of our ordinary life and permitted us a brush with an authentic, exotic place. The kachina's connection with that vacation, the last we took as a family, was probably its most powerful association for me for years, and it can prompt several narratives about my past, as it did above. So part of its significance is that it "tells" about me and my past. It is a nostalgic object that suggests the loss of childhood, and in the "intimate distance" between the present and the past, the adult and the child, lies its power to make meaning.[3] The kachina prompts me to formulate a narrative to bridge that distance, and in this way it allows me to be a tourist of my own life.[4] The kachina helped me begin to construct the narrative of my life, a narrative of authentic experiences I could revisit through telling it.

The kachina also signifies Hopi culture; as part of my childhood doll collection, it "represented" one of many exotic cultures, in the same way that the

Figure 5.2. Souvenir Navajo weaver.

Author's "collection."

doll wearing a sari in my collection represented India. The kachina domesticated my experience of "otherness";[5] when it became part of the interior of my
childhood room, it reflected the interior of my childish mind. In buying the
kachina for me, I think my parents were trying to "furnish" both my room and
my mind, suggesting that I incorporate something "Indian" into my white,
bourgeois self. This primitive presence in my childhood room also spoke to my
capacity to outgrow my own primitive state. In a kind of magical logic, incorporating this "other" would contribute to my own growing power.

But I think I was also aware that the kachina signified another narrative, about the Hopi family who had used it and my relation to them. I vaguely perceived that there was something inequitable going on in the transaction I had been a part of. What had prompted the Hopi family to sell the kachina? What circumstances might lead my family to sell my dolls? I was very dimly aware that this situation was somehow connected to a shameful history of white exploitation of Indian people; the transaction seemed illicit. Furthermore, the kachina seemed to have a life and a history: from its origins in the Hopi family, it had briefly, sadly, fallen into the state of being a commodity, and we had rescued it. Although as tourists we constantly saw evidence that we were in the land of the Indians, we never met any; this transaction was as close as I would come to an encounter with any "natives."

Since I acquired it, the kachina has stayed with me, still a loaded presence, like a troubling foster child. It now "lives" in my Brooklyn apartment, where I have arranged a number of souvenirs and family "heirlooms" to suggest an "Indian corner" in a nineteenth-century gentleman's library. It seems that the only way I can remain comfortable with this object is to frame it within a context that creates an ironic distance even as it creates a narrative about "me."

It is in some ways easier for me to discuss the Navajo weaver doll. Unlike the kachina, it does not narrate an authentic southwestern experience of mine. The only personal narrative I can attach to it is how it was given to me. It was at one time, probably, a trace of someone's trip to the Southwest, but now it has become disassociated from that narrative. Nevertheless, it is still a souvenir; it was made to be a souvenir and came already loaded with a narrative that recapitulates the attractions of the Southwest. First it represents Indian artisan labor, a major attraction since the turn of the century. Along with the "olla maiden," Indian artisans (mainly potters, weavers, and silversmiths) have been central icons in the creation of the Southwest as a cultural region. Indian arts and crafts have signified authenticity to generations of non-Indian Americans and are a vital part of the region's economy.[6] The souvenir doll "tells" about the production of Navajo weavings. It replicates in miniature the typical iconography of Navajo weavers: a scene of domestic industry, with the product near completion. (Other steps in the production of weavings, such as shearing the wool, carding, spinning, or dyeing, were almost never depicted in the tourist literature. Certainly the spectacle of a weaver *buying* yarn to weave was never shown.) The miniaturization of the weaver aestheticizes and eternalizes the labor depicted and suggests that this is antiquated, primitive labor, frozen and cut off from modernity and lived experience.[7]

In addition, the object has a wonderful "meta" aspect: the sticker on the bottom guarantees that the object, which *represents* Indian hand labor, was "hand made by an American Indian." I love that it's a sticker, too, a mechanically reproduced label added to a handmade object to assure the buyer of its authenticity. Although the object shows evidence of handwork, the sticker effectively separates out that quality and then reapplies it to the object by means of some adhesive. This process speaks about how the characteristics of "authenticity" have always been defined and maintained by non-Indians. Who put the sticker there? By what authority? The sticker prompts questions about how the object was produced. Who wove the blanket? Was it the same person who made the doll? Was he or she Navajo? Was the souvenir produced on an assembly line, with one person making the weaving, one the doll, and another assembling them? What about the distinction between the "handmade" and the "mass-produced"? What kind of craft or labor is making souvenirs? What does this say about the value of Native American labor? Why does the assurance of handcraft add value? The final irony is that the doll has no hands. I like to think it's a joke, a refusal by the person who made the doll to capitulate totally in being reduced to a pair of hands.

"Handmade . . ."

Of all Indian-made objects and products, the souvenir is the lowliest. Anthropologist Nancy Parezo distinguishes the different external markets for Indian arts and crafts in descending order of value: ethnographic/archeological specimens; fine art; crafts ("home decorations and gifts"); and finally souvenirs.[8] Although any object can serve as a souvenir, Parezo refers here to objects produced for tourist markets. The characteristics of these objects contradict what is valuable in the other markets: the singular, the handmade, the "detailed." Parezo says souvenirs "require simplification and mass production, since the extra expense of the addition of time-consuming, intricate details brings no economic return. . . . Indeed monies obtained from souvenirs are considered by makers as wages."[9] Wage labor does not signify authenticity; wage labor is "alienated" labor. In contrast, Indian artisanal labor signifies a kind of authenticity based on the idea that the primitive artisan thinks with his or her hands, that the mark of the hand is "honorific" in a world of mass-produced goods.[10] Indian craftwork seems to be an unmediated form of production, in which the artisan is bound by tradition and nature rather than capitalist markets. In fact, for the last hundred years and more Native American craftspeople in the Southwest have been participating in the marketplace, responding to the demands of tourists and collectors.

The influences of these markets have been well documented, but the idea that something is handmade by an American Indian prompts a kind of willful blindness, a fantasy of the auratic magic of such objects.[11] The production of objects intended for sale to tourists admits that Indian people are engaged with the marketplace. It suggests that Indians can actually "see" tourists, that they are not inward looking or blind to modernity.

In her essay "How 'They' See 'Us': Native American Images of Tourists," folklorist Deirdre Evans-Pritchard notes that Native Americans have observed closely the significance of their exchanges with whites. She finds that jokes Native Americans tell about tourists and anthropologists often hinge on the whites' desire to commodify Indian cultures: "Reifying culture is fundamental to cultural tourism and fits well with the general sense in Indian folklore that the whiteman is a slave to consumerism."[12] The Hopi filmmaker Victor Masayesva, Jr., has often addressed this tendency to reify, to turn the abstract into the material or concrete, in the markets for Indian arts and crafts. His short film *Pott Starr* (1990) begins with an image of an "olla maiden" going to fill her olla with water at a stream.[13] As she walks, she is replaced by an animated olla with arms and legs. The joke is that Indian women are objectified but also that Indian-crafted objects are subjectified, animated by the culture they supposedly "embody." This tendency to animate Indian-crafted objects is evident in the touristic expectation that Indian objects "tell stories." Evans-Pritchard notes that many artisans use symbols to create an aesthetic effect, but they will sometimes tell a tourist a story associated with a work, because this is what the tourist expects.[14] This expectation may derive from the ethnographic approach to objects as metonymic, or *representative* of cultures (like the dolls in my childhood collection), but it also suggests a fantasy of playing Indian: the tourist can reanimate the object by retelling the Indian's story. Later in *Pott Starr* the animated olla is seen walking in downtown Santa Fe. The camera then follows a white woman in cowboy boots, Navajo-style skirt, and concha belt. She approaches the Native American vendors under the portal of the Palace of the Governors. We see her hand, with red polished nails and turquoise rings, reaching down from the top of the screen in slow motion. Then we see her from the vendor's point of view, bending and reaching—not looking at the camera, but at the objects, which are out of sight. Finally we see that the woman is reaching for an olla, which disappears in a flash. In addition to parodying the grasping, consuming white tourist or collector who refuses to see Indian subjectivity, the scene suggests that what she desires is, ultimately, unavailable.

The question of what tourists desire is compelling. In her poem "The

Living Exhibit Under the Museum's Portal," Nora Naranjo-Morse suggests that what tourists want is confirmation of what they already know. "Visitors looking for mementos to take home, / that will remind them of the curiously / silent Indians, wrapped tightly in colorful / shawls, just like in the post-cards."[15] Tourists buy souvenirs from Indians arranged in a "living exhibit," who look just like Indians seen on picture postcards, which can serve as souvenirs themselves. Such representations of Indians circulate in what Guy Debord has called a "spectacle," "a social relation among people, mediated by images."[16] In the spectacle of Indian artisanal labor, touristic desire is created and fulfilled in a self-perpetuating, repetitive cycle, and as the "represented," Indians are "curiously silent."

In the touristic economy, the tourist is mobile and spectating, and everything the tourist sees is subject to appropriation. Photography allows this almost literally, but the purchase of goods is redolent of an exchange with the natives—even if what is purchased is not of native manufacture. In the cultural as well as monetary economy of tourism, shopping is an important activity. It drives the economic engine of the industry, but it also recapitulates a

Figure 5.3. Still from Victor Masayesva, Jr.'s, video *Pott Starr* (1990).
Courtesy of Electronic Arts Intermix, New York, http://www.eai.org.

powerful cultural narrative of exploration, contact, and exchange with alien beings. In the Southwest, the Columbian exchange and its historical consequences are lurking within this narrative. What is the wish to reenact this exchange, culturally speaking? An imperialist power play? A longing for authenticity? For contact with the other? With the self? A nostalgic wish for wholeness?[17] Probably each of these longings comes into play at some point.

More and more I agree with sociologist Dean MacCannell's assertion that touring is a trope for a modern state of being, that "'the tourist' is one of the best models available for modern-man-in-general."[18] The desiring, roving, spectating, consuming tourist is the embodiment of the late capitalist individual. Touring is a performance of "life," inscribed within consumer capitalism. The meaning of this performance only becomes clear upon returning home, at which point the tourist begins to construct a narrative of the experience. Stewart notes that souvenirs "allow one to be a tourist of one's own life."[19] One tours the museum, or collection, of one's experiences: an interior furnished with souvenirs, a life collected, inspected, cataloged, interpreted, and finally narrated. In the process of narration, the self is performed; it is a performance of re-collected experience. This may be why other people's souvenirs hold no appeal. Detached from their narratives, they fail to signify authenticity. Signification is emptied out, and they are material reminders of the tenuous and ephemeral ways we construct our sense of self.

". . . By an American Indian"

Which brings me to the Indian Arts and Crafts Act of 1990. The act was passed by the House and Senate on October 27, 1990, and George Bush signed it on November 29. Cosponsored by Senator Ben Nighthorse Campbell (Republican-Colorado) and then Representative Jon Kyl (Republican-Arizona), the act expands the powers of the Indian Arts and Crafts Board (IACB), an agency of the U.S. Department of the Interior, and directs the IACB to promote the economic welfare of Indians through development and expansion of markets for arts and crafts. In addition, it mandates the IACB to create and administer a system of trademarks and to set standards of "'genuineness and quality.'" But the crux of the law makes it illegal "to offer or display for sale or sell a good, with or without a Government trademark, in a manner that falsely suggests it is Indian produced, an Indian product, or the product of a particular Indian or Indian tribe or Indian arts and crafts organization, resident within the United States."[20] The act imposes big fines if the law is broken: a first-time individual offense can result in a $250,000 fine and five years imprisonment; for an entity such as a corporation the first-offense fine is $1 million. Subsequent fines start from $1 million for an individual and $5 million for a nonindividual offender.[21]

In support of this bill, Senator Nighthorse Campbell explained that Indian art is "the only ethnic art form in the United States that is badly plagiarized. . . . Arts and crafts are one of the most important industries on reservations. This is also a consumer protection bill: when people buy Indian art they have a right to know that an Indian made it."[22] Indeed, a lot of money is at stake: American Indian–style arts and crafts earn an estimated $1 billion a year, and 10 percent of that is siphoned off by fake products.[23] If "handmade by an American Indian" is the standard trope for authenticity, the trope for inauthenticity is "made in Taiwan"—or Hong Kong or Indonesia or Mexico.

The intent may be benign, but the Indian Arts and Crafts Act is very troubling in the way it codifies Indian identity. The act defines "Indian" as "any individual who is a member of an Indian tribe; or for the purpose of this section is certified as an Indian artisan by an Indian tribe." "Indian tribe" is defined as a federally or state-recognized Indian tribe, band, nation, Alaska native village, or another organized group or community.[24] One of the problems with this definition is that many Native Americans are not registered with any tribe. Most critics of the act cite instances in which someone is Indian by blood but not officially certified. For example, the artist Kay WalkingStick has pointed out that some tribes recognize matrilineal descent (like the Hopi), some patrilineal (like the Salish). If a person had a Hopi father and a Salish mother and was born off the Salish reservation, that person could register with neither tribe.[25] Furthermore, even though the act leaves the certification of artisans and questions of membership up to the discretion of each tribe, the history of regulating tribal membership is complicated and riven by racism, corruption, and resistance. For example, to be a member of the Cherokee tribe, one has to have the enrollment number of an ancestor who registered as a Cherokee with the federal government at the turn of the century. For many reasons, not all Cherokees at the turn of the century did this.[26]

One of the most cogent responses to the act came from the artist Jimmie Durham, who identifies himself as Cherokee but lacks an enrollment number. Two of his exhibitions scheduled for 1991 were canceled because the institutions were worried about being prosecuted under the new law. Durham recognized that the terms of authentic Indian identity, as well as the definitions of authenticity in the Indian art market, have long been in the hands of the colonizers, and the Indian Arts and Crafts Act serves to enforce those terms and that tradition. In response to the act, Durham wrote an open letter in which he declared that "authenticity is a racist concept which functions to keep us enclosed in 'our world' (in our place) for the comfort of a dominant society."[27]

Cultural products made by Indians are authenticated not just in terms of whether a particular individual made them (as are objects in the non-Indian art markets); the ethnic identity of the maker must also be authenticated. This is the particular aim of the Indian Arts and Crafts Act, and the regulations, which went into effect in 1996, make it clear that this identity is tied to race. The regulations state that if an artisan is not a certified member of a tribe, he or she can be certified by a tribe as a "non-member Indian artisan." In order to be so certified, the artist must be of the "Indian lineage" of a tribe.[28] Also, someone who is not a certified member or a "non-member Indian artisan" may describe him- or herself as of "Indian descent, Native American descent," or tribal descent.[29] Furthermore, in its response to the public commentary on the regulations, the Indian Arts and Crafts Board specified that someone's "adoption by an 'Indian spiritual leader' or tribal member does not necessarily make that person a member of a recognized tribe."[30] The key terms here are *ancestry* and *descent*. Blood is the authenticating factor in Indian identity.

Why is this problematic? I think mainly for the reasons Jimmie Durham suggested, that racial identities are restrictive and easily controlled by others. Indian artists, like most people, are forever negotiating between what Werner Sollors has called achieved and ascribed identities,[31] but in the art markets the identity "Indian artist" is defined by ethnicity and tradition, both of which are conceived of as inheritable, or ascribed. Nora Naranjo-Morse also comments on this dilemma in the poem "Mud Woman's First Encounter with the World of Money and Business." She writes about selling her figures to a gallery owner, who asks, "Who is your family? / Are any of them well known in the Indian art world?"[32] Here Naranjo-Morse confronts the market's demand for blood. As she has pointed out in an interview, this line of questioning boils down to: "Are you sellable?"[33] She questions the relevance of her descent to the work under negotiation and recognizes that the object is being evaluated not in terms of her labor and talent, but in terms of the exact quality of her "Indianness." The other question Naranjo-Morse implies is, Would any gallery owner ever put such questions to an Anglo artist?

This conception of an inheritable Indian artistic tradition rests on the notion of race as inescapable and telling. The markets for Indian art demand blood as the mark of authenticity and operate on the assumption that "blood will out." No matter how "individualistic" or "nontraditional" the object, it will tell on its maker. In the words of Clara Lee Tanner in the 1988 book *Beyond Tradition:* "Even the most contemporary work usually includes some hint of heritage."[34] In the ethnic art market, Indian blood signifies the inescapable, the natural—and the market's demand for it naturalizes tradition as a kind of timeless inheritable magic. For most of this century Indian artists and artisans have not been recognized as historical agents; instead the market insists that they do what they do naturally and that artists, dealers, and collectors are participating not in a real market, but in a kind of benign magical exchange, in which a mystical essence that has rubbed off on the object from the caress of an Indian hand can be accumulated by the buyer. In these exchanges, the object of desire represents continuity and perhaps a connection with an imagined "other" and past. This continuity is represented by a racialized notion of tradition rather than by any notion of tradition as a function of human history, as a process that is complicated by conflict and disruptions.

Which brings me back to the problem of reification. In addition to the racialized notion of authenticity, Jimmie Durham has argued that the European conception of identity is tied to ownership. "European culture's emphasis on the sovereign subject and its private property is alien to a Native American concept of the self as an integral part of a social body whose history and knowledge are inscribed across a particular body of land."[35] The image of the "sovereign subject and its private property" brings to mind the tourist and his or her souvenirs, subject to the possessive gaze and interpretation of the self. And in the markets for Indian arts and crafts identity becomes a commodity. Thus the Indian Arts and Crafts Act calls for a system of trademarking to ensure authenticity. As a reporter in *The Albuquerque Tribune* noted, after a meeting held by the Indian Arts and Crafts Association in 1997 to discuss the law, "Copyright, trademarks and the issue of intellectual property emerged as keys to controlling ownership of symbols, designs and cultural heritage."[36] The possibility of a Navajo trademark is already under discussion in the Navajo Tourism Department.[37] Behind these discussions about "cultural heritage" and authenticity lie notions of culture and identity in which "culture" is a kind of inheritable property, but it is property that can't be disposed of or even controlled (except by the government) because it is tied to race.[38]

Because tradition and culture are racialized in the markets for Indian arts and crafts, objects that circulate in those markets become less metonymic and more synecdochic, like trophies. As I have tried to show, not only are Indian people objectified, but also Indian-crafted objects are "subjectified," or animated by ethnicity. The Luiseño artist James Luna has addressed issues of objectification and subjectivity in many of his works. In a 1986 installation called *Artifact Piece* he exhibited himself, sedated on barbiturates, in a museum case. In addition to a display of "artifacts" from his life, the scars on his body were annotated.[39] This, he seems to be saying, is where the objectification and appropriation of Indian culture leads you. What kind of "cultural property" is this? The exhibit also speaks about Native Americans as part of the tourist spectacle. He serves himself up for the touristic gaze but in a way that makes the voyeurism of this gaze clear and uncomfortable for the viewer. Is he a trophy of the hunt? A souvenir? But even as he offers himself as an artifact or trophy, he also recapitulates a kind of touristic narrative inside the case. The scars and artifacts are souvenirs of his life; they construct a narrative of his life. But his "present absence" complicates matters. He is a living human "subject," but he is drugged, unable to narrate the souvenirs himself. He seems to be enacting a fear that lurks in the souvenir, in horror stories such as "The Monkey's Paw," in which Susan Stewart notes, "The danger of the souvenir lies in its unfamiliarity, in our difficulty in subjecting it to interpretation. There is always the possibility that reverie's signification will go out of control here, that the object itself will take charge, awakening some dormant capacity for destruction."[40] Luna presents the uncomfortable possibility that the object might reanimate itself and assert its subjectivity as a historical agent, wreaking revenge for the violence done to it.

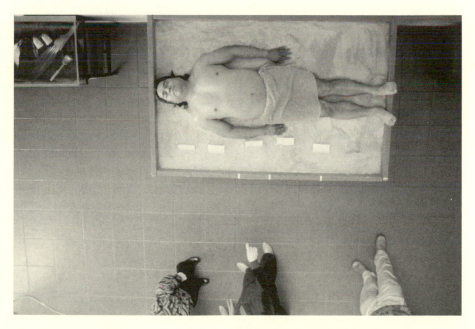

Figure 5.4. James Luna, *The Artifact Piece* (detail), 1986, San Diego Museum of Man.

In his 1993 short film, *History of the Luiseño People*, Luna probes the question of Indian identity further.[41] Nothing much happens in the film; it simply shows Luna at home on the La Jolla reservation making phone calls to friends and relatives on Christmas Day. As he talks on the phone, he smokes cigarettes and consumes the better part of a six-pack of beer. We hear only his side of the phone conversations. A TV in the room is showing the movie *White Christmas*. The film refuses all the stereotypes of Indians. Luna is emphatically not being picturesque. The film offers an unsatisfactory encounter with an "Indian." As a tourist, the viewer is seeing into the "back regions" of the attraction, but the spectacle fails, and the viewer becomes a voyeur.[42] This encounter won't leave the tourist with a souvenir or even a narrative. Instead Luna shows us someone who looks like a poor American. While the film addresses the real problems of poverty and alcoholism among Native Americans, Luna is also concerned with questions of identity and representation. He does not present himself as "representative"; it's impossible to generalize about the identity the film presents; what we see is much too specific. He is one man in a particular historical situation.

Figure 5.5. Nora Naranjo-Morse, *A Pueblo Woman's Clothesline*, 1994, Heard Museum, Phoenix, Arizona.

I'd like to conclude with an image of one more object that is "handmade by an American Indian." Nora Naranjo-Morse's *A Pueblo Woman's Clothesline* (1994) also speaks to a notion of identity that is situated in the world as it is. The *Clothesline* is rooted in the ground, but the flags it flies are constantly changing. It suggests the texture of a Pueblo woman's life as it is actually lived and the kind of domestic and political labor that has not "traditionally" appeared in the marketplace. The object escapes commodification. Like James Luna's *Artifact Piece* or the arrangement of souvenirs in my living room, the *Clothesline* offers narratives of endless variation that speak about ownership and commodification and the body. But Naranjo-Morse's piece makes the point that identity is situated within history and that it is negotiated and performed every single day.

Notes

The epigraph at the beginning of this chapter is from Susan Pearce, *Museums, Objects, and Collections: A Cultural Study* (Leicester: Leicester University Press, 1992), 72.

1. I have written about the significance of this kachina at greater length in an article, "Re-Collections of a Texan Girlhood," *Journal of the American Studies Association of Texas* 28 (October 1997): 1–13. Thanks to *JASAT* editor John Tisdale for permission to republish passages from the article.
2. Susan Stewart, *On Longing: Narratives of the Miniature, the Gigantic, the Souvenir, the Collection* (Durham, N.C.: Duke University Press, 1993), 135.
3. Ibid., 140.
4. Ibid., 146.
5. Ibid., 134.
6. Leah Dilworth, "The Spectacle of Indian Artisanal Labor," in *Imagining Indians in the Southwest: Persistent Visions of a Primitive Past* (Washington, D.C.: Smithsonian Institution Press, 1996): 125–72.
7. Stewart, *On Longing*, 144.
8. Nancy Parezo, "A Multitude of Markets," *Journal of the Southwest* 32 (winter 1990): 563–75.
9. Ibid., 572.
10. Thorstein Veblen, *The Theory of the Leisure Class* (New York: Penguin, 1986): 161.
11. For influences of markets on Indian crafts, see J. J. Brody, "The Creative Consumer: Survival, Revival and Invention in Southwest Indian Arts," in *Ethnic and Tourist Arts: Cultural Expressions from the Fourth World*, ed. Nelson H. H. Graburn (Berkeley: University of California Press, 1976), 70–83; and Molly H. Mullin, "Consuming the American Southwest: Culture, Art, and Difference" (Ph.D. diss., Duke University, 1993).
12. Deirdre Evans-Pritchard, "How 'They' See 'Us': Native American Images of Tourists," *Annals of Tourism Research* 16 (1989): 92.
13. Victor Masayesva, Jr., *Pott Starr*, videocassette, 6 min., IS Productions, Hotevilla, Ariz., 1990.
14. Evans-Pritchard, "How 'They' See 'Us,'" 95.

15. Nora Naranjo-Morse, *Mud Woman: Poems from the Clay* (Tucson: University of Arizona Press, 1992): 29–30.

16. Guy Debord, *Society of the Spectacle* (Detroit: Red and Black, 1983), 4.

17. Susan Stewart considers these longings in relation to the body and notes that according to Baudrillard, the exotic object is linked to the "anteriority" of childhood and its toys (*On Longing*, 146).

18. Dean MacCannell, *The Tourist: A New Theory of the Leisure Class* (New York: Schocken Books, 1989), 1.

19. Stewart, *On Longing*, 146.

20. *Indian Arts and Crafts Act of 1990, U.S. Code*, vol. 25, sec. 305a (1999).

21. Gail K. Sheffield, *The Arbitrary Indian: The Indian Arts and Crafts Act of 1990* (Norman: University of Oklahoma Press, 1997), 12.

22. Michelle Quinn, "Ethnic Litmus Test a Problem for American Indian Artists; Arts," *Los Angeles Times*, 18 June 1992, Home Edition, F1.

23. These estimates were quoted in ibid., 1; and T. D. Mobley-Martinez, "Indians to Act on Fake Art," *Albuquerque Tribune*, 25 January 1997, A1.

24. Sheffield, *The Arbitrary Indian*, 13.

25. Kay WalkingStick, "Indian Arts and Crafts Act: Counterpoint," in *Native American Expressive Culture* (Washington, D.C.: Akwekon Press and National Museum of the American Indian, 1994), 116.

26. Ibid., 115–16.

27. Richard Shiff, "The Necessity of Jimmie Durham's Jokes," *Art Journal* 51 (fall 1992): 75–76.

28. *Code of Federal Regulations*, Title 25, part 309.4 (a) (1).

29. Ibid., 309.3 (c).

30. Indian Arts and Crafts Board, "Protection for Products of Indian Art and Craftsmanship," *Federal Register* [on-line] 61, no. 204 (October 1996): 54553, wais.access.gpo.gov, quoted in Ron McCoy, "Federal Indian Arts and Crafts Regulations Take Effect," *American Indian Art Magazine* 22 (spring 1997): 88.

31. Werner Sollors, *Beyond Ethnicity: Consent and Descent in American Culture* (New York: Oxford University Press, 1986), 5–6.

32. Naranjo-Morse, *Mud Woman*, 35.

33. Stephen Trimble, "Brown Earth and Laughter: The Clay People of Nora Naranjo-Morse," *American Indian Art* 12 (autumn 1987): 64.

34. Clara Lee Tanner, introduction to *Beyond Tradition: Contemporary Indian Art and Its Evolution*, by Jerry D. Jacka (Flagstaff, Ariz.: Northland Publishing, 1988), 36.

35. Shiff, "Jimmie Durham's Jokes," 76.

36. Mobley-Martinez, "Indians to Act on Fake Art," A1.

37. Duane A. Beyal, "Tourism Office Hosts Unique Forum to Examine Arts and Crafts Issues," *Navajo Times*, 14 May 1998, A2. However, as of May 2000, the Indian Arts and Crafts Board has not finalized the regulations on trademarking under the act.

38. As of May 2000, the Indian Arts and Crafts Board, the entity charged with enforcing the Indian Arts and Crafts Act of 1990, had not prosecuted any cases under the act due to budgetary restrictions. Matt Kelley, "Tribes: Gov't Not Enforcing Laws," 17 May 2000, Associated Press Online, <http://dailynewsyahoo.com/h/ap/20000517/pl/indian_knock-offs_1.html>, 18 May 2000.

39. Carla Roberts, "Object, Subject, Practitioner: Native Americans and Cultural Institutions," *Native American Expressive Culture* (Washington, D.C.: Akwekon Press,

1994), 24. See also Lucy Lippard, *Mixed Blessings: New Art in Multicultural America* (New York: Pantheon Books, 1990), 198.

40. Stewart, *On Longing,* 148.

41. James Luna, *History of the Luiseño People,* videocassette, 27 min., dir. Isaac Artenstein, 1993. When I saw this movie for the first time, at the Margaret Mead Film Festival at the American Museum of Natural History in 1994, it was listed in the program as *I've Always Wanted to Be an American Indian,* which is also the title of a photo essay by Luna. The photographs in the essay depict places on the La Jolla reservation along with demographic statistics about the people who live on the reservation. I still like this title for the film best. See James Luna, "I've Always Wanted to Be an American Indian," *Art Journal* 51 (fall 1992): 18–27.

Many thanks to Emelia Seubert, assistant curator, Film and Video Center, National Museum of the American Indian, Smithsonian Institution, for screening this and other films for me.

42. MacCannell, *The Tourist,* 94–96.

EXCHANGING PLACES
VIRTUAL TOURISM, VICARIOUS TRAVEL, AND THE CONSUMPTION OF SOUTHWESTERN INDIAN ARTIFACTS ━

ERIKA MARIE BSUMEK

G race Nicholson, a Pasadena-based dealer in ethnographic arts and crafts from Asia, Mexico, and the United States, managed to build an extremely successful business by collecting items in Japan, China, Mexico, and from American Indian artisans (or Indian traders) who lived in remote regions of the American West. Although she is currently remembered as an expert on Pomoan Indian baskets and Northwest Coast Indian culture, Nicholson also traveled extensively in the Southwest. While there, she collected Indian-made baskets, blankets, jewelry, pottery, and other items to sell to museum curators, ethnologists, and middle- to upper-class consumers from her shop, Grace Nicholson's Treasure Shop of Oriental and Western Art. As her reputation grew, she established a thriving mail-order business and devised strategies for how best to fulfill the desires of virtual tourists and to perpetuate middle-class consumer demands for, in this case, southwestern Indian artifacts.[1]

Today the World Wide Web promises users seemingly unlimited information and a variety of "virtual experiences." One can "surf" Hawaiian beaches or "chat" with a Tibetan Lama via a computer. Web video cameras provide images of urban street scenes or rural farm life in "real time" to the deskbound. One can, in essence, travel virtually anywhere without ever leaving home. Those wishing to visit the American Southwest, for instance, can log on to innumerable sites that feature Arizona sunsets, popular regional art galleries, or the Navajo Nation itself. Web site sojourners can also conveniently shop for blankets made by Navajo weavers or ceramic vessels crafted by Santa Clara potters through their home computers.

Although we tend to think of virtual tourism as an activity of the late-twentieth and early-twenty-first centuries, middle- to upper-class Americans have been going on "virtual tours" of the American Southwest for at least a century. Beginning in the late nineteenth century, many Americans traveled to the Southwest via the Atchison, Topeka, and Santa Fe Railway (AT&SF) to see the region that was home to Zuni, Hopi, Taos, Navajo, Tewa, and other American Indian groups. Through a heavily promoted tourist campaign, the AT&SF managed to create a romantic fantasy rich in its "radiant vision of Indian life."[2] In later decades, automobiles altered the tourist experience. Individual drivers had the freedom to travel to Indian pueblos, view ceremonial dances on feast days, and then move on to their next destination. Successive generations of tourists sought "authentic" experiences with "primitive" Indian peoples that continually fueled the powerful market forces that drove the region's tourist industry.[3] Yet many other Americans chose an alternative mode of travel. While still in search of "genuine" representations of American Indian life, early virtual tourists traveled not by rail or automobile. Instead they journeyed through their consumption of Southwestern Indian artifacts, the ethnographic details associated with their origin, and the experiences one might have to go through in order to acquire them from American Indians.

These virtual tourists traveled by voyages made by others and through the objects they obtained. The consumption of experiences and goods was meant to reflect the status of those who could afford to buy them. Virtual tourists purchased seemingly unusual ethnographic items that suggested adventure. The collection of ethnographic objects themselves was not a new phenomenon. In the sixteenth, seventeenth, eighteenth and early nineteenth centuries, explorers and wealthy men of European heritage assembled an array of artifacts from non-Western peoples that they deemed "curiosities."[4] Wealthy male collectors of earlier generations had hunted for, among other things, spears, clubs, masks, and other forms of weaponry.[5] By contrast, early-twentieth-century virtual tourists tended to be middle- to upper-class women in search of items that acclaimed their class status and represented "authentic experience" at the same time.[6] By 1900, as married American women with disposable income became fascinated with the Southwest and the indigenous peoples who lived there, they began to gather the baskets, blankets, pottery, and jewelry made by American Indians and appropriated these items for domestic decorative purposes.[7] The adventures that another individual, usually a dealer in Indian-made artifacts, had experienced in the process of obtaining the goods were essential to the commercial transactions that personified virtual tourism. Virtual tourism enabled middle-class women to obtain unique decorative items *and* adventure while, at the same time, avoiding both the perils and difficulties that often accompanied firsthand tourist experiences. Through their consumption of Indian-made goods, virtual tourists experienced the American Southwest. This "experience" separated them from those who shopped in department stores for decorative accessories. As a result, virtual tourists came to value the act of consumption as much as the ideology that stimulated such consumerism. In short, virtual tourism made the hobby of home decoration a transcendent adventure.

Grace Nicholson: Dealer in Southwestern Artifacts

Navajo traders, hotel managers, curio store owners, and dealers in American Indian arts and crafts produced a significant amount of publicity to spark the interest of potential tourists. The AT&SF, the most well-known promoter of travel and tourism in the Southwest, went to great lengths to present the public with images of "primitive" Navajos, Hopis, Zunis, and Puebloan peoples in calendars and magazine articles and through a variety of visually striking advertisements. In 1915 they even named a passenger train that traveled from Chicago to Los Angeles "The Navajo."[8] "The Navajo" generated much excitement and reminded potential passengers of the connections between American Indians, travel, and the Southwest. Fred Harvey, the famous hotelier, hired ethnologists, artists, and writers to produce promotional pamphlets and to chaperone tourists on "Indian detours" to Navajo, Hopi, Zuni, or other Pueblo reservations.[9] Well-known Indian traders Lorenzo Hubbell and John Bradford Moore produced their famous catalogs of Navajo rugs and silverware and marketed their ability to coordinate tours of "Indian country."[10] A. F. Spiegelberg of Santa Fe, the Benham brothers of Albuquerque, and countless other curio store owners placed ads in national magazines in order to sell Navajo, Hopi, and Pueblo goods to potential visitors. Finally, dealer Grace Nicholson was an important member of the larger network of southwestern tourist-related businesses. As a successful dealer in Indian-made goods, Nicholson kept her large craftsman-style bungalow in Pasadena well stocked with Indian-made products.

In order to do so, she established ties with the Hubbells, the Moores, and the Spiegelbergs. She also corresponded with representatives of the Harvey Company, utilized the AT&SF for shipping, and traveled extensively throughout the region.[11]

Despite the fact that Nicholson was one of the most influential dealers of Indian arts and crafts of the era, relatively little is known about her. Born in Philadelphia on December 31, 1877, she moved to California in 1901. In

Figure 6.1. Interior of Grace Nicholson's home/showroom. Nicholson carefully crafted her home displays so that clients might easily understand how to use baskets, blankets, and ceramic vases in their own homes. Grace Nicholson Collection, vol. 56, photo scrapbooks.

This item is reproduced by permission of the Huntington Library, San Marino, California.

early 1902 she began purchasing Indian-made products for ethnological exhibits and to sell to individual clients. By 1905 Nicholson had begun to deal in American Indian artifacts from northwestern and southwestern tribes. As a result, she traveled to Indian reservations in Washington, Oregon, California, Arizona, and New Mexico on buying trips. While there, she formed lasting relationships with American Indian artisans and engaged in ethnological research. As was common practice of the time, once she had obtained Indian-made goods, Nicholson worked out of her home in Pasadena.

Nicholson capitalized on the connection between her home and her work by selling Indian-made goods to be used as decorations out of her residence, which became a highly designed shop. Lorenzo Hubbell, trader to the Navajo and Hopi and successful businessman, also used the practice of decorating

Figure 6.2. Grace Nicholson's home office, letter books, and business records shared shelf space with Indian baskets. Grace Nicholson Collection, vol. 56, photo scrapbooks.

This item is reproduced by permission of the Huntington Library, San Marino, California.

his home as a salesroom. The elaborately decorated Harvey Hotels in Albuquerque (the Alvarado Hotel), Gallup (El Navajo), and at the Grand Canyon (the Hopi House) were, in all likelihood, major influences on Hubbell and Nicholson. The Fred Harvey Company had hired famed designer Mary Colter to decorate the Alvarado and the Hopi House to show tourists how they could use Indian-made goods as decorative accessories.[12] By decorating the interior of the Alvarado Hotel or Grace Nicholson's home-based Treasure Shop with Navajo products, entrepreneurs such as Harvey, Hubbell, and Nicholson relied upon an established marketing technique. As early as the 1850s, urban hotels provided visitors with "model interiors." When hotels exhibited furniture and paintings or featured interior design theme parlors, consumers were able to, as scholar Katherine Grier has illustrated, "translate the room making information that such interiors provided" in terms of class, style, and use.[13] From 1900 throughout the late 1930s, Nicholson used decorative schemes to help clients view how goods could be displayed in their own homes. Such displays were especially useful in helping her to sell goods made by American Indians. Over time, she developed a reputation as an expert on American Indian goods and culture, became a skilled interior design consultant, and cultivated a flourishing mail-order business. Her customers sought her advice on the placement of articles as well as the ethnographic details that governed their use and manufacture among indigenous peoples.

The character of Nicholson's business reflected the extent of her experience in the Southwest and her connections to American Indian craftsmen and craftswomen. Nicholson utilized Pomo baskets as wall hangings, while Navajo blankets covered floors, windows, and walls or served as makeshift doors. She kept photographs and paintings of American Indians available for customer perusal, and she used traditional markers of middle-class domestic taste, such as crystal chandeliers, silk curtains, and high-quality and highly stylized paisley print tablecloths, as background accessories.

For those unable to shop in person, Nicholson sent photographs depicting the store's interior and her stock. Or she sent shipments of baskets, blankets, and jewelry for the customers' inspection. Customers were instructed to keep what they liked and return the rest with payment.[14]

Nicholson claimed to sell experiences along with "western art treasures" from the confines of her bungalow. Her baskets, blankets, and jewelry assembled and represented her adventurous encounters with American Indians. Nicholson used her home to illustrate that domesticity, decoration, and authentic experience were complementary concepts. Whereas the Fred Harvey Company hoped to provide tourists with a home away from home when they decorated hotels with Indian-made goods, Nicholson sought to send the trappings of her travels to those unable or unwilling to make the trip themselves.

Nicholson produced elaborate brochures that included photos of her goods and her home/shop. She used the larger tourist network to distribute these brochures among actual and virtual tourists—those who were traveling to the Southwest or wished to do so. Possible wayfarers to southern California, for instance, were issued an "informal invitation" to purchase Apache, Hopi, Maricopa, Pima, Navajo, Hupa, Mission, Pomo, and other Indian-made and ethnographic objects at Grace Nicholson's famed Treasure House of Oriental and Western Art in Pasadena.

Just east of the Maryland Hotel, Nicholson invited tourists who were "lovers of Indian objects" to stop by her "ATTRACTIVE SALESROOM . . .

Figure 6.3. Nicholson utilized modern fabrics, such as this paisley print tablecloth, to highlight her stock of handmade Indian wares. Grace Nicholson Collection, vol. 56, photo scrapbooks.

This item is reproduced by permission of the Huntington Library, San Marino, California.

to view her notable collection" of merchandise. The brochures that found their way into the parlors of the less mobile also made it easy for virtual tourists to buy Indian-made goods. Nicholson met the needs of virtual tourists by assembling an assortment of elaborately designed baskets, bold silver jewelry, and graphically striking blankets, which she shipped via the AT&SF railroad to her customers who lived outside of Los Angeles. Her own promotional literature bragged that "every visitor pronounces Miss Nicholson's the most Notable, Beautiful and Unique Shop they ever visited." Nicholson advertised that the store was the perfect place for real and virtual tourists who had an interest in American Indian goods: "If you have a Hobby," reminded Nicholson, "consult this shop."[15]

By selling Indian arts and crafts as items of interior design and decoration, Hubbell, Harvey, and Nicholson all attempted to appeal to those parties, most often women, who were in charge of decorating the home. It has been suggested that men and boys have had a tendency to collect "representations of the male world such as cigar bands and arrowheads," whereas women and girls favored "dolls, flowers and valentines" as collectibles. Gendered behavior has also influenced patterns not only of what men and women collect, but how they go about acquiring such goods. Historically, male collectors, according to Steven Gelber, have actively pursued objects, whereas female hobbyists were "passive recipients."[16] The behavior of Nicholson's clients reveals that virtual tourists had their own way of gathering objects of their desire. To buy an article from Grace Nicholson was not a passive act of consumption, but an act of vicarious travel. Her clients may not have hunted down objects in person as often as their male counterparts, but they did pay someone—a woman, nonetheless—to do so for them. By designing her shop to appeal to women, Nicholson reaffirmed that the hobbies of home decoration and the collection of American Indian artifacts were complementary. In doing so, she made the consumption of Navajo saddle blankets, Apache baskets, and feathered Pomo hairpins a leisure activity that she consciously geared toward women.

Middle- to upper-class women merged the hobbies of home decoration and the collection of Indian-made goods with vicarious travel. As a result, virtual tourism appeared to occur within the gender-appropriate forum of the home and may be one of the reasons why virtual tourism as related to the consumption of Indian-made items has received little attention. Tourists did visit Pasadena to shop for goods, but housebound housewives in search of unique decorative items also purchased goods from Grace Nicholson. These "virtual tourists" contributed considerably to her success. Between 1910 and 1920 Grace Nicholson built an extremely lucrative business as a dealer in American Indian artifacts, and by 1916 she claimed to have sold at least twenty thousand American Indian objects.[17]

At a time when shopping was an uncontested leisure activity for middle- to upper-class American women, Nicholson was able to manipulate the meanings of the goods she sold through a multilayered process of exchange.[18] For her own records and use, she kept a series of "Indian notebooks" in which she documented the number of people who lived in the villages she visited, the kinds of designs that were most often used on different baskets or blankets, and the craft techniques individual artists employed.[19] Nicholson was particularly interested in the lives and cultures of indigenous artisans—especially as they related to the production of goods. Regarding the manufacture of Navajo wedding baskets, for instance, Nicholson documented that "while a real Navajo is weaving a basket she is untouched and avoided by members of her family."[20] Nicholson watched American Indian craftsmen and craftswomen whenever

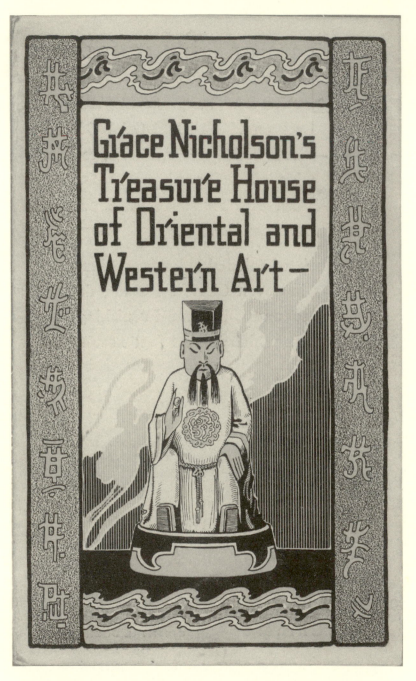

Figure 6.4. Front plate from Nicholson's Treasure Shop brochure. Nicholson Collection, addenda, box 2.

This item is reproduced by permission of the Huntington Library, San Marino, California.

possible, documented what she saw, and, when possible, paid American Indians directly for the products of their labor, which she sold to white consumers for a handsome profit. The crucial aspect of virtual tourism, however, occurred when Nicholson exchanged her experiences with the housebound in addition to stories, ethnographic details, and photographs of American Indians when she shipped the merchandise. Thus shoppers purchased not only what they perceived to be rare American Indian artifacts, they also literally bought a piece of the American Southwest and the ethnographic expertise and adventure that went along with its acquisition. The combination they consumed reaffirmed their social status as, at most, adventurous and worldly women or, at least, disillusioned consumers who were tired of standard department store wares.[21]

When Nicholson traveled, she carefully recorded, in written and photographic forms, where she purchased the goods, who their makers were, and what the goods' patterns and symbols signified according to tribal beliefs. These customs reveal Nicholson's sensitivity to modern business practice and demonstrate her respect for American Indian artisans. At a time when individual efforts were usually subsumed under tribal affiliations, Nicholson's behavior was rare.[22] The photographs and written descriptions were also a meaningful part of the exchange: the more detailed the package, the more value the goods had for consumers. For instance, in 1912 Nicholson sent Mrs. Frank S. Ford a large number of southwestern American Indian artifacts, as well as the stories associated with their use and acquisition. Grace Nicholson authenticated the items she sent to Mrs. Ford by providing information about the baskets such as, "This basket is known as the medicine basket. The little black dots at the ends . . . are supposed to represent the various homes of the spiderwoman, who according to Navajo lore is responsible for the population of the world."[23] In the end, Mrs. Ford paid almost $500 for a collection of forty-two artifacts made by Navajo, Hopi, and Pueblo Indians. The fact that Mrs. Ford spent so much money on the objects indicates she had money to spend on goods that had a particular ethnographic meaning and a large enough home to accommodate them. Her consumption operated as an index of her class, her preferred leisure activity, and her own personal taste.

Although she collected much of her own data, Nicholson also consulted other dealers for information that she passed on to her clients. In 1906, Nicholson asked a dealer in southwestern Indian goods from Santa Fe, A. F. Spiegelberg, to share any knowledge he might have about Navajo ceremonial baskets. He replied that designs on the baskets usually included "spider sorrow crosses," that "the spiderwoman is accredited by Indians of the Southwest for the population of the globe," and that the "little squares on the corner of the crosses" represented "the houses [where] she deposited some of her children" who came to populate the earth. He added, "This basket is used at childbirth."[24] Nicholson often paraphrased and sent such details to clients—as she had for Mrs. Ford—including the symbolic details that she believed Mrs. Ford might find interesting.

Mrs. Jesse Metcalf of Providence, Rhode Island, also shopped at Grace Nicholson's store in Pasadena via mail in 1913. Grace Nicholson sent Mrs. Metcalf a collection of Navajo silver pieces and informed her client that "the workmanship is very different by comparison with the modern stuff made for tourists."[25] Clearly Mrs. Ford and Mrs. Metcalf were not like most tourists, nor did they wish to be classed with them. They desired goods that were not specifically made for "modern tourists," goods that had ethnographic value. Usually such products could only be found in remote areas.

In addition to Mrs. Metcalf, Nicholson had other clients in Providence. Mrs. W. S. Radeke, for instance, found out about Nicholson's store and services from Mrs. William G. Baker. This kind of networking helped Grace Nicholson establish a growing body of clients. Nicholson sent Mrs. Radeke seven Navajo bracelets ranging in price from $6 to $10 each. She also sent concha belts, necklaces, earrings, rings, and Navajo blankets. In total, Mrs. Radeke spent over $300 on Navajo goods. Mrs. Radeke was assured of their quality when Grace Nicholson informed her that if she didn't wish to keep all of the goods she had sent, Mrs. Baker, the woman who arranged contact between Grace Nicholson and Radeke, would present such items to a museum or an art school. She also informed her client that some of the items were very "scarce" and that the "old Navajo [blanket I] selected to send you on account of [the] variety of design used." In addition, Grace Nicholson informed her that "the Chimayo [blanket] with the Brazil wood dye is a lost art" and that "the silver is all genuine old Navajo Indian make."[26] She closed the letter with, "Of course, I have hundreds of other very rare antique art objects which Mrs. Baker wishes you might see personally. If you come to California this winter I could have the pleasure of showing them to you. If that is not possible, I could express them to you for your consideration."[27] Such information allowed virtual tourists to travel to a place, the Southwest, and a time, the past, that existed mostly in the imagination of Nicholson's clients. Virtual tourists, it seems, wanted to experience the period before the Southwest was flooded with "average" tourists who purchased simply curios from American Indians. Ironically, Nicholson sold, and virtual tourists collected, a form of Indian culture that was supposedly untouched by the same modern impulses that allowed people such as Nicholson to travel to the region in the early twentieth century.

Nicholson's success proves that the endeavors of virtual tourism and consumerism were relatively common forms of entertainment and leisure among middle- and upper-class women in the early 1900s. Although there is no profile of Nicholson's average client, her business records do reveal one common feature that many of the women shared: marriage.[28] It was this feature that both enabled virtual tourism and threatened to limit its ties to consumerism. By and large, married women seem to have had less opportunity, or were less willing, to take part in long-distance southwestern tours than single men or women of the same class—unless their husbands also had the desire to travel. Yet marriage did not deter their desire to consume the goods made by southwestern Indians. In some cases, marital status even sparked their desire to buy Indian-made goods and to get away from home. On a particular gloomy day in the winter of 1918, Mrs. Mary C. Jones of Pittsburgh wrote to Grace that "it is a miserable day as far as weather goes . . . the kind of day to give me the blues." The dreary weather made Mrs. Jones consider the possibility of adding to her decorative scheme *and* dream of traveling to the Southwest. "I was going to send for a rug for my Indian room," stated Jones, "but now that there is a prospect of my going out [to California] soon, I think I shall wait." Jones already had two Indian, most likely Navajo rugs, which she claimed "do not look at all badly on the floor for the time being." After giving Nicholson an extensive set of measurements for the size of rug she wanted to buy, Mrs. Jones then revealed that she wasn't actually sure when, or if, she would be able to travel to Pasadena. Although she and Mr. Jones had toured extensively together, it was difficult for her to venture out on her own. In order to travel to southern California, she needed a reason other than leisure. Jones told Nicholson that she might be able to leave Pittsburgh by midsummer "as the theosophic Convention will be . . . held in July." Jones then confided to Nicholson that "I am a little out of touch with the society, but I have not said this to Mr. Jones, as I am keeping that—I mean the Convention—as an excuse to get to California during the summer."[29] Mrs. Mary Jones had to carefully plan a trip if it were to be a leisure activity—even if that might mean traveling at a time when most tourists stayed away from southern California—and hide the true nature of her trip. Touring the Southwest and shopping for Indian rugs were apparently not good enough reasons for her to justify leaving Pittsburgh in the winter of 1918. The reality of her situation led her to dream, on particularly dreary days, of going to California. Luckily Nicholson was there to send her Indian rugs and stories of their acquisition to lift her spirits and transform her immediate environment. The strikingly personal nature of the correspondence between Nicholson and Mrs. Jones also reveals how invested many vicarious travelers became in their quest for virtual tourism—many counted Nicholson as collector, friend, and confidant.

Clients continually sought Nicholson's friendship and advice. W. T. Coatsworth of Buffalo asked Nicholson to send her information and photographs of a large Indian basket she might use as *the* key decorative item on her mantelpiece. She then requested additional advice on how to preserve the baskets she had already purchased. She concluded by stating that shopping via mail had its drawbacks—especially in January in Buffalo. She, like others, wished instead that she could be shopping in California instead of weathering the colder climate of the Northeast.[30]

The assemblage, sale, and consumption of Indian-made materials reflected a layered interaction in which two of the main participants, the dealer and the consumer, reinvented the meaning of the goods. For example, Nicholson wanted to sell only "old," "scarce," "lost," and "rare" pieces to her clients—pieces that they couldn't easily obtain even if they were to go on a standard southwestern tour—for the obvious reasons that she could charge more for such items and because the difficulty of obtaining such goods verified their authenticity. Thus Nicholson's efforts appeared to be worth the amount the consumers paid. Nicholson herself also gained a certain amount of status as the purveyor of goods. She earned her reputation as an expert but also won the sympathies of individuals who didn't want to be lumped in, either physically or mentally, with an ever increasing number of working- and middle-class "modern" tourists.[31] Hundreds of women had the desire to travel in the Southwest; those who were either unable to go or simply found it distasteful to travel as an "average tourist" traveled vicariously through Nicholson.

Becoming a Vessel of Experience

In this exchange, Indian-made goods no longer represented simply what their producers intended. Rather, they became imbued with consumer belief about their symbolism. Nicholson added additional meanings to the goods by traveling in order to get them and then selling the experience as part of the package. To sell the goods she purchased from southwestern American Indians, Nicholson chronicled her experiences while traveling. Such information was used to prove that her career as a dealer was, indeed, one filled with authentic experiences.

Proof of both authenticity and adventure pleased one of Nicholson's wealthiest clients, Mrs. Florence Osgood Rand Lang (1862–1945) of Montclair, New Jersey. Mrs. Lang was a collector of ethnographic materials and an ideal customer for Nicholson. At the urging of her mother, Annie V. Rand, Florence purchased tens of thousands of dollars' worth of Indian artifacts from Nicholson for her personal use. These artifacts would eventually form the basis for the Montclair Art Museum's collection of American Indian arts and crafts.[32] As was her custom, Grace Nicholson carefully noted significant details that enhanced the authenticity of the artifacts and the encounters she, as an adventurous professional, had to go through to acquire them. For example, she made sure to point out that the Navajo silverware she sent Mrs. Lang in October of 1912 was "secured direct from Navajos, who live far away from the Railroad." She added, "I spent the last two months of my trip in New Mexico, and Arizona, visiting nearly every out of the way trading post and crossing and re-crossing the Navajo Reservation a number of times." And as was her trademark, she also included photographs of the Navajo craftswomen and craftsmen who had made the material she was sending to Mrs. Lang.[33]

The photographs, and the assurance that the Navajos she traded with "lived far from the railroad," eliminated any questions Mrs. Lang might have about either the authenticity of the items she was purchasing or the adventure one might go through in order to get them. Mrs. Lang was interested in southwestern Indians but decided, for unknown reasons, not to go on a collecting tour of her own.[34] Instead she traveled extensively in Europe, summered in Nantucket, wintered in Pasadena, and patronized Grace Nicholson's shop in the meantime. To Mrs. Lang the items in her collection represented bona fide southwestern American Indians, ethnographic expertise, and a form of adventure that she sought but did not have the time or patience to experience.[35]

Similar stories of acquisition and affirmations of authenticity were common in Nicholson's correspondence with the rest of her clients and illustrate the distance between vicarious and actual tourists. These themes appeared in various forms: in her claims that items were secured direct from American Indians, in her extensive documentation of the myths associated with the goods, in the photographs she took of the producers, and in the stories she told her clients of her experiences while searching out the items sold in her shop. The adventures Nicholson reported included camping, hiking, viewing ceremonial dances, participating in Indian rituals, and crisscrossing large sections of the American West. Average tourists traveled to a real if often prepackaged version of "Indian country"; vicarious tourists did not. Instead they might one-up the average tourist by paying someone else to undergo the hardships of finding "out-of-the-way" places and "scarce" materials for them. They still "toured" but only through another's words and actions and, most importantly, through the materials that embodied them.

As a vessel of experience, both Nicholson and her goods offered virtual tourists a much less challenging form of adventure, replete with all the spoils

Figure 6.5 This photograph is typical of the kind that Nicholson sent or showed to clients who sought ethnographic knowledge as well as handmade items. Navajo Indians at loom. Grace Nicholson Collection, vol. 56, photo scrapbooks.

This item is reproduced by permission of the Huntington Library, San Marino, California.

of a tour and none of the hardship. Those who wished to obtain southwestern Indian goods but wanted to avoid the bad food, uncomfortable beds, tiring hikes, and actual contact with American Indians purchased a sterilized and semischolarly experience through Nicholson. Nicholson knew that many of her clients may have wanted Navajo rugs or Santa Clara pottery for their living rooms, but she also knew that many were uninterested in or afraid of the more graphic details of American Indian life. Accordingly, she provided clients with a narrative of consumption that was rich with ethnographic detail. For instance, Nicholson commonly told buyers that the design of the Navajo medicine basket "was symbolic," that a Navajo basket was made out of "twigs of the sumac (ki or chil chin) . . . a triple incision is made into the butt end of the twig, one part is held between the teeth while the other two are torn off with the fingers," or that "it is explained by the Medicine Men of the present day that the 'thunder stones' were used by them in certain secret ceremonies, for producing lightning and accompanying rain."[36] These were the kind of details that purchasers might relate to visitors to entertain and/or impress them. But Nicholson also methodically withheld information from her clients regarding the less creative or mystical details of life on American Indian reservations. In doing so, she transformed her experiences with southwestern Indians into a narrative fit for middle- to upper-class consumers.

Thus the "tourist" narrative that Nicholson constructed was heavily edited. For instance, while traveling throughout Navajo and Pueblo country in the summer of 1912, she confided to her close personal friend Alice Phromm:

> Between you and I this has been one of the hardest trips I've made this summer. Lost in weight . . . Mr. H. [Hartman] and I wanted to visit the adjoining Pueblos so went to Oraibi with a one armed government official and he succeeded in getting us accommodated [sic] at the Government building—en route we killed an enormous rattle snake, and I have the 8 tailfins.

Referring to the most difficult part of the trip, Nicholson continued, "I was disappointed with the Pueblo as it is so filthy and the Indians are in dreadful shape with trachoma . . . a serious contagious eye trouble." Nicholson may have wanted to hide news of this disease, which Navajos also suffered from, as clients were already prone to return goods if they had any strange characteristics. In many instances, Nicholson began "bathing" Indian baskets in gasoline before shipping them to clients in order to rid them of odors and/or sanitize them.[37]

In the same letter Nicholson informed her friend of another frightening and difficult experience that she did not share with her clients. After attending a "disappointing" Flute Dance, Nicholson traveled an additional eighteen miles to attend the same ceremony again at Wishangnovi and Shipaulovi. "At the later place," she told Phromm, "I had an unusual experience."

> On this trip I'd been wearing my Thubehon turquoise necklace. It has caught the Indians' eye and is often a means of opening conversation. Mr. Ladd was in some house and Mr. H. [Hartman] was near taking pictures. A young Indian admired my necklace and went in the doorway of his house and beckoned me. I had been inquiring for some small katchina baskets. He said he had some and pointed to the west room—I entered and was about to pass him when I noticed the room darken. He had closed the door quietly and fastened it inside with a nail. I gave him one look and demanded that he open the door. I tell you I hunted up my party in a jiffy.[38]

It is unclear exactly what Nicholson began to fear when the unnamed Indian shut the door. Whether she feared that he would take the necklace, or make a pass—or something worse—at her, even with her assistant, Mr. Carol Hartman, nearby, Nicholson clearly felt threatened.

Although Nicholson faithfully recounted the more antiseptic details of her travels and ethnological data to consumers, she never mentioned the poisonous snakes, poverty, disease, and potentially threatening behavior that were also part of her experiences. As a businesswoman she selected details that would enhance the value of southwestern Indian-made goods. Stories recounting safe adventure, photographs, and ethnographic details authenticated purchases and were qualities her clients desired, whereas disease, danger, and despair were not. The type of details Nicholson sent to purchasers along with products reinforced to the consumers that they were buying authentic, handcrafted items made by the nonthreatening, healthy, and picturesque peoples depicted in the common tourist literature. This occurred despite the fact that her clients voiced their desire to avoid the "average" tourist experience.

Virtual Tourism and Its Consequences

Nicholson managed to build a highly successful business that catered to actual and virtual tourists, and her prosperity can be attributed to the fact that her occupation tapped into, and reinforced, both contemporary style and the leisure activities of women. But Nicholson did more than tap into current trends—she also supported young women who wished to turn their interest in arts and crafts into a moneymaking enterprise. In 1931, for instance, when she endowed a scholarship at Scripps College to be awarded to young women art students, Nicholson demonstrated her desire to share some of the wealth she had accumulated in support of younger women who might wish to receive formal training in the field of art and thus, perhaps, actively pursue their own adventures.

Regardless of whether or not the young women of Scripps College were successful in actively experiencing life's adventures on their own, the virtual tourists of the 1900s who had hired Nicholson to tour and collect for them established trends that would be continued by cultural tourists of later generations. These women sought out specific forms of cultural entertainment through the consumption of American Indian culture. They consumed "old," rare," and scarce" items that had been made by indigenous Americans they imagined to be physically healthy—if supposedly disappearing—as a form of recreation. In this sense, virtual tourism, like contemporary cultural tourism, served a multiplicity of needs for its participants. First, virtual tourism enabled middle- and upper-class women to distance themselves from both the average tourists and the real American Indians of the Southwest that they might have actually come into contact with had they gone on a southwestern tour. The distance between virtual tourists, average tourists, and actual American Indians demarcated their class status. Mrs. Lang, for instance, who had the status of wealth and privilege, didn't need to go on collecting tours as she could afford to pay Nicholson to do it for her. The status that accompanied being able to pay someone to travel was especially important for women who were often unable, even if they were willing, to travel. In all cases, buying a "secondhand" experience allowed them to consume the trappings of adventure and style without sacrificing the authenticity of the items they purchased for their personal comfort and status. Thus their class afforded them the opportunity to straddle the worlds of "true womanhood" that dictated the gender-appropriate behavior of devoted housewifery and the emerging "cult of personality" that encouraged women to display their own personality through their hobbies or in their decorative schemes. As an agent of both vicarious travel and consumerism, Grace Nicholson enabled virtual tourists to walk between the worlds of wife and adventurer by wrapping the goods she sold in a blanket of ethnographic detail and authentic experience while conjuring the transcendent aspects of shopping and travel.[39]

As an adventurous, unmarried businesswoman, Nicholson profited from the concept of virtual tourism, and her clients reaped the benefits of the practice. Not surprisingly, however, a relatively high price accompanied the consumption that gave breath to the virtual tourist experience. The demand for Indian-made goods to be used as markers of class, leisure, and personality had a unique effect on American Indians of the Southwest, particularly the Navajo. Because "old," "rare" and "scarce" goods were the most popular, important ceremonial goods began to disappear from the reservations. Bertha Little, one of Nicholson's contacts on the Navajo Reservation, told Nicholson in 1907 that old Navajo wedding baskets, like the one sold to Mrs. Ford, "are very scarce and when the singings [ceremonies] are held the Indians often borrow baskets from each other, the traders, or missionaries or anyone else who is fortunate enough to have one." As the supply of key ceremonial objects left the reservation, certain objects became more and more difficult for Navajo Indians to make or to find. In fact, today old Navajo wedding baskets have all but disappeared from the reservation. Thus the consumption of Indian-made goods was more than a benign practice that afforded women of a certain class a tool for displaying status or escaping the confines of their homes: it also worked to deprive southwestern Indians of some of their most important cultural vessels.

Notes

1. Sally McLendon, "Pomo Baskets: The Legacy of William and Mary Benson," *Native Peoples: The Arts and Lifeways* (fall 1990), 26–33, and "Collecting Pomoan Baskets, 1889–1939," *Museum Anthropology: Journal of the Council for Museum Anthropology* (June 1993): 49–59; Douglas Cole, *Captured Heritage: The Scramble for Northwest Coast Artifacts* (Norman: University of Oklahoma Press, 1985), 236–37; Nicholson's most profitable period occurred between 1912 and 1934. *Grace Nicholson Summary Report*, Grace Nicholson Collection (GNC), Box 12, Folder 10, Huntington Library, San Marino, Calif.

2. T. C. McLuhan, *Dream Tracks: The Railroad and the American Indian, 1890–1930* (New York: Harry N. Abrams, 1985), 19.

3. On automobile tourism, see Phoebe Kropp's essay in this collection. Marta Weigle, "'Insisted on Authenticity': Harveycar Indian Detours, 1925–1931," in *The Great Southwest of the Fred Harvey Company and the Santa Fe Railway*, eds. Marta Weigle and Barbara Babcock (Phoenix: Heard Museum, 1996), 47; Curtis M. Hinsley, Jr., "Authoring Authenticity," *Journal of the Southwest* 32 (winter 1990): 462.

4. Nicholas Thomas, "Licensed Curiosity: Cook's Pacific Voyages," and Anthony Alan Shelton, "Cabinets of Transgression: Renaissance Collections and the Incorporation of the New World," in *The Cultures of Collecting*, eds. John Elsner and Roger Cardinal (London: Reakin Books, 1994), 116–136, 177–203.

5. Nicholas Thomas, *Entangled Objects: Exchange, Material Culture, and Colonization in the Pacific* (Cambridge, Mass.: Harvard University Press, 1991), 126; Cole, *Captured Heritage*, 12.

6. I am borrowing the idea of authentic experience from T. J. Jackson Lears, *No Place of Grace: Antimodernism and the Transformation of American Culture, 1880–1920* (Chicago: University of Chicago Press, 1981), 5. By the late nineteenth century, Lears suggests, "for the educated bourgeoisie, authentic experience of any sort seemed ever more elusive; life seemed increasingly confined to the airless parlor of material comfort and moral complacency." But unlike those who he describes as wanting to shatter their confinement, I propose that virtual tourists found a way to circumvent it. They sought out "authentic experience" via shopping for items that conjured a different time, a different place, and a different people.

7. Erika M. Bsumek, "Making 'Indian Made': The Production, Consumption, and Construction of Navajo Ethnic Identity, 1880–1935" (Ph.D. diss., Rutgers, State University of New Jersey, 2000), 112–33. Molly H. Mullins illustrates how some educated and elite white women used American Indian arts and crafts as a way to "study" American Indian culture. Molly H. Mullins, *Culture in the Marketplace: Gender, Art, and Value in the American Southwest* (Durham, N.C.: Duke University Press, 2001), 63–67.

8. Weigle and Babcock, *The Great Southwest*, xv.

9. Diana F. Pardue, "Marketing Ethnography: The Fred Harvey Indian Department and George A. Dorsey," in Weigle and Babcock, *The Great Southwest*, 102–8.

10. David Brugge, *Hubbell Trading Post: National Historic Site* (Tucson, Ariz.: Southwest Parks and Monuments Association, 1993), 28; Frank McNitt, *The Indian Traders* (Norman: University of Oklahoma Press, 1962), 210; Bsumek, "Making 'Indian Made,' 79–84."

11. Nicholson made a number of important collecting trips to the Southwest. She visited and corresponded with Hubbell, Spiegelberg, Moore, and the Benham brothers. See J. L. Hubbell to Grace Nicholson, 3 October 1903, and A. F. Spiegelberg to Carol Hartman (Nicholson's assistant), 1 October 1906, GNC. In 1912, Nicholson went on an extensive tour of the Southwest. See Nicholson Letterbook, 1912, GNC. She also traveled to the area prior to 1912 on shorter trips.

12. Virginia L. Grattan, *Mary Colter: Builder Upon the Red Earth* (Grand Canyon, Ariz.: Grand Canyon History Association, 1992), 8. The Indian interiors at Harvey Hotels were designed to merchandise Indian-made goods.

13. Katherine Grier, *Culture and Comfort: Parlor Making and Middle-Class Identity, 1850–1930* (Washington, D.C.: Smithsonian Institution Press, 1988), 33.

14. Nicholson to Mrs. Radeke, Providence, R.I., 1 November 1912, Nicholson Letterbook, 1912. My analysis does not include all of Nicholson's business transactions but rather locates certain patterns and behaviors that typified the exchanges between Nicholson and her customers.

15. Capitalization as in the original document "Grace Nicholson's Treasure House of Oriental and Western Art, Circa 1929," addenda, box 2, GNC, Huntington Library.

16. Steven M. Gelber, *Hobbies: Leisure and the Culture of Work in America* (New York: Columbia University Press, 1999), 101.

17. Summary Report, GNC, 2. Joan M. Jensen, *One Foot in the Rockies: Women and Creativity in the Modern American West* (Albuquerque: University of New Mexico Press, 1995), 61–66, 116. Jensen indicates Nicholson was part of a network of women who collected information on American Indians.

18. Elaine S. Abelson asserts that shopping was the primary form of women's leisure during the late nineteenth and early twentieth century. Elaine Abelson, *When Ladies Go A-Thieving: Middle-Class Shoplifters in the Victorian Department Store* (New York: Oxford University Press, 1989), 21; Victoria De Grazia and Ellen Furlough, eds., *The Sex of Things: Gender and Consumption in Historical Perspective* (Berkeley: University of California Press), 1996.

19. 1912, Indian Notebook, GNC.
20. Ibid.
21. Using Indian goods to decorate one's home had become a trend by the 1920s. Erika Marie Bsumek, "Making 'Indian Made'"; see especially chapter 3.
22. Molly Mullins, "The Patronage of Difference: Making Indian Art Art, Not Ethnology," in *The Traffic in Culture: Refiguring Art and Anthropology*, eds. George E. Marcus and Fred R. Myers (Berkeley: University of California Press, 1995), 179. Mullins reports that there were a few "patrons" of Indian art who worked with individual Indian artists, but identifying artists with the goods that they made was not common practice in the early twentieth century. Nicholson occasionally attributed pieces to artisans and is unique in this regard.
23. Nicholson to Mrs. Frank S. Ford, 1912, Nicholson Letterbook, 1912, pp. 81–84, GNC.
24. A. F. Spiegelberg to Mr. Carol Hartman, 1 October 1906, GNC.
25. Grace Nicholson to Mrs. Jesse Metcalf, 21 October 1913. Mrs. Metcalf was delighted with Nicholson's work and purchased an additional $251.50 worth of Indian goods in 1913. Another item sent to Metcalf was an "old Spanish shawl for $150.00." This bumps up the total cost of goods Metcalf purchased from Nicholson to $361.50. Nicholson Letterbook, 1912, p. 99, GNC.
26. Nicholson to Mrs. Radeke, Nicholson Letterbook, 1912, p. 107, GNC.
27. Grace Nicholson to Mrs. Radeke, 32 Prospect St., Providence, R.I., 1 November 1912, Nicholson Letterbook, pp. 107–8, GNC.
28. Out of the individuals for whom there was data, more than 50 percent were women and only one, Matilda Coxe Stevenson, represented an institution (GNC).
29. Mary C. Jones to Grace Nicholson, ca. 1918, GNC.
30. W. T. Coatsworth to Grace Nicholson, 14 November 1910, Buffalo, N.Y., GNC.
31. On early-twentieth-century tourism see Hal Rothman, *Devil's Bargains: Tourism in the Twentieth-Century West* (Lawrence: University Press of Kansas, 1998); Cindy S. Aron, *Working at Play: A History of Vacations in the United States* (New York: Oxford University Press, 1999), 223–28; and Dona Brown, *Inventing New England: Regional Tourism in the Nineteenth Century* (Washington, D.C.: Smithsonian Institution Press, 1995), 210. Brown reveals that as work patterns changed, so too did patterns of leisure. More and more middle- and working-class individuals began to tour, and tour packages became increasingly popular. As this occurred, Nicholson's status increased as she offered wealthy consumers the adventure associated with "off the beaten track" tours and a prepackaged experience.
32. Eventually Lang allowed her private collection to be viewed by the public when she donated it to the Montclair Art Museum (MAM) in 1931 in memory of her mother, who had been cofounder of this museum. She also gave $50,000 to the building fund.
33. Nicholson Letterbook, 1912, p. 101, GNC. Mrs. Lang was the heir to the Rand-Ingersoll machinery fortune. She was a supporter of women's suffrage and a member of the Daughters of the American Revolution, the Altruist Society, and many other women's organizations. Although she did not belong to Nicholson's average class of clients, her behavior was not significantly different from theirs. In fact, most of Nicholson's clients sought to emulate wealthy individuals like the Langs. On Nicholson sending photographs of items and artifacts to Lang, see Nicholson to Lang, 16 January 1914, Lang Collection, MAM.
34. The Langs "wintered" in Pasadena. I have found no evidence that they ever went on "Indian tours" themselves.
35. Mr. and Mrs. Lang often delayed traveling to California because traveling conditions were sometimes troublesome. In 1918, for instance, she wrote to Nicholson that they "finally decided not to go to California this year on account of the poor travelling facilities." Mrs.

Lang to Miss Grace Nicholson, 1 April 1918, MAM. Although the Langs did travel to California, I have not found any evidence they spent considerable time in New Mexico, Arizona, or other southwestern destinations that were considered more adventurous than Pasadena. Additional correspondence from Nicholson to Lang is peppered with ethnographic details. See Nicholson to Lang, 10 November 1911, 11 November 1912, 20 October 1913, and many other dates (MAM).

36. Medicine basket quote comes from Nicholson Letterbook, 1912, p. 79, GNC. Quote about twigs comes from Grace Nicholson, *Indian Notes*, 1912, p. 66, GNC. Quote regarding the "modern medicine men" comes from 11 March 1913 letter from Grace Nicholson to Mrs. Lang, Lang Collection, MAM.

37. Nicholson to Alice Phromm, 26 August 1912, GNC; Robert A. Trennert, *White Man's Medicine: Government Doctors and the Navajo, 1863–1955* (Albuquerque: University of New Mexico Press, 1998), 48, 165, 209. Nicholson often advised clients on how to use gasoline as a way to kill germs and odors.

38. Nicholson to Alice Phromm, 26 August 1912, GNC.

39. On the transcendent aspects of consumption of handmade arts and crafts, see Lears, *No Place of Grace*, 91–96.

APPROPRIATE CULTURAL TOURISM— CAN IT EXIST? SEARCHING FOR AN ANSWER

THREE ARIZONA CASE STUDIES ⟞

WILLIAM L. BRYAN, JR.

Tourism is big business and getting bigger. It's the second-largest industry in the Southwest. Visitors and spending are up. Consolidation is the
wave of the future. Internet bookings are soaring and fundamentally changing the world of tourism marketing. More frequent, yet shorter getaways and
more adventure travel are becoming the norm. Travelers want more
thoughtful and more active vacations. Cultural enrichment tourism is rapidly gaining in popularity.

One could go on with such banner headlines and pronouncements. They
are found in most travel newsletters and are expounded upon by travel spe-
cialists, futurists, and travel trend experts in the marketplace. What does this
all really mean to the tourism industry and to the rest of us who at one time
or another are vacation travelers? What does this mean to the natural environment in which so many tourism activities take place? What does it mean
to communities where these tourism endeavors are carried out? And most
importantly, concerning the subject of this essay, what does it mean to the
growing cultural tourism sector of the economy in the American Southwest?
Exploring this topic in detail is most daunting and perhaps too ambitious for
this essay. Nevertheless, here I focus on three different cultural tourism
endeavors that are operating in Arizona. None should be viewed as successes
or failures unless we are clear on how success is defined. Instead these are
daring experiments by individuals and organizations wanting to create interactive, cross-cultural, and authentic experiences that are enriching, educational, and fun for the engaged traveler. At the same time, these experiments

are trying to be environmentally responsible and accountable to the communities in which they occur. But with these endeavors is a bottom line for each individual/institution: they must be profitable. In other words, these endeavors are steeped in the principles of capitalism.

Although the intent may be honorable, it is indeed difficult to create and grow sustainable cultural tourism enterprises in an industry that is basically extractive by nature, where volume is key and where, in most cases, bigger is better. Traditional tourism success in Arizona has always been measured by the number of people who visit the Grand Canyon during a given year (over 4.9 million), the number of people who come to Arizona as tourists on an annual basis (over 30 million), and the rate of growth from year to year in those numbers. Tourism is a low-margin business, which means volume is all-important for it to be profitable. Furthermore, most tourism enterprises pay only lip service to environmental and community accountability. Ecotourism is more often a marketing ploy than a significant characteristic of tourism activities.[1] Most importantly, the bottom line is inviolate. Don't for a moment think differently.

Can appropriate tourism endeavors really exist that are nonexploitive of community and environment, are renewable, and can replenish the environment and communities in which they occur? Perhaps. We at Off the Beaten Path[2] try to select such programs and activities. Our primary focus for the last fifteen years has been to create and provide custom experiences for clients in the regions where we operate. We then design journeys based on client interests and at the same time try to integrate our agenda concerning community and environmental accountability. Despite laudable attempts, more often than not the ideal is shortchanged. However, the three southwestern business activities described in this essay are examples of great efforts to create and maintain appropriate cultural endeavors. These entities are Coyote Pass Hospitality in Tsaile, Arizona; the La Ruta Program being developed by La Ruta de Sonora Ecotourism Association in Ajo; and the Sonoran Institute in Tucson. Various farm and ranch recreation enterprises are also being developed and implemented by many southeastern Arizona ranchers.

Appropriate Cultural Tourism

Appropriate tourism embodies leisure-time activities that are governed by the uniqueness of the human and natural environments within which the activity takes place. Furthermore, appropriate tourism intertwines recreation and education in ways that enhance and maintain a sustainable local economy and a quality natural and human environment.

Ecotourism

According to the Ecotourism Society, ecotourism is responsible travel to natural areas that conserves the environment and improves the well-being of local people.

As we look at the above-mentioned commercial tourism enterprises, particular emphasis is given to how each endeavor addresses four salient operating issues that underlie the appropriate tourism specialty travel industry. These issues are

1. Tourism as an inherently extractive industry;
2. The dominance of volume in defining basic tourism practices;
3. The issue of pricing;
4. The struggle to develop and adhere to tourism standards.

First, a brief elaboration on these four topics.

Tourism as an inherently extractive industry

Simply put, outdoor tourism endeavors, in most instances, take more than they give to the human and natural resources utilized in the recreational experience. Fishing, hiking, horseback riding, mountain biking, camping, and sightseeing in national parks and other parks all fall into this category. The same can be said to be true with most cultural recreational experiences, such as visiting a Native American tribe or a Hutterite or Amish community, spending time on a working ranch, or reliving romantic fantasies of rural life in small southwestern ranching communities.

The prevailing paradigm is, how can one recreate as cheaply as possible? This way of thinking primarily focuses on monetary costs, yet rarely on environmental and community costs. And it derives from what we all learned when we were young—that is any form of outdoor recreation should be done for free or close to it. This attitude is particularly prevalent in the western part of the United States, where public lands and wildlife are basic parts of the equation. Recreating at the expense of communities, ecosystems, or species is something about which we historically have given very little thought. In a cultural tourism context, human and cultural resources are there to be engaged and utilized as inexpensively as possible. In many ways, it is a logical extension of traditional Christian mythology, where natural resources are there for people to use as we see fit.

The dominance of volume in defining tourism practices

Volume has historically been a key ingredient in the tourism economy and thus is important for profitable tourism endeavors. This is highlighted by state tourism bureaus or chambers of commerce when they gauge the success of the tourism sector. Volume statistics at state and national parks are viewed as strong indicators of how successful tourism is in a given time period—the more the better. Only recently has resource capacity in regard to numbers of people been given much attention in the tourism world.[3] Limits on multi-day river trips in the Grand Canyon and how visitors are regulated on the valley floor of Canyon de Chelly are the exception rather than the norm in managing capacity on public lands.[4]

However, in the private sector, limits on volume frequently are not only accepted, but are often seen as opportunities to extend profit margins. For example, when you go on safari at Animal Kingdom (Walt Disney World) for $44, your safari touring vehicle leaves at intervals that allow visitors to never see those who are ahead or behind them, giving the impression that they are seeing animals "on their own" and in an exclusive manner. Another example is ultra-exclusive Necker Island in the British Virgin Islands, which has twelve rooms that are only rented to one party at a time. This exclusive trip costs a total of $12,000 to $16,000 a day (all inclusive for six days). Outfitters working on private land at Vermejo Park near Raton, New Mexico, and Jicarilla Apache in Dulce, New Mexico, where hunter numbers can be strictly controlled, get at least $10,000 per hunter for a trophy elk hunt. In contrast, an outfitted elk expedition on public lands costs $2,800 to $3,200 per six-day hunt. The best fly-fishing in the West is usually found on private water, where there are limits on how many fishermen can fish a stream at any one time; daily rod fees can be as much as $300 a day.

These examples all demonstrate that private entrepreneurs have long since discovered the value of exclusivity, where the highest-quality outdoor experiences occur with fewer numbers of people, and that a growing number of people are willing to pay the corresponding price.

Ironically, on public lands, where the private sector operates as permitted concessionaires or commercial outfitters, tourism companies have had a much harder time accepting limits on resource capacity. For example, in Yellowstone National Park most private concessionaires are opposed to restrictions on volume during Yellowstone's winter season, where 1,500 to 2,000 snowmobiles a day are not uncommon, creating more air pollution on a daily basis than automobiles create in the park during a summer season. There are some exceptions where the private sector operating on public lands has accepted the concept of resource capacity. The limited number of permittees allowed to float the Colorado River through the Grand Canyon is a good example. The same is true on the Middle Fork of the Salmon River. Limits on outfitted backcountry use in most national parks are generally accepted as well. Unfortunately, private enterprise rarely takes the lead in helping determine such limits but more frequently sees them as a threat to doing business.

Low volumes and limited capacity are crucial to high-quality cultural tourism experiences. Ideal sizes for small groups experiencing cultural tourism endeavors are no more than fourteen to sixteen people, whereas most profitable group tour enterprises work with twenty to forty people at any given time. These larger sizes are essential in making trips "affordable" and at the same time profitable. So an inherent problem arises. Can one have affordable yet profitable cultural tourism operating in small communities or fragile environments? Or is it inevitable that cultural tours in the twenty- to forty-person range are the only ones that can profitably exist, thereby dictating that cultural activities are usually contrived experiences with the entertainment component dominating educational efforts and cross-cultural interactions?

The issue of pricing

If one assumes that sustainable cultural tourism requires interactive experiences in very small group situations, what sector of the public can afford such experiences, and will they purchase tours where appropriate cultural tourism practices are seriously attempted? Does this doom cultural tours to become elitist experiences that only those who are willing to spend $250 to $350 per person a day can afford? Can such tours accommodate all the needs of elite tourists, particularly their demands of high-quality accommodations and costly dietary preferences? Aren't people who truly want a sustainable tourism experience those who value human interactions, traditional meals, meeting with elders, spending a day with a rancher doing chores? Are these people used to spending $300 per person or more a day for their recreational experience? Doesn't this reality contradict the belief that appropriate cultural tourism should be cheap and affordable? Isn't it also true that most of us have the impression that cross-cultural exchanges are less costly than high-technology recreational experiences? Therefore a presumption is made that an in-depth visit with a Navajo family or being part of a ranching family's daily life should be much less expensive than playing golf at a major destination resort in Phoenix or river rafting through the Grand Canyon.

Unfortunately, it doesn't work that way. Looking at the accompanying costing sheets (table 1) and their pricing for a possible cultural tourism small group tour in the Four Corners area of the Southwest, one can readily see why such an experience is a lot more expensive per person than if it were a large bus tour. In the table I tried to incorporate realistic pricing for both fixed and variable costs and fair wages for expedition leaders and community resource people. No doubt, some community costs are omitted and most likely never accounted for.

Table 7.1

Possible Costing for Hypothetical Four Corners Journey

Number Participants			12	36
Fixed Costs				
Guides' Fees & Expenses	Rate/Day ($)	# Days		
Guide 1 fee	200.00	9	1,800.00	1,800.00
Guide 2 fee	200.00	9	1,800.00	
Guide 1 expenses			900.00	900.00
Guide 2 expenses			900.00	
Guides' airfare			700.00	350.00
Transportation	Rate/Day ($)	# Days		
2 Vans (fee, gas, insurance)	250.00	9	2,250.00	
Motor coach				4,800.00
Driver room, gratuity				700.00
Resource People				
Local guide, Mesa Verde NP Includes entrance fee			400.00	900.00
Will Tsosie— 2 day tours	$25/person/day		600.00	1,800.00[*]
Total Fixed Costs			$9,350.00	$9,450.00
Fixed Cost per Person			$779.17	$262.50
Variable Costs (per Person, Net)				
Day 1: Arrive Durango				
1/2 twin hotel, w/tax			47.00	47.00
Dinner			25.00	25.00
Day 2: Mesa Verde				
1/2 twin hotel, w/tax			47.00	47.00
Meals			40.00	40.00

Table 7.1 *(continued)*

Day 3: Ute Mt./Hovenweep/Bluff

Ute Mountain Tour	30.00	30.00
$^1/_2$ twin hotel, w/tax	47.00	47.00
Hovenweep entrance fee	5.00	5.00
Meals	40.00	40.00

Day 4: San Juan Float

$^1/_2$ twin hotel, w/tax	30.00	30.00
Meals	25.00	25.00
San Juan Float, inc. lunch, gratuity	87.00	87.00

Day 5: Jeep Tour, Monument Valley

$^1/_2$ twin hotel, w/tax	30.00	30.00
Jeep tour, inc. lunch, gratuity	90.00	90.00
Meals	25.00	25.00

Day 6: Coyote Pass Hospitality/Chinle

$^1/_2$ twin hotel, w/tax	50.00	50.00
Meals	45.00	45.00

Day 7: Jeep Tour, Canyon de Chelly

$^1/_2$ twin hotel, w/tax	50.00	50.00
Meals	42.00	42.00
Jeep tour, inc. gratuity	45.00	45.00

Day 8: To Durango

$^1/_2$ twin hotel, w/tax	70.00	70.00
Meals	35.00	35.00

Day 9: Departure

Miscellaneous Charges per Person	74.00	54.00

Subtotal per Person	979.00	959.00
Fixed Costs per Person (16 passengers)	779.17	262.50

Total Cost per Person (net)		$1,758.17		$1,221.50
	25%	2,344.22	25%	1,628.67
Gross profit		7,032.67		14,658.00
	30%	2,511.67	30%	1,745.00
Gross profit		9,042.00		18,846.00
	35%	2,704.87	35%	1,879.23
Gross profit		11,360.46		23,678.31
Selling price		$2,695.00		$1,925.00

Profit at 35% Gross Profit

10 passengers @ $2,695/person:	$9,368.33
30 passengers @ $1,925/person:	$21,105.00

Notes

Fixed costs: Stay the same regardless of group size.

Table 7.1 *(continued)*

Variable costs: Vary depending on group size.

Lodging costs: Reflect double occupancy, lodging, tax, and net price of likely accommodations used on this tour.

Meal costs: Breakfasts are excluded; lunch and dinner costs reflect amounts likely to be incurred on this tour.

Markup: Varies depending on the tour company; anywhere from a low of 25 percent to a high of 45 percent. Markup for domestic trips is rarely above 40 percent. Here 35 percent is used because marketing costs are not accounted for in fixed trip costs.

*The total from 36 people x $25 per person x 2 days is probably too large. Will Tsosie would probably settle for a lower price.

Specifically, if the group size is twelve, the cost per person is $2,695 for a nine-day trip. This assumes a 35-percent markup and nets $11,360 gross profit to the tour operator. For a group of thirty-six visitors (a bus tour), the price for the same trip would be $1,895 and the tour operator has a gross profit of $23,678, again assuming the 35-percent markup. If the numbers of actual paying customers on the journey are lower than these "full" numbers, margins change. But the change is less dramatic in the bus tour scenario (see table 1).

In looking at these cost sheets, one can ascertain that the larger the group, the more affordable the per person price. Therein lies the dilemma. Is appropriate cultural tourism with small group sizes practical only for the most affluent? Do such tourism endeavors exacerbate the growing problem of classism in our society? Or do we need to look at cultural tourism and tourism in general in fundamentally different ways?

One other aspect of price and profitability is that frequently the local cultural tourism host or provider is an individual well trained in how to interact effectively in cross-cultural situations. But in most third world and developing nations these professional resource suppliers are being paid on a daily basis substantially more than other vendors in their communities. Furthermore, their daily wage is based in part on their knowledge of communal resources. Therefore a complex issue arises as to whether their preferred role in the community is appropriate and what, if any, costs should be allocated to maintaining and nourishing and in some cases replenishing communal resources. If only the guides or hosts benefit economically in developing communities, is it truly appropriate cultural tourism?

The struggle to develop and adhere to tourism standards

The concept of standards concerning the delivery of services in the tourism economic sector has not been a high priority among the business community.

Standards that have been created and implemented have been initiated by insurance companies and regulatory agencies. For example, a backcountry horse outfitter operating in a national forest or park comes under guidelines developed by the U.S. Forest Service or the National Park Service. They also operate under the insurance carrier guidelines from whom they get their liability insurance. Very little comes by way of a private association or organization of outfitters. Most associations pay lip service to the standards issue. There are exceptions, like the river rafting industry, where, because of strong competition in the marketplace, river outfitter associations such as the Fishing Outfitters Association of Montana (FOAM) have been very active in creating, implementing, and policing their own standards. But with natural history or cultural interpreters, associations such as the Natural History Interpretive Association have only voluntary standards that are not seriously adhered to or enforced. Therefore the idea of developing, implementing, and being held accountable to standards in the appropriate cultural tourism world is in essence nonexistent. It is up to the deliverer to follow his or her own code of ethics. This means that caveat emptor—buyer beware—must be the consumer's watchword.

Where accommodations and related services are concerned, the star rating system in Europe is well known in the tourism industry and taken very seriously by overnight guests. In the United States, AAA and Mobile Guide ratings and customer-oriented newsletters like the "Hideaway Report," "The Angler's Guide," and "Passport" provide some evaluation and assessment. Condé Nast Traveler also tends to be consumer oriented in critiquing accommodations and services. But most rating systems are arbitrary and don't come close to having clear and consistent standards in their assessments or categorization of services. As a result, their usefulness is not taken as seriously as the star system and is rarely considered in trip planning by most travelers.

Coyote Pass Hospitality

"A unique experience awaits you. A very special doorway is now open for you. This entry leads to a remarkable cultural experience—something that has not been available at any other place or at any other time. This is your opportunity to participate in a once-in-a-lifetime journey into the world of the Navajo People."

This is the opening paragraph describing Coyote Pass Hospitality, the brainchild of Will Tsosie, a traditional Navajo and devoted ambassador of the Navajo culture. Will, with his extended family, wants his guests to experience his way of living, culture, and environment—and to do so on his terms.

Coyote Pass Hospitality has been in operation since 1992.[5] Totally dedicated to appropriate cultural tourism, Will Tsosie and his family work hard to establish situations where there are cross-cultural understandings. They first get to understand the guests' perspective and then assist them in learning and integrating the traditional Navajo view into their world of thought and life. As their brochure says, "Your guides (Will Tsosie and family) will shepherd you through many facets of Navajo life—oral tradition, ethnographic interpretation, ceremonies, herbology, and philosophy. Sit with a rug weaver while she works or watch a silversmith at his craft. You may expand your knowledge to include neighboring tribes; our guides are most knowledgeable about other Native American cultures of the Southwest."

Coyote Pass Hospitality explores the countryside, visiting many archeological sites and learning about the Anasazi, from whom some believe the Navajo descend. This is done by visiting various ruins in the vicinity of Chinle. At the same time, the traveler also experiences the scenic vistas of the immediate area in which Coyote Pass Hospitality works, including the spectacular mountains and hills of Lukachukai. One can even spend time with part of the Tsosie family, who raise sheep during the summer in the mountain country. When appropriate, Will wants the visitor to experience life as a Native American. Often he and his guides will allow the visitor to experience Navajo traditions such as dances, songs, food, and even staying as guests in hogans. Coyote Pass Hospitality also is willing to take a client to visit the Zuni, Hopi, Acoma, or Rio Grande Pueblos. One also has the opportunity to have a traditional meal with Will's family. Sometimes guests are encouraged to venture forth with family members, collect various edibles found growing in the nearby area, bring them back, and help in food preparation for the evening meal. Blue corn pancakes, fry bread, berries, and various meats and legumes are specialties. At all times, Will engages guests in conversation, trying to draw them out so they can have the opportunity to learn about Navajo religion, politics, ceremonies, economic development strategies, and even the premises and intentions of cultural tourism as practiced by Coyote Pass Hospitality.

Although most of Coyote Pass Hospitality's activities involve cultural interactions and sightseeing, the Tsosies are very careful not to overly impact fragile environmental areas and cultural sites. They are particularly concerned about sharing with guests why it is important to leave artifacts as they are and why certain areas can't be visited. However, an important issue is, what is the appropriate size of the group with which it is best to work? Will prefers to work with groups in the four- to fifteen-person range. Nonetheless, he is frequently asked to be a step-on guide for larger groups that want to spend part of a day or more learning about Navajo history and culture.

Also, the Tsosies feel constant pressure about the issue of money. Currently Will's price is $100 a night, double occupancy. He then charges $20 per hour for his time. Larger groups often can offer a better price to Will than his small-group daily rate.

Will struggles with issues related to how he allocates portions of his fees to other members of his family and to the community. On the other hand, some consumers suggest that perhaps he is charging too much. So, what price guidelines are there? Who helps Will come up with a fair rate? There aren't other operations like Coyote Pass Hospitality in the nearby area—let alone on Navajo lands or in southwestern Indian country. There are large commercial tours, but nothing like the cultural immersion Will tries to provide his guests. Pricing, for all intents and purposes, is solely a somewhat extraneous marketplace factor rather than the issue of providing a livable wage for the Tsosie family. However, if the market targeted is on a tight budget, does this livable wage get compromised?

A particularly sensitive topic is that the Tsosie family is financially benefiting from a willingness to share their knowledge about tribal community and customs, which is a Navajo communal resource and not the exclusive property of the Tsosie family. One must inevitably ask the question, is this an extractive service? Can one realistically incorporate into a "per person price" the appropriate costs of using communal resources owned by the Navajo Nation?

Another dilemma Coyote Pass Hospitality faces is that guest agendas often are inconsistent with their own views and standards concerning cross-cultural experiences and education. Some guests want to go to ceremonies where non-Indians aren't allowed. Others want to do Vision Quests under the guidance of a Navajo. This "wanna-be" mentality is often quite prevalent among those who wish to visit tribal members. Frequently confronted with these aspirations, Will finds himself tested—should he be accommodating to such requests or hold firm to his own standards? A short article in *National Geographic Traveler* titled "Native for a Night" states, "If you ever wanted to be a Native American, Will Tsosie, a Navajo, gives you an overnight opportunity."[6] It can be very tempting to let customers dictate how you present yourself when they are willing to pay good money for a contrived entertainment-type experience. It is easy to ask, "Why not?" especially given the modest existence that sustains the Tsosie family and the fact that there is no formal peer accountability process among those tribal members involved in cultural tourism.

Continually confronted by guests wanting to take away something—an experience, a picture, an artifact, a one-way interaction—Will often asks, what do we Navajo get in return? What does the Tsosie family get in return? As one writer said of the Coyote Pass Hospitality experience, "Few visitors will come away without an intimate view and deepened respect for the profoundly esthetic and spiritual nature of Navajo life. And, for himself and his clan, Will Tsosie reminds you, 'It is a two-way street, the world also comes to us.'"[7] Will wishes the "two-way street" was an easier concept for all in the cultural tourism business to grasp. But it is a lonely path to follow, as there isn't an organized group of cultural tourism suppliers in southwestern Indian country where one can talk through these dilemmas or where opportunities exist to help one another be accountable to such standards. The Arizona Indian Business Association can be supportive and even honored Coyote Pass Hospitality in 1997 as the outstanding Indian-owned business in Arizona. The Native American Business Resource Center at Northern Arizona University has been particularly helpful as well. Nonetheless, the demands of larger groups, intermediaries demanding lower prices, and the incessant demands for Anglo-type amenities are and will continue to be difficult pressures associated with cultural tourism.

Since there are no operating standards or codes of ethics for sustainable cultural tourism among the Navajo, it is up to Will and his family to decide from what standards they wish to work. Cultural and environmental accountability is something that is theirs alone with which to reckon. When actions stray, it is family pressure and Will's traditional way of life that provide the proper balance.

La Ruta de Sonora

Founded in 1997, La Ruta de Sonora has worked hard to develop a unique model for appropriate cultural tourism in the Southwest. Although still in the early stages of operation, La Ruta formed as an economic development project with roots in cultural tourism and ecotourism. This project was the creation of the multicultural La Ruta de Sonora Ecotourism Association out of Ajo, Arizona, and the nonprofit Sonoran Institute based in Tucson.[8] A tricultural project, it involves the communities of Baja, California, and Sonora, Mexico; the rural Anglo communities of southwestern Arizona; and the Tohono O'odham Nation.

The region in which La Ruta operates has been traditionally an economically depressed area. However, industrial tourism along with small tourism endeavors that are accountable to communities are beginning to make inroads into this region. For example, the community of Puerto Peñasco on the Sea of Cortez is fast becoming a weekend mecca for partygoers from Tucson and Phoenix. Tourism enterprises being developed around this trend are created with little thought given to sustainability perspectives involving community and environment. In the midst of such tourism activities, the nascent La Ruta has emerged, according to its brochure, to "create and package specialized tours, themed itineraries, and custom trips for visitors who want to explore this unique region. It is committed to providing guests with authentic adventure experiences at affordable prices, while creating ecotourism economies that directly benefit local enterprises and entrepreneurs. It encourages the sustainability of local customs, traditions, and cultures by promoting local values and a natural resource conservation ethic."

The bicultural regions where La Ruta is operating provide three major attractions—desert, heritage, and sea experiences. The Sonoran Desert experience involves traveling through the Tohono O'odham Nation and visiting Ajo, a historic company mining town; Organ Pipe Cactus National Monument; Cabeza Prieta National Wildlife Refuge; and the Mexican National Park: Reserva del Pinacate. The heritage experience follows the trade routes of the ancient Hohokum Indians and the trails of Jesuit missionaries and Father Kino during the late 1600s and early 1700s.

The sea experience focuses on the upper Gulf of California, the Colorado River Delta, and the Sea of Cortez. One can visit small Sonoran coastal villages and spend time at several nature-based outdoor laboratories, including El Golfo de Santa Clara Field Station (used by many high schools in the Southwest) and Centro Intercultural de Estudias de Desiertos y Océanos, a cultural center for the study of deserts and oceans. La Ruta allows visitors to combine any of these experiences and will package them in ways that best meet guests' interests and needs.

Although both group and custom La Ruta departures are already ongoing, there is still plenty of work to be done to perfect La Ruta as a working model for appropriate cultural tourism. Exhaustive efforts have been spent making sure those tourism activities being promoted are ones that are sustainable to both the communities and environments in which La Ruta operates. At the same time, both communities and environments must continue to maintain their attractiveness to an upmarket traveling clientele over the long term and provide meaningful employment to local hosts and guides and meaningful tourism experiences for the traveler. To do this, sustained efforts have been made to gain acceptance of La Ruta in the various communities in which it is operating. This includes working with local governments, tribal councils, and officials. La Ruta has worked hard developing a certification program for its hosts, leaders, and interpreters. It also has developed a code of ethics for its travelers.[9]

La Ruta had the opportunity to be extremely thorough in its early planning thanks to several nonprofit grants that provided the necessary capital to make sure the program developed in a sustainable and accountable manner.

That is why concerns about volume, affordability, and standards have been at the forefront of La Ruta's planning.

Nevertheless, La Ruta faces many dilemmas. The fact that it originates from a nonprofit institution has provided the luxury to spend more time developing the La Ruta experience than would have been realistic if La Ruta were developed from the for-profit sector. Another issue concerns La Ruta's current commitment to work with local and tribal governments as it goes about developing its products. Too much local bureaucracy has resulted in a long and dubious history of working with tribal governments in Indian country on private-sector endeavors. Also, when working through tribal governments, one often works only with those who are in favor with the current leadership, which can change on a regular two- or four-year basis. La Ruta faces the predicament of working either with the Tohono O'odham government or just with entrepreneurial members of the tribe. If La Ruta chooses individual entrepreneurs, similar to Will Tsosie and Coyote Pass Hospitality, does this inevitably put La Ruta at odds with tribal government? It didn't in the case of Will Tsosie, since the tribe saw tourism as a relatively low economic development priority at that time. Another problem is that if La Ruta helps train such entrepreneurs as Will Tsosie on Tohono O'odham through their certification program, the potential exists for these individuals to economically benefit from communal resources and culture. These dilemmas also can arise in working with local governmental entities in Sonora and Baja, Mexico, and southwestern Arizona as well. There is no clear answer on how best to address issues of accountability, equity, and self-sufficiency when developing an appropriate cultural tourism endeavor like La Ruta. But in the long run, working with people who are a part of the private sector may have longer-term positive impacts to communities than working primarily through their governments.

Affordability has been a very important issue for La Ruta. What really is an affordable cultural tourism experience? Is it affordable because La Ruta has been subsidized? Is it affordable because local guides and hosts are paid less than they should be? Or should very little profit margin be built into the price? For whom is the La Ruta experience designed? Is it for the people who can afford actual costs, or is it for people who want the La Ruta experience but can't afford the real costs and therefore need a subsidized experience? Eventually La Ruta needs to evolve toward a for-profit, cooperative entity where profit margins in the 30- to 35-percent range are expected and where local guides and hosts involved are making a good living wage, not only in the context of their community, but in the professional tourism world as well.

Table 2 shows a "mock" La Ruta group trip that has been itemized and priced in an attempt to account for community costs and fair local wages.

One can readily see that "affordability" comes when the trip is priced with motor-coach-type volumes (thirty to thirty-six passengers) and not at the ten- to twelve-passenger level. This "typical" excursion is a relatively expensive trip. Therefore, is it affordable to the market La Ruta wants to reach, or do costs have to be lowered? If so, at the expense of whom?

Table 7.2

Possible Costing for Hypothetical La Ruta Tricultural Journey

Number of Participants			12	36
Fixed Costs				
Guide Fee & Expenses	**Rate/Day**	**# Days**		
Guide 1 fee	200.00	10	2,000.00	2,000.00
Guide 2 fee	200.00	10	2,000.00	
Guide 1 expenses			1,100.00	1,100.00
Guide 2 expenses			1,100.00	
Guides' airfare			700.00	350.00
Transportation				
Maxivan(s)	120/day/van		2,400.00	
Motor coach	350/day			4,800.00
Bus driver gratuity/lodging				850.00
Mexican insurance			250.00	250.00
Resource People				
10 resource people days for 12 passengers	175/day		1,750.00	
14 resource people days for 25+ passengers	175/day			2,450.00
Miscellaneous Expenses				
Park entrance fees ($20/person estimated)			240.00	720.00
Total Fixed Costs			$11,540.00	$12,520.00
Fixed Cost per Person			$961.67	$347.78
Variable Costs (per Person, Net)				
Day 1: Tucson				
½ twin hotel, w/tax			64.80	64.80
Dinner			30.00	30.00
Day 2: To Sells				
½ twin hotel, w/tax		37.80	37.80	
Meals			34.00	34.00

Table 7.2 (*continued*)

Day 3: Sells

¹/₂ twin hotel, w/tax	37.80	37.80
Meals	42.00	42.00
Local community donation	20.00	20.00

Day 4: To Ajo

¹/₂ twin hotel, w/tax	37.80	37.80
Meals	42.00	42.00
Mine tour	10.00	10.00

Day 5: To Puerto Peñasco

¹/₂ twin hotel, w/tax	64.80	64.80
Meals	37.00	37.00
Pinacate tour		

Day 6: Puerto Peñasco

¹/₂ twin hotel, w/tax	64.80	64.80
Meals	37.00	37.00
Sea of Cortez boat trip	60.00	60.00

Day 7: Puerto Peñasco

¹/₂ twin hotel, w/tax	64.80	64.80
Meals	37.00	37.00
CEDO donation	20.00	20.00

Day 8: To Magdalena

¹/₂ twin hotel, w/tax	54.00	54.00
Meals	37.00	37.00
Mission entrance fee (2 missions)	10.00	10.00

Day 9: Return to Tucson

¹/₂ twin hotel, w/tax	64.80	64.80
Meals	52.00	52.00
Mission entrance fee (2 missions)	10.00	10.00

Day 10: Depart Tucson

Breakfast included	—	—
Miscellaneous Charges per Person	67.00	47.00

Subtotal per Person	$1,036.40	$1,016.40
Fixed Costs per Person	$961.67	$347.78

Total Cost (per Person, Net)		$1,998.07		$1,364.18
	25%	2,664.09	25%	1,818.90
Gross Profit		7,992.27		16,370.13
	30%	2,854.38	30%	1,948.83
Gross Profit		10,275.77		21,047.31
	35%	3,073.95	35%	2,098.74
Gross Profit		12,910.58		26,444.06
Selling Price		$3,075.00		$2,095.00

Table 7.2 *(continued)*

   Profit at 35% gross profit

10 passengers @ $3,075/person:	$10,769.33
30 passengers @ $2,095/person:	$21,924.67

Notes

Fixed costs: These costs stay the same regardless of group size.
Variable costs: Vary depending on group size.
Lodging costs: Reflect double occupancy, lodging, tax, and net price of likely accommodations used on this tour.
Meal costs: Breakfasts are excluded; lunch and dinner costs reflect amounts likely to be incurred on this tour.
Markup: Varies depending on the tour company; anywhere from a low of 25 percent to a high of 45 percent. Markup for domestic trips is rarely above 40 percent. Here 35 percent is used because marketing costs are not accounted for in fixed trip costs.

It is most gratifying to know that La Ruta is working hard at developing a certification process for its local and regional guides. It is also laudable that they have developed a strong code of ethics for La Ruta visitors. However, that is only part of the overall experience where standards must be considered. This type of thinking and preparation must also extend to accommodations, food, infrastructure in parks, and the all-important safety issue.

Meaningful standards in these areas can only come once it is clear who is the La Ruta visitor. Is it the visitor who is looking for a total immersion experience in the cultures and the environment in which La Ruta operates? Is it for people who already care, want to know more, but can only afford subsidized rates? Or is it for the visitors who want to learn and enjoy themselves but at the same time have a guarantee of certain standards pertaining to accommodations, food, and amenities in parks and cultural areas and feel that they can be reasonably safe in the process of experiencing the La Ruta program? If the market is the latter, how far does one go to make sure accommodations are up to their standards and that issues of private bathrooms and cleanliness are addressed? Must La Ruta provide safe sanctuaries for these visitors? In other words, must visitors go from one "safe sanctuary" to another on a La Ruta tour so as to guarantee personal safety? La Ruta has to continually work on this aspect of traveler standards while trying to best define who is the potential La Ruta visitor. This is made all the more difficult because of the definition of what constitutes an appropriate cultural tourism experience. A totally sanitized experience becomes contrived. Authenticity can be easily sacrificed to ensure the "right" accommodations and that visitors will be "safe." So, where is the common ground? Where does La Ruta meet the visitor halfway so that all agendas are achieved in ways that are sustainable and accountable? Obviously just having highly trained guides who have gone through a rigorous certification process for La Ruta cannot alone speak to these issues. But it is certainly a great start.

Despite unresolved difficulties, La Ruta needs as much support, help, and direction as possible in the overall appropriate cultural tourism world. It is a very significant ongoing experiment that hasn't been easy to develop, as La Ruta leaders often feel alone in what in actuality is an innovative process in cultural tourism.

Ranch Recreation in Southeastern Arizona

In today's urban world, the old-time Arizona family ranch operation—the western ranch archetype—is a cultural and economic entity that is fast becoming an anachronistic economic segment of the New West. The multigenerational family ranch is rapidly disappearing as an economic and cultural way of life as agriculture becomes more global and corporate in character. Having always lived on the margin/frontier, the western rancher is increasingly abandoning his or her way of life to subdivisions, sprawl, and other tentacles of a rapidly increasing urban society.

One could argue "so be it"—that it is just an economic fact of life. But some believe that the cowboy is a vital part of western history who symbolizes independence, freedom, the frontier, hard work, and all of what the romantic West is envisioned to be. Never mind the fact that the cowboy image is somewhat tainted due to the historic mistreatment of land and indigenous cultures by some ranchers. That, too, is a somber chapter of western history. Regardless, the southeastern Arizona ranching way of life as it is known today is in serious jeopardy, and from both a cultural and economic perspective, it is not at all clear what the future holds.

No La Ruta experiment is under way for the southeastern Arizona rancher and tourism. But several Will Tsosie types are looking at ranch recreation as a way to supplement their income so as to continue their ranching way of life in a changing climate, economy, and environment.

In a state where tourism is a huge industry and the population is rapidly increasing, many southeastern Arizona ranchers wonder what adjustments in their daily ranch routine might be necessary to accommodate a modest amount of tourist-related activities.

County extension agencies, universities, travel promotion units, economic development groups, and even conservation groups have been pursuing and promoting, in one form or another, the working ranch vacation experience as a viable economic alternative for southeastern Arizona ranchers to supplement their incomes. Such a tourism experience is defined as a destination vacation at a working farm or ranch where guests participate in working farm/ranch activities as a form of pleasure, learning, and relaxation. Guests usually ride horses, hike, do farm/ranch chores, learn the history of the area, and have an interactive experience with the ranching family. However, a working ranch's primary source of income is from farm and ranch endeavors, not taking in guests. This differs from a guest ranch vacation experience, where the ranch's primary economic objective is offering its guests a western experience. Activities are similar, but the primary source of income at a guest ranch is its paying guests, not ranching or farming.

To the economically strapped rancher who may have already explored other income options, including spouses working in town, selling parts of the ranch, or going into substantial debt, the working ranch vacation endeavor deserves a closer look. The Drydens of Black Rock Ranch[10] in Thatcher, Arizona; the Monzingos of the ZR Hereford Ranch[11] outside of Benson; the Holders of the Anchor Ranch[12] outside of Safford; and the Riggs[13] outside of Willcox are all examples of ranch families pursuing the working ranch recreation concept to supplement their income. While unorganized, these ranch families are economic pioneers to many in southeastern Arizona who are considering providing similar appropriate tourism experiences to guests willing to come to their ranches. Unfortunately, there is no La Ruta type organization helping them position themselves to get into this business. County extension agents and travel promotion entities are providing encouragement, but this is done more in a sporadic manner or on a onetime consulting basis. None of the realities of such a new business concept and strategy are being systematically or holistically examined. Neither is the basic tenet that first and foremost one needs to determine whether there is a viable market for such tourism experiences and whether the market is willing to choose to embrace a working ranch vacation in southeastern Arizona at the appropriate time and for the appropriate price.

To many ranchers, the fantasy of bringing in $250 to $300 a day per person (as some high-end dude ranches do) has one dreaming of a quick fix. The reality is that $100 to $175 a day per person for a working ranch stay (except for hunters) is more realistic. Also, many ranchers are not trained to be good entertainers or interpreters, and many do not have hospitality as a strong suit. Many don't have the experience or aptitude for cross-cultural communication. Some blanch at the thought of having to talk to people who might have radically different views on the Endangered Species Act or on immigration laws and policies. Many can't see how they could sincerely welcome a vegetarian into their daily ranch life, let alone someone who insists on having a private bathroom and relatively fancy accommodations. However, there are those who understand that this is the real world and enjoy communicating with people with diverse points of view who come from very different backgrounds. They see a critical need to not only teach themselves, but also educate paying guests on the basic facts of ranch life. Many enjoy the opportunity to welcome visitors and see this as not only a viable economic way of supplementing their income, but as an important cross-cultural exchange that not only enriches their ways of thinking and living, but also could reposition the southeastern Arizona ranch entity as a viable and healthy part of the state's economy over the next fifty years.

Ranchers anticipating taking in guests understand the volume issue. They realize they can't take more than one to four families or couples at a time. But often they have no idea what price their guests should pay. Can they get $150 to $200 a day per person for a three-day stay? If so, what kind of product needs to be developed so that such a price can be attained? Would such a product be too expensive to develop and overly compromise the daily authentic ranch experience?

Before becoming overly enthusiastic about working ranch vacations, one must address the question of whether there is a viable market that can be targeted for such an experience in southeastern Arizona. Most likely, there is adequate consumer demand for such a product, but it is not well defined, nurtured, and analyzed so that one can determine how best to reach out and successfully market to potential customers. In a time when more and more travelers want authentic, meaningful experiences during their vacation and are more than willing to pay for this to occur, they don't usually know that such experiences could be found on a working ranch. The Drydens, Monzingos, Holders, and Riggs are on their own to identify and develop the market, establish product and pricing, and adhere to operating standards that they define. No one is helping these people in a consistent and thorough manner. To increase the difficulty of their task, they have little or no working capital to adequately position themselves in the marketplace. If county extension services, travel promotion groups, and agricultural groups want these ranch families of southeastern Arizona to have viable farm and ranch recreation enterprises, substantial infrastructure development must occur. That takes sizable capital investments or grants, much like what La Ruta has enjoyed.

Unfortunately, this is not happening in Arizona or in other Rocky Mountain states where farm and ranch recreation has been promoted as an appropriate cultural tourism endeavor that can play a meaningful role in sustaining the farm/ranch way of life. The travel promotion unit of the Department of Commerce in Montana, Travel Montana, spent six years holding one-day seminars every winter throughout the state, educating over a thousand farmers and ranchers in farm and ranch recreation. Idaho has sponsored similar programs, as has Wyoming. In the extension program at the University of Wyoming, a research program sponsored by the U.S. Department of Agriculture[14] has been working on the most cost-effective ways to market farm and ranch recreation. Although the project's scope was limited by the U.S. Department of Agriculture due to a tight budget, this project holds some promise for marketing farm and ranch recreation through a large Web site on the Internet. However, all of these small efforts are not part of an integrated, sustainable, and ongoing strategy that would lead to creation of an ongoing and vibrant appropriate tourism industry for those whose life for generations has been farming and ranching.

Farm and ranch recreation in southeastern Arizona and in other Rocky Mountain states could be a significant, appropriate tourism enterprise. But onetime promotion seminars and education programs won't do much more than cause struggling ranchers to raise their hopes over a possible source of income that cannot materialize unless a significant, comprehensive, and coordinated effort is developed. This must include identifying what appropriate cultural tourism standards are necessary in ranch recreation, defining a market, and then making sure the market knows about those ranch recreation experiences that best fit that market niche. One cannot develop any kind of appropriate cultural tourism experience, let alone a ranch recreation experience, and assume that visitors will then come in sufficient numbers, pay a fair price, and have the type of meaningful experience that is essential to cultural and economic sustainability.

Conclusion

All three of these working experiments in appropriate cultural tourism are laudable in and of themselves. However, as the general tourism sector of the economy continues to expand rapidly, little thought is being given to direction, strategic planning, environmental and community appropriateness, or social equity issues. Despite rising levels of income, mobility, and accessibility in the populations of developed nations, tourism enterprises are increasingly dominated by corporate "bottom line" philosophy. Consider the Alaska cruise tourist industry: some 600,000 people took cruises in 1999, compared to 334,000 in 1994 and only 38,000 in 1972. Cruise companies such as Princess, Carnival, and Holland America have created this contrived expedition experience so as to fill their large cruise ships in the summer, as they understand that they are at capacity in the winter in the Caribbean and off the coasts of Central America. These corporations even have their own tourism shops in places such as Juneau and Ketchikan so that when passengers go ashore, such companies can have onshore profit centers as well. Once the cruise season is over, the shops close and those who manage them relocate to their shops in the Caribbean and Central America. Therefore southeastern Alaska in the summer has become nothing more than a corporate theme park for industrial tourism, not unlike what is occurring in Las Vegas, Orlando, Branson, and Anaheim. Volume, corporate profits, and dividends to shareholders are suddenly dominating what used to be a highly individualistic "mom-and-pop" industry with some semblance of authenticity and legitimate cross-cultural interactions.

Furthermore, consolidation is emerging as the prevalent corporate strategy of the present-day specialty travel world. Roll ups and mergers of adventure travel companies are taking place at an alarming rate in areas of the tourism sector, where $20-million to $50-million companies were large. Now many of these companies are being rolled up into $500-million to $700-million corporate entities, with the names of Grand Expeditions[15] and Far & Wide[16] beginning to dominate the upmarket specialty travel landscape. Owner-managers and family businesses have given way to CEOs, COOs, IPOs, and trading on the NASDAQ. While all this is occurring, little thought is being given to where tourism as an industry is headed. Programs at Southwestern, Great Basin, and Northern Rockies universities are not addressing issues such as the definition of appropriate tourism and investigation of tourism's environmental and social impacts. Rather, university tourism programs are more apt to be found in MBA programs, hotel management schools, or business research institutes, some of which are funded with state tourism promotion tax dollars.

No institutes or think tanks of tourism policy in the West are looking in constructively critical ways at tourism trends in states such as Arizona, where tourism is a $12-billion-a-year industry. Few in the industry are debating over the makeup of the ideal tourist. Furthermore, no extensive networks or organizations are currently operating where Coyote Pass Hospitality, La Ruta, and ranchers can go to receive support, advice, and direction in the areas of appropriateness, accountability, sustainability, and standards. The basically extractive nature of tourism and how its undesirable effects might be mitigated are not being addressed in any systematic manner. Only a few programs in institutions of higher learning are examining issues of justice and equity as they relate to tourism practices. Also, only a beginning investigation exists on issues of resource capacity as they relate to public and/or private lands.

Such endeavors as Coyote Pass Hospitality, La Ruta, and working ranch vacations need networks and organizations where they can interact and build upon one another's experiences so that issues of volume, pricing, and standards are adequately developed and so markets for such entities are more clearly defined, as are the strategies to reach such markets. More institutions like The Ecotourism Society, the Sonoran Institute, and tourism public policy programs should be started at universities. As industrial tourism continues at its cancerous rate of growth, the concept of appropriate cultural tourism could easily fade into the catacombs of a large corporate and capitalistic culture where the bottom line rules all. That is why the real-life experiments of Coyote Pass Hospitality, La Ruta, and farm and ranch recreation need to be given the opportunity and support to thrive and be duplicated.

Notes

1. Perhaps this is changing somewhat, in part due to the efforts of The Ecotourism Society (PO Box 755, North Bennington, Vt. 05257, (802) 447-2121, www.ecotourism.org). The concept of ecotourism is thoroughly reviewed in Martha Honey's *Ecotourism and Sustainable Development: Who Owns Paradise?* (Washington, D.C.: Island Press, 1999) and Hal Rothman's *Devil's Bargains: Tourism in the Twentieth-Century West* (Lawrence: University Press of Kansas, 1998).

2. Based in Bozeman, Montana, Off the Beaten Path operates in the desert Southwest, the Rockies, and Alaska, providing exceptional experiences to travelers. See www.offthebeatenpath.com.

3. A good example of this emerging interest was reflected at the 1999 Congress on Recreation and Resource Capacity, 29 November–2 December 1999, Snowmass, Colorado (www.cnr.colostate.edu/nrrt/capacity).

4. River use since 1980 in the Grand Canyon is limited by a maximum number of user days between May 1 and September 30 (115,500). Valley floor visits in Canyon de Chelly are limited to guided tours only. Additionally, the tours must be led by a Navajo tribal member.

5. The address, phone number, and Web site for Coyote Pass Hospitality are Box 91-B, Tsaile, Ariz. 86556, (520) 724-3383, *www.navajocentral.org*.

6. *National Geographic Traveler*, "Nature for a Night" (November–December 1993).

7. Will Tsosie, personal communication to the author.

8. The address, phone, and Web site for La Ruta de Sonora are PO Box 699, Ajo, Ariz. 85321, (800) 806-0766, www.laruta.org. The address, phone, and Web site for the Sonoran Institute are 7650 E. Broadway, Suite 203, Tucson, Ariz. 85710, (520) 290-0828, www.sonoran.org.

9. Code of Ethics for La Ruta Visitors:

   1. The earth and the sea are fragile. Respect them.
   2. Leave only footprints. Take only photographs.
   3. Respect others' customs, manners, and cultures.
   4. Ask permission before photographing anyone.
   5. Always follow designated trails and roadways.

6. As you travel, remember to reduce, recycle, and reuse.

7. Support the people, products, and services of La Ruta.

10. Black Rock Ranch Wilderness Retreat, PO Box 543, Thatcher, Ariz. 85552, (520) 428-6481.

11. ZR Hereford Ranch, PO Box 2225, Benson, Ariz. 85602, (520) 586-3509.

12. Anchor Ranch, 128 E. 19th Street, Safford, Ariz. 85546, (520) 428-0033.

13. Jim and Jana Riggs, Crossed J Ranch, HCR2 Box 6303, Willcox, Ariz. 85643, (520) 824-3369.

14. Project Title: Farm/Ranch Recreation Partnership Systems Enhance Rural Development and the Environment. Funded by USDA Fund for Rural America Project. Project head: Jeff Powell, Department of Renewable Resources, University of Wyoming, PO Box 3355, Laramie, Wyo. 82071-3355, (307) 766-5164.

15. Grand Expeditions: www.grandexpeditions.com.

16. Far & Wide: www.farandwide.com.

REDUCING THE IMPACTS OF TOURISM THROUGH CROSS-CULTURAL PLANNING ━

SUSAN GUYETTE AND DAVID WHITE

People often find tourism problematic: economic exploitation and environmental impacts are of concern to residents of tourist destinations as well as to outside observers. Specifically in regard to cultural tourism, a frequent criticism is that tourism damages or destroys cultural authenticity. Such outcomes are common, and the literature on tourism is rife with examples.[1] Even so, negative results are not inevitable—positive results are possible.

Some "adverse effects" have existed primarily in the academic imagination or in the imaginations of other elites who value certain idealized images of cultural others. As a result, people sometimes sense "inauthenticity" or "spurious" culture whenever what they encounter diverges from their ideals. Situations involving cultural change are particularly susceptible to such perceptions. Questions of authenticity can be examined in a more fruitful manner by focusing on the social construction of authenticity and recognizing that there are multiple levels of social presentation of reality. Yet "commercialization" may still be seen as the simple divide between "genuine" and "spurious."[2]

The argument that commercialization equates with the inauthentic is alluring, but ultimately it is unsustainable. The notion of commoditization has structural inconsistencies (things not intended for market exchange nonetheless find their way into markets, and the increased consumption stimulated by mass production also creates a demand for customized products). Even more importantly, market systems are pervaded by externalities, including socially constructed values and preferences.[3] The more important questions relative to authenticity may focus less on commercialization and more on the fabric of social relations between producers and consumers. In other words, genuinely negative results occur when touristic reality is constructed mostly by the purveyors and consumers and when tourism develops without substantive, informed, empowered involvement of the "host" population.

Cross-cultural planning, an interdisciplinary approach informed both by anthropology and by planning, provides methods that allow host communities to anticipate the potential effects of touristic development. They can thus reduce or avoid the negative cultural or environmental effects and increase or maximize the positive benefits, even while attempting to establish or modify social relationships between the host community and their touristic audience.

Who Does Cross-Cultural Planning and Why

Cross-cultural planning incorporates cultural considerations so local groups can more effectively manage tourism in keeping with their own values. Planning is useful for anticipating outcomes. Without an understanding of what may happen as a result of tourism, it is impossible for a community to identify the appropriate actions that would maximize positive gain while minimizing negative impacts.

Planning methods discussed here focus on small-scale, rural, and culturally diverse communities. A rigidly dichotomous view of cultural tourism, in which "guests" are sophisticated affluent members of powerful industrialized western societies and "hosts" are naive poverty-stricken members of powerless underdeveloped nonwestern societies, is clearly outmoded. On a global basis, to some extent, and especially among such host communities within the western United States, host communities have potential access to the decision-making process, and they have various ways to affect tourism development so that benefits accrue to them. Yet host communities are internally diverse, and issues within communities often prevent a unified approach to development.

The authors have been involved in cross-cultural planning efforts for nearly twenty years. Susan Guyette was senior planner and tourism director for the Eight Northern Indian Pueblos Council—a consortium consisting of the pueblos of Taos, Picuris, San Juan, Santa Clara, San Ildefonso, Nambe, Pojoaque, and Tesuque, all in northern New Mexico—from 1986 to 1990. In 1990, Guyette started a private consulting firm, providing a variety of planning services to American Indian tribes and non-Indian communities nationwide, as well as in the southwestern United States. David White has worked with Guyette on several projects, beginning in 1992. Although initiatives for tourism planning continue to originate within state or local governments, most of the projects we have worked on were conceived by tribal or community groups. In nearly all cases, tourism was already under way and our projects were conceived to help mitigate negative impacts. Contracts are often issued directly by the tribes but occasionally by state agencies or other groups. Funding for such efforts comes from diverse sources: some projects are federally funded through the Administration for Native Americans or other agencies (tribes compete for grant funding), but others are self-funded through tribal economic ventures.

In the past, tribes have had little influence on tourism development. Much still remains to be accomplished if the industry is ever to be characterized as one in which Indian people have an equitable share in the economic benefits and do not suffer disproportionately from adverse environmental effects. Indian culture has been an integral part of southwestern tourism since its beginning in the late 1800s. Travelers by rail—and later, by automobile—sought cultural arts and crafts as souvenirs and for decoration. Although Indian people contributed significantly to the growth of the economy through tourism, they derived little direct benefit from this industry for three-quarters of the twentieth century. Their products were undervalued in direct exchange with the artists, and accrued value went primarily to non-Indian middlemen. Government efforts to revive and initiate Indian arts and crafts during the first half of the twentieth century succeeded in creating a much-expanded market but did little or nothing to rectify the disproportionate sharing of the benefits.

Mainstream tourism development has been based on "growth pole theory," an idea that development of a relatively few dynamic factors in geographic clusters (generally urban centers) will spread over time or "trickle down" to the rest of the spatial system.[4] Much of the nation's economic resources thus went into urban infrastructure development, yet this type of development did not spread enterprise or wealth to Indian reservations and rarely to rural communities. The goal to maximize per capita income had negative impacts on rural communities, with decreased reliance on agriculture, animal husbandry, and other means of local production. In many cases quality of life did not increase, but rather decreased with a shift toward reliance on per capita income. In terms of tourism gain, urban centers secured the largest share of expenditures while rural areas provided the "attractions."

During the 1970s and 1980s, statewide promotional efforts increasingly used images of Indian culture. A growing feeling among American Indian people of being "used" for tourism, further heightened by the day-to-day poverty rooted in unemployment rates often ranging from 50 percent to 80 percent in tribal communities, created unrest and the determination to gain an equitable share in the industry. Tourism is a leading industry in the Southwest, and it represents a potentially important economic alternative for those tribes choosing to participate. Yet to secure benefits for entire communities, as well as for select artists and their families, community attitudes toward tourism and culture had to be addressed.

Although the inequities of tourism were strongly felt, communities saw positive benefits as well. For example, tourism stimulated a pottery revival in the early twentieth century due to creation of market demand. In general, Pueblo people considered this to be beneficial to their communities: it promoted retention of a highly valued cultural craft and one that—unlike wage labor—involved the cooperative efforts of extended family groups, in securing and processing the clay and in making and painting the pottery. At the same time, some young potters have expressed concern over the static image of Indian pottery that results from market demand for older, traditional styles. They find it a challenge to uphold their image of Pueblo culture as always evolving and changing.

As American Indian people become increasingly determined to share the visitation experience on their own terms and to shift the inequities of the past, planning has become an important tool for them. Tourism is seen as having played an important role in shaping the cultural contact process, with impacts both positive and negative. Tourism often impacts privacy for cultural practice and personal privacy in homes. Physical impacts to tribal lands are high, and funds are not available to provide the basic tourism services necessary to reduce negative impacts. Exposing youth to new value systems is an impact of tourism still often expressed as a concern. Although tourism sometimes damages older structures when visitors climb on them or tour buses shake the ground, tourism also provided an impetus to preserve older structures. Tourism has stimulated the making of cultural arts and present-day learning among younger generations, and tourism often encourages cultural pride in youth.[5]

Negative results of tourism development may include displacement of community residents, disruption of the social structure, diminished local economic opportunity, and exploitation of local arts and culture as well as environmental damage. Since communities are choosing to engage in tourism as an alternative to high unemployment rates, the challenge is to develop a methodology for working *with* communities in overcoming such problems. Tribes find the situation complicated and the decisions difficult. If jobs are not created within the community, out-migration is high. The loss of youth impacts cultural continuance in devastating ways. Given these hard choices, tribes in New Mexico are organizing and communicating their needs to shift the balance to a more equitable situation. The $4-billion tourism industry is the leading source of employment in New Mexico,[6] after government, and with visitation to tribal lands at ten million persons,[7] this opportunity is one of the few promising avenues for tribal employment. Many tribes are considering tourism as a development option, yet hold protection of their culture as a first concern. There is a need for a participative, holistic approach to planning, addressing carrying capacity and control of tourism development and incorporating cultural sustainability into the planning process.[8]

It is important to understand that tribal economies include both internal and external markets. Internal/external boundaries are carefully delineated within communities. Certain items produced for ceremonial use may be sold within a tribe or among closely related tribes. Such items are not sold in the tourist trade, which instead emphasizes items such as pottery, sculpture, and paintings. Ceremonial or symbolic boundaries (e.g., permissible motifs on pottery) are also defined as appropriate or inappropriate for items sold in the tourist trade.

Although tourism has been used largely by mainstream America as an economic opportunity, Indian tribes are very cautious about using culture for economic benefit. This is the key reason why some tribes remain divided internally about the extent to which it is appropriate to participate in a tourism industry. Indian people often stress the importance of culture being respected and protected, but opinions differ on whether efforts are best spent on cultural self-esteem or also on educating the non-Indian public about Indian culture. The insistence on respect and protection of culture may not be readily understandable to an American public unaware of past contempt for Indian culture and unfamiliar with the extent to which the U.S. government prohibited indigenous religious practice, suppressed Indian language and dress, and attempted to destroy the Indian sense of identity. Educating the public on such matters is often a primary motive for development of tourism ventures among Indian communities. Tourism can be a means of reviving, expanding, and reinforcing traditions if developed and managed carefully. Cross-cultural methods can be used to protect cultural values while creating a more equitable exchange with non-Indian tourists. In order to demonstrate this, we will briefly discuss some key aspects of cross-cultural planning and then move on to examples of tribal planning efforts.

Cultural Tourism Defined

We do not see tourism as a phenomenon peculiar to industrial societies; we agree, instead, with Dennison Nash,[9] who suggests that tourism can be found among hunters and gatherers and among horticulturalists. Similarly, Turner and Turner[10] have observed touristic motives involved in medieval pilgrimages. We define cultural tourism as an exchange of information on lifeways, customs, beliefs, values, language, views of the environment, and other cultural resources. This exchange is always uneven; the challenge in planning for cultural tourism is to ensure that the exchange takes place as equitably as possible, in a manner seen as appropriate by members of the host community. As one Hispanic community organizer commented, "The easiest thing for people to learn from each other is bad habits." Too often, as a result of little or poor planning, people hosting cultural tourism have learned undesirable behaviors from their guests while being subjected to demands that they divulge sensitive or private cultural information to those same guests. With careful planning, community members (especially young people) can be shielded from inappropriate guest behavior while maintaining control over the information they wish their guests to be given as a result of the exchange.

Cross-Cultural Planning: Principles and Approaches

The exchange definition of cultural tourism points the way to planning processes addressing potential gains and negative impacts, creating a more equitable outcome from tourism. This is a critical point for resolving the usual love/hate relationship with tourism. Optimists, and those with existing economic interests in tourism, tend to focus on the potential gains: they want to move ahead quickly with development and tap markets as soon as possible. Those who oppose tourism tend to be reserved about change, particularly when that change could impact culture. Those who are cautious are very important in the planning process, as they can see the potential negative impacts. By valuing the opinions of more conservative members of a group, demonstrating respect for their knowledge and working to create comfort for them, proponents of a change can often move a project forward that otherwise would have been stalled.

In relation to economic development strategy, culturally appropriate tourism development is guided by three important factors: *form*, *scale*, and *timing*. Tourism development can be enhanced while retaining *forms* of the traditional economy, such as cottage industry in the arts and recreation enterprises. In the Southwest, these may already be tourism enterprises: entrepreneurial activities oriented toward tourists have existed for at least a century and a half. Keeping *scale* appropriate is essential; large-scale development can disrupt an entire community, whereas small-scale development is more easily absorbed. *Timing* is important to remember in allowing development at a pace that enables planning and intervention to reduce negative impacts. Phasing development is critical in creating a regional-level development strategy, and small tourism businesses may gradually network to create a larger-scale enterprise or link via a regional itinerary. It is of course true that American Indian people cannot entirely control tourism development, yet tribal sovereignty confers a degree of control over projects on reservation lands that far exceeds the influence of non-Indian communities over developments in their midst.

Tourism planning is a systematic process of identifying opportunities and threats in the future environment and of formulating policies based on organizational resources and goals for operations in that environment over a relatively long term.[11] Tourism is about connection. A tourism scenario can be well managed, with a low number of visitors (and therefore a low impact) and encouragement of the community members' stores and cottage industries to produce arts, traditional foods, other items of tourist interest, and culturally appropriate demonstrations. Awareness in the planning process is essential. Whenever two or more cultures come together, the potential for cultural change is high. Traditional communities tend to fear the threat of their traditions being altered. Sensitive cultural tourism development starts with a respect of fears that culture will be changed.

Steps in Tourism Planning and Development

Six major steps in tourism development are important if communities are to create an equitable exchange: (1) key issue identification, (2) policy formation, (3) planning and strategy, (4) etiquette definition, (5) business development, and (6) training of community members and promotion of their businesses.

1. Key Issue Identification

Defining key issues about tourism allows community members to express their concerns. If accomplished through a broadly based community participation process, key issue definition tends to create alignment within the community and resolve internal conflict because community members feel listened to. Statewide tourism planning with the twenty-two Indian tribes of New Mexico (example 1) and with Zuni Pueblo (example 2) demonstrates how key issue identification can lead to community-based tourism strategies.

EXAMPLE 1: Strategic Plan of the New Mexico Indian Tourism Association

With the formation of the New Mexico Indian Tourism Association (NMITA) in 1990, tribes in New Mexico organized regionally and statewide to communicate needs and issues to the tourism industry as well as to state agencies. A statewide tourism planning process completed in 1998[12] reflects the first time all twenty-two tribes have been systematically interviewed to determine needs, future directions, and opinion on tourism policy. Key issues, needs, and strategies were defined as well as an action plan for assistance. All tribes conveyed the feeling of being "used" by the State of New Mexico for tourism purposes without receiving a fair share of tourism revenues to cover the costs of serving as hosts. Privacy impacts, cultural barriers, and infrastructure needs are communicated in the plan as well as difficulties experienced in managing tourism.

NMITA's Strategic Plan identified gaps in services as well as needs for tracking visitors. This plan is now being used to secure additional resources for the tribes and to improve policy at the state level. Based on the plan, NMITA is conducting valuable trainings with the tourism industry, such as "Visioning Native Cultures," which intends to correct cultural misconceptions and to educate tourism providers about effective ways of working with tribes.

EXAMPLE 2: Benefits of Managing Tourism at Zuni Pueblo, New Mexico

Zuni people and their ancestors have been involved in tourism for thousands of years. Prior to the coming of the Spanish, Zuni people played a predominantly proactive role in managing visitors through a complex system of trade relationships. After Spanish and American contact, however, a shift occurred to a more reactive stance toward outsiders in Zuni. In recent years, most of the benefits of the exchange accrued to outsiders. Now the key question asked at Zuni is, "What will Zuni's role be in the future—will it be proactive or reactive?"

The issue of sustainability in tourism requires an active role in setting limits, expanding opportunity, and protecting environmental and cultural resources. To address community concerns over tourism impacts, Zuni completed a strategic plan for managing tourism in 2001, assessing cultural privacy and site protection needs as well as identifying potential job creation through tourism. As an outcome of the planning process, Zuni created: (1) a staffed tourism program, (2) a visitor's guide to teach respectful visitation etiquette, and (3) a tour program to contain visitation to culturally sensitive areas. The tribe is planning a cultural facility to house educational exhibits, an expanded tour program, an arts business, art classes, and a small business development center. Although the new complex will be supported largely through tours and art sales, cultural benefits will include revitalization of several decreasing art traditions, such as the pottery-making tradition. Because 90 percent of jobs at Zuni are tourism- and art-sales-related, the community is now aligned for more effective management.

2. Policy Formation

Policy formation is critical in maintaining community support for tourism development. Is the community divided on the issue? Is there a way to design a solution that includes everybody's interests? Is there a means of benefiting from tourism while minimizing negative impacts? One policy-based solution to reducing negative impacts is situating tourism enterprises away from tribal lands. Development of the Hotel Santa Fe by the Pueblo of Picuris (example 3) is an excellent model of policy formation leading to off-reservation development.

EXAMPLE 3: The Hotel Santa Fe

A tourism success story is the development of the Hotel Santa Fe in downtown Santa Fe by Picuris, a small pueblo in northern New Mexico. This is a large, joint venture in which Picuris is 51 percent owner. Picuris was able to use the 1974 Indian Financial Act to obtain a guaranteed loan to initiate this development, considered a model economic development project nationally. Few tribes have purchased urban land and developed economically in an area outside their reservation. Some might find a small poetic justice in the fact that Santa Fe, seat of government for Spanish colonialism of the Puebloan Rio Grande drainage, has now been commercially "colonized" by one of the pueblos that took active leadership in the Pueblo Revolt of 1680. One important success of this hotel venture is tribal ownership of the hotel gallery as of fall 1991, an outlet where Picuris members can sell their handcrafted Indian art items.

There is still a lack of jobs for local people since the distance from the pueblo to the hotel is 120 miles round trip, over winding mountain roads. Now that the outlet for sales in Santa Fe is owned, training situated in Picuris is resulting in creation of employment within the pueblo. The hotel project merges cultural preservation with economic sustainability, as the potential of tapping the Santa Fe tourism market creates sales for artisans living on-reservation at Picuris.

3. Planning and Strategy

Several types of planning may be involved in tourism development. A strategic plan, whether it is local or organizational (as described above in example 1), identifies key issues, positive benefits, potential negative impacts, development strategies, and specific projects. Strategic planning is a process of problem analysis.[13] Protecting the privacy of community members is likely to be a tourism planning priority. A regional tourism plan, as in example 4, identifies resources and how they can be linked. A land use plan, as described for Pojoaque Pueblo (example 5), is essential for deciding areas or "zoning" for different uses, such as housing, agriculture, commercial, and sacred activities. Pojoaque's planning process led to managed development along the highway, away from residential areas. This type of plan helps protect culturally sensitive areas and manage visitors to achieve the lowest impact possible from tourism. A marketing plan or promotional strategy is essential for targeting a desirable audience. Effective promotion requires knowing the characteristics of the intended audience and how to attract them. A business plan is essential for locating business niches and successful enterprise development through estimation of income potential and expenditures.

EXAMPLE 4: Regional Planning among the Northern Pueblos, New Mexico

Prior to a regional tourism planning process completed in 1987,[14] tribes in the region (Nambe, Pojoaque, San Ildefonso, San Juan, Santa Clara, Picuris, Taos, and Tesuque) perceived themselves in competition with one another. A needs assessment conducted with tribal governments identified key issues and strategies to work cooperatively with the tourism industry. As an outcome, the tribes now sponsor a promotional vehicle for their region. The Visitor's Guide to the Northern Pueblos, first published in 1988, is fifty-six full-color pages with a distribution of one hundred thousand annually to promote Pueblo businesses and artwork. Itineraries in the guide link reservation businesses, greatly increasing referrals to Pueblo businesses and visitor expenditures on-reservation. Etiquette, as defined by the communities, educates visitors on respectful behavior. The guide reaches visitors when they plan their vacation as the State of New Mexico distributes it to tourists inquiring about Indian culture. The rate of business formation has doubled in the recent years of the guide, from forty-five Indian-owned businesses to ninety-one relating to tourism.

EXAMPLE 5: Land Use Planning at Pojoaque Pueblo

Pojoaque Pueblo paved the way for managed development by designating allocations for different land uses in 1988.[15] The pueblo's new business development is situated in a commercial zone along Highway 285, a prime route for tourists but distant from residential areas, therefore minimizing privacy impacts. Prior to the definition of a commercial zone, the pueblo owned one business, a supermarket; business formation has accelerated, with a new total of eighteen businesses, including a casino. Land use planning encourages one-step consensus on uses of tribal lands rather than the slower and less coordinated project-by-project method.

Land use planning enhanced the cultural revitalization process by allocating three acres for a cultural center. Strategic planning also guides development of the Poeh Cultural Center and Museum, an important site for visitor education about the Tewa region. Community participation ensured that a priority mission of the center would be teaching cultural arts to Tewa people. A strong secondary focus is on providing educational programs for the public. A percentage of casino profits is reinvested into cultural center projects, thus supporting cultural revitalization efforts. Such reinvestment reduces the extractive nature of tourism.

4. Etiquette Definition

Whether or not cultural tourists recognize the need for observation of special etiquette depends on whether they see themselves simply as consumers or understand that they are guests participating in a relationship that carries mutual obligations. Some southwestern visitors have had a misconception that dances were "performances" staged for their benefit; accordingly, they sometimes wore inappropriately skimpy clothing or applauded at the end of a dance. Southwestern American Indian people are adamant that tourists are guests rather than "customers," and not only the Hopi but other Pueblos as well have banned non-Indian attendance at dances after inappropriate behavior by guests.

It would seem that most cultural tourists want to behave appropriately during their visits, but often they lack the awareness that would allow them to do so and, in ignorance, are rude (if they do not want to behave appropriately, they will likely find their consumerist goals frustrated). Thus if they understand that dances are religious in nature, they can adjust their behavior and dress accordingly. Etiquette definition can be part of a larger visitor education program that teaches visitors how to be respectful of local culture. An effective means of educating visitors is to distribute a tribally approved statement of etiquette as visitors enter the community. Etiquette definition played a key role in the development of a regional-level tourism plan coordinated by the Eight Northern Indian Pueblos in New Mexico (example 4, above).

5, 6. Business Development, Training, and Promotion

These steps may easily be overlooked, especially if a community remains uncomfortable about the notion that tourism is a business. Yet these are essential elements if tourism is to appropriately serve the community. Promotion may be most effective through a regional effort (see examples 1 and 4). Business development is very important in order to maximize potential benefits, and training of employees is necessary if the tourism exchange is to meet expectations on both sides. Identifying locally or Indian-owned businesses, their needs for growth, and promotional needs is essential for communities to profit equitably from tourism.

Analysis of the Existing Tourism System

Before designing a tourism plan, it is necessary to identify the sorts of infrastructure, facilities, and amenities already available. A "tourism system" model[16] can be used, expanding the basic system of attractions, services, and transportation to include cultural components as well. Interrelatedness and cooperation between elements of a tourism system are essential for success. Major system components must be linked, to function complementarily. This approach creates both financial and visitor satisfaction gains.

Needs Assessment and Inventory of Resources

Needs assessment is a critical step in planning. A local needs assessment can (1) gather community opinion on whether tourism is desired, acceptable types of tourism, and concerns about tourism; (2) identify existing businesses in the region; (3) analyze business forms that have developed spontaneously and succeeded over time; (4) identify existing skills and training needs; (5) determine needs for business expansion; and (6) establish rapport with local businesses.

SWOT Analysis

Identifying strengths, weaknesses, opportunities, and threats is called a *SWOT* analysis. Strengths are resources to build upon. Seeing collective strengths and how these could be enhanced often inspires community members. Weaknesses are areas in need of improvement, and it is important to consider how these may be overcome. Areas of opportunity are building blocks for future benefits. Opportunity definition creates enthusiasm and moves a community toward a proactive stance. Change can be threatening, and tourism development in particular can impair privacy and threaten the sense of tradition. Identification of threats allows impact-reducing strategies to be devised. SWOT analysis is a useful technique in gaining the opinion of all segments of the community and in resolving mixed feelings regarding tourism.

Projecting Positive Gains and Negative Impacts

Tourism is often a controversial sort of development. Without extreme care, negative impacts to traditional communities can outweigh positive gains. Preparing a list of anticipated positive gains and negative impacts can guide each development effort and overall planning. Cultural costs and benefits can be analyzed by means of a matrix like that shown in table 1.[17] Such matrices also can be used to stimulate creation of scenarios with the community. This is a useful technique for examining potential outcomes, possible impacts, and strategies for development. The community can then decide which scenario has the best cultural and environmental fit.

Tourism Goals and Objectives

Ambivalence or lack of agreement in the community may lead to a lack of planning, which in turn causes negative impacts. Community involvement is the only way to gain alignment for taking action to mitigate negative impacts. Once needs are determined, goals and objectives can be formulated by the community. The more focused the planning, the greater the potential benefits.

Table 8.1. **Projecting Positive Gain and Negative Impact of Tourism on Local Culture**

Cultural Domains	Potential Positive Gain	Potential Negative Impacts
Economic	Increased # jobs Increased sales of locally produced items	Costs of providing basic services to visitors can exceed profits if local businesses are not developed to encourage expenditures
Kinship	Increase of family-owned and -operated businesses Increase of arts and crafts production, family cohesiveness in cooperative efforts	Increased contact with outside cultures may influence youth toward acculturation
Religious	Increased interest in traditional activities, value placed by youthas a result of outside interest and respect	Visitor influx may interfere with religious practice, privacy

Political	Increase of income for local government operations	Disruption in the pattern of local income distribution (especially in an egalitarian community)
	Opportunity for leadership	
Ecosystem	Tourism development can initiate "zoning" and protection of fragile or sacred areas and prevent mixed uses	Negative environmental impacts if planning is not conducted to protect areas and contain visitors
		Water usage and infrastructure wear

Cultural Boundaries Analysis

Many indigenous cultures find it important to define information that can be exchanged and that which must be protected. Defining cultural boundaries at the beginning of a cultural tourism project is one way to minimize the sharing of inappropriate information. Often those who oppose tourism are afraid that secret information will be shared; this is an important and valid concern. Different topics can be assessed according to kinds of information that can be shared with different markets. In this way, both internal and external markets can be included. For example, a tribe might hold certain information completely to themselves, while another set of information might be shared with people of a related tribe, and still other information might be shared with people from outside the region or from different cultures. This process is directly applicable to (1) defining text for museum exhibits or interpretive presentations, (2) creating the format and content for festivals, or (3) creating itineraries defining tourist stops.

Creating Economic Equity in the Exchange

Achieving economic equity in cultural tourism depends upon one basic factor: visitors must purchase goods and services from the host community in order for that community to see economic benefits. An important concept utilized in measuring regional tourism impact is the regional income multiplier. An income multiplier is a factor by which sales are multiplied in order to estimate the impact on incomes.[18] Tourism income multipliers tend to fall within the range of 0.4 to 0.8; for example, a $100 expenditure is likely to increase local incomes by $40 to $80. The income multiplier will tend to be lower in a rural area than in an urban area, yet it will be higher when tourists buy products requiring considerable local labor in production, such as arts and crafts. Four ways of raising an income multiplier are

Increasing the amount of tourist expenditure directly in the region;
Increasing purchase of goods and services produced locally;
Increasing the expenditures of local income in the local region; and
Extending the visitor length of stay.

Restaurants, grocery stores, gas stations, and other service industries increase multiplier effects.

Packaging and Identifying Strategies for Cooperation

One of the most important things to learn about the tourism industry is how it regards possible attractions. Ideally, the industry wants a prepaid tour package, sometimes called a "product," which is available for outright purchase. If such packages are not available, the most important development step a community can accomplish is the printing of itineraries that show travelers how to link different stops within the reservation region. In particular, travelers need to know distance and time to allow between stops, types of products they will find at a stop, and approximately how long each stop may take. Creating an itinerary involves defining a theme, identifying components that create the desired educational experience, and linking the elements in an interesting way. Itineraries create synergy; that is, the end result is more than the sum of its parts. Itineraries secure an audience for smaller attractions, and every stop on a tour gains more than its share would have been if working in isolation. An example of a tribe developing a tourism package as well as managing visitors effectively is the tour at Acoma Pueblo.

EXAMPLE 6: Tourism Management at Acoma Pueblo

Acoma Pueblo consists of new Acoma settlements, a casino along Interstate 40, HUD housing developments, and Sky City, the ceremonial heart of the community still occupied by a number of elders and families. The ancient mesa settlement referred to as Sky City is situated in a fragile desert environment. Physical impacts to the old village and structures, privacy impacts interfering with cultural practice, and environmental damage to the mesa were high from tourist visitation until 1987. Once the pueblo implemented a managed tourism program and shuttle transportation with step-on guides, negative impacts decreased dramatically. To increase employment, the visitor center rents outdoor booth space to local artists. The visitor center also provides museum exhibits that appropriately address visitor curiosity about the history and culture of Acoma Pueblo.

Creating a Regional Network for Tourism

Tourism is highly dependent on linkages that constitute an entire trip for the traveler. Thus cooperation is the single most important factor in tourism. A visitor does not travel several thousand miles to visit one attraction; instead, the tourist looks for a series of interesting stops and needs to know how to link them. Tourism potential is high for most tribes and rural areas if approached on a regional basis. Visitors need to be told how they can link several stops for a total vacation, and they need to know travel times as well as places for lodging and meal service. Developing a vacation concept in the form of a visitor's guide or a set of itineraries is important even if tour packages are not available to visitors. Literally, the word *tourism* reflects the stop as part of a larger itinerary.

Too often, regional units are defined by political entities, and then agency personnel are puzzled as to why small businesses or microenterprises within the region do not seem to cooperate. A foundation of common interest and a common style of conducting business must be developed for people to see themselves as a region. Having a culture in common can lead to the desire to form a regional unit. Creating effective regional tourism may mean working on a microlevel first and gradually developing a common regional vision through inputs of many small enterprises. This is a very different process than governments bringing together experts to determine an economic development goal for the region they administer. As tribes in the Southwest are increasingly developing tourism goals and linking their own businesses, the balance in the tourism equation is becoming more equitable.

Designing Promotion

Conducting market research is an essential first step in targeting promotional efforts. It is critical to understand present visitors as well as the characteristics of those desired. Visitors want to know what they can do and what they cannot; they want to feel comfortable and want to know how they can contribute to the people they are visiting. Frequently visitors will spend more dollars in a local community when they know the importance of those tourism dollars to the local economy and when they are guided as to where to spend their dollars. Training businesses on cross-cultural expectations is critical for successful tourism development. The most effective promotional effort reaches visitors as they plan their vacation. Cooperative promotional efforts can be accomplished on intertribal or intercommunity levels in conjunction with major industries, state and federal governments, and at a multistate regional level.

Developing an Action Plan

The best tourism planning will accomplish nothing without an action plan to guide its implementation. As the community shapes an action plan identifying steps, resources, personnel, and time frames, a proactive stance is taken in the tourism equation. When plans are developed by outside interests, scale often exceeds community capacities, and timing is usually structured for the quickest economic return rather than taking community needs into account. The key to a successful plan is how well it identifies and incorporates the community perspective on an appropriate development process.

Conclusion

Tourism is nothing new in the Southwest. If we consider Anasazi society and culture and look at centers of ceremony and exchange such as Chaco Canyon, we cannot avoid thinking about the diverse visitors and tradesmen who came to New Mexico from the Colorado River and beyond, from Mexico, and from other directions as well. We cannot avoid wondering about the "performances" that surely took place at Chaco Canyon, performances that presented, dramatized, elaborated, and recontextualized group identities of both visitors and hosts into emergent trade relations.[19] Packaging and staging of culture seems to have been an integral part of human group interactions for thousands of years. It is important to ask who has the right to decide which sorts of packaging and staging are problematic and which are not. Tribal communities must decide for themselves when a particular form of exchange does or does not uphold and benefit their culture and their values. The cross-cultural planning method outlined here supports and strengthens such decisions.

Cultural tourism, poorly planned, can have a wide variety of adverse effects. Well planned, it has the potential to help create a community-sustaining economy and to assist in overcoming stereotypes and prejudices. The idea of exchange is fundamental to the development of respectful cultural tourism. Cultural tourism is a linking between cultural groups to exchange cultural resources and experiences. Economic development through tourism presents an era of opportunity for many tribes and rural areas. But for the exchange in tourism to be fair, communities cannot continue to "tag along" and pretend their involvement is not commercial. Effective tourism development involves engaging in a dialogue, defining and communicating needs, planning and managing. Tribes must decide what they are willing to provide to visitors, and tourists must understand that what their hosts offer them is as valuable as what they are asked to pay.

Cultural bias in the tourism industry must continually be identified and addressed. The tourist industry's view of a "tourism product" implies something to be bought and sold, or a commoditization of culture. This view contrasts sharply with what is viewed in an exchange-based economy as the value of hospitality. To traditional communities, hospitality is not something to be merely bought and sold. It involves the exchange of friendship and a sharing of cultural knowledge. Understanding this different worldview is important if visitors are to gain insight into the host culture and its values.

Before tribal governments began to launch economic development efforts in the 1980s, artists were the main beneficiaries of tourism within tribal economies. Yet artists themselves did not have direct access to markets and often were exploited by urban galleries that paid too small a price for their beautiful and well-made artwork. Because Indian art expresses a rich cultural symbolism, certain arts are ceremonial and not to be sold. Many issues around the sale of art therefore need to be resolved on an ongoing basis for participation in the marketplace to continue. Since Indian art is a main avenue to further appreciation of Indian culture and a significant source of income generation for many tribal families, this factor becomes even more critical.

Many sensitive issues must continue to be resolved. Members of the New Mexico Indian Tourism Association often report ways in which the mainstream tourism trade makes insensitive requests from tribal members. Such requests indicate a need to educate both tourism representatives and other non-Indians. For example, tribal members are often asked to wear ceremonial dress while working in tourism-related activities. Asking for traditional clothing to be used in this way is an inappropriate request, as it is not to be worn outside of a ceremonial context. Educational efforts by NMITA are helping to reduce the frequency of such incidents.

The future of tourism may have many beneficial possibilities. "Virtual tourism," via the Internet, may provide additional outlets for indigenous products while at the same time educating the public without the liability of physical impacts from their actual presence. Already the Indian Pueblo Cultural Center in Albuquerque, the Eight Northern Indian Pueblos, and the Poeh Center at Pojoaque Pueblo are using Web sites to educate and assist potential visitors. Dewailly asks whether a combination of virtual and tactile reality approaches could give mass tourism greater sustainability.[20] Certainly the Internet is a valuable resource for sharing information about appropriate behavior, community goals, and sources of local products before the visitor arrives. The Internet can also facilitate the sale of products to visitors after they leave, continuing the economic benefits without the physical intrusion.

Increasing visitor understanding of Indian people as ongoing cultures is essential for respect in the exchange. Due to the stereotypes of American Indians promoted on television and particularly abroad, there is a tendency for other ethnic groups to regard Indian cultures as remnants of the past. This can be very damaging, particularly to young people, who find themselves sandwiched between stereotypes and living realities. New Mexico Indian communities clearly express a need to promote new images of Indian people as also living in the present and the future, and many of the communities are seeing a growing role for cultural tourism in promoting this alternative view.

Notes

1. Regarding cultural inauthenticity, see Daniel Boorstin, *The Image: A Guide to Pseudo-events in America* (New York: Harper and Row 1964); D. MacCannell, "Staged Authenticity: Arrangements of Social Space in Tourist Settings," *American Journal of Sociology* 79 (1973): 589–603; S. Papson, "Spuriousness and Tourism: Politics of Two Canadian Provincial Governments," *Annals of Tourism Research* 8 (1981): 220–35; Richard Handler, "On Sociocultural Discontinuity: Nationalism and Cultural Objectification in Quebec," *Current Anthropology* 25 (1984): 55–71; "On Having a Culture: Nationalism and the Preservation of Quebec's Patrimoine," in *Objects and Others: Essays on Museums and Material Culture,* ed. G. W. Stocking (Madison: University of Wisconsin Press, 1985), 127–217; and Richard Handler, *Nationalism and the Politics of Culture in Quebec* (Madison: University of Wisconsin Press, 1988); and R. Handler and J. Linnekin, "Tradition, Genuine or Spurious," *Journal of American Folklore* 97 (1984): 273–90. For various cases involving adverse environmental and economic consequences of tourism, see the papers in Valene L. Smith, ed., *Hosts and Guests: The Anthropology of Tourism* (Philadelphia: University of Pennsylvania Press, 1980).
2. See Peter L. Berger and Thomas Luckmann, *The Social Construction of Reality: A Treatise in the Sociology of Knowledge* (Garden City, N.Y.: Doubleday and Company, 1966), for the basic concepts of "social construction of reality." MacCannell, in *The Tourist: A New Theory of the Leisure Class* (New York: Schocken Books, 1976), has promoted a Goffmanesque version of authenticity as a notion that is constructed in a half-dozen front and back "stages"; MacCannell disputes Boorstin's notion that tourists seek the inauthentic, but he remains convinced that "the dividing line between structure genuine and spurious is the realm of the commercial" (155). For an explicit discussion of both authenticity and anthropological accounts as socially constructed, see Nelson H. H. Graburn, "Tourism, Modernity, and Nostalgia," in *The Future of Anthropology: Its Relevance to the Contemporary World,* eds. Akbar Ahmed and Chris Shore (London: Athlone, 1995),

158–78. We agree with Erik Cohen ("Authenticity and Commoditization in Tourism," *Annals of Tourism Research* 15 [1988]: 371–86) that authenticity is flexible, negotiable, and sometimes multivocal.

3. See M. Estellie Smith, *Trade and Trade-Offs: Using Resources, Making Choices, and Taking Risks* (Prospect Heights, Ill.: Waveland Press, 2000), passim and especially 197, 203–4, 207, 217, re the sociocultural dimensions of market systems. Recognition that cultural meanings are negotiated in a variety of settings leads to fundamental questions about the presumed dichotomy between "spurious" and "genuine" culture (see Smith, "The Process of Sociocultural Continuity," with CA comments, *Current Anthropology* 23, no. 2 [1982]: 127–42; and Benita J. Howell, "Weighing the Risks and Rewards of Involvement in Cultural Conservation and Heritage Tourism," *Current Anthropology* 53, no. 2 [1994]: 150–59).

4. The Department of Commerce, in *Native American Multi-Cultural Tourism Development* (Washington, D.C.: Government Printing Office, 1994), emphasizes potential community benefits if tourism planning addresses community concerns.

5. Niles M. Hansen, *Development from Above: The Centre-Down Development Paradigm* (New York: John Wiley and Sons, 1981), 27.

6. New Mexico Department of Tourism, *1996 Conversion Study*, manuscript report, prepared by Southwest Planning and Marketing, Santa Fe, N.Mex., 1997.

7. Susan Guyette, *Strategic Plan of the New Mexico Indian Tourism Association*, manuscript report, prepared by Santa Fe Planning and Research, Santa Fe, N.Mex., 1998.

8. Richard Butler, "Sustainable Tourism: A State-of-the-Art Review," *Tourism Geographies* 1, no. 1 (1999): 7–25.

9. Dennison Nash, "Tourism as an Anthropological Subject," *Current Anthropology* 22, no. 5 (1981): 461–81.

10. Victor and Edith Turner, *Image and Pilgrimage in Christian Culture: Anthropological Perspectives* (New York: Columbia University Press, 1978.

11. George A. Steiner, "Formal Strategic Planning in the United States Today," *Long Range Planning* 16, no. 3 (1983): 12–17.

12. Guyette, *Strategic Plan of the New Mexico Indian Tourism Association*.

13. Richard W. Rider, "Making Strategic Planning and Political Strategy," *Long Range Planning* 16 (1983): 73–81.

14. Susan Guyette, *Regional Economic Development Plan*, manuscript report, prepared for Eight Northern Indian Pueblos Council by Santa Fe Planning and Research, Santa Fe, N.Mex., 1996.

15. W. C. Kruger and Associates, *Pueblo of Pojoaque: Community Development Plan*, Albuquerque, N.Mex., 1988.

16. Clare Gunn, *Tourism Planning: Basics, Concepts, Cases* (Washington, D.C.: Taylor and Francis, 1994).

17. Susan Guyette, *Planning for Balanced Development: A Guide for Native American and Rural Communities* (Santa Fe, N.Mex.: Clear Light Publishers, 1996).

18. United States Department of Commerce, *Tourism USA* (Washington, D.C.: United States Travel and Tourism Administration and the Economic Development Administration, 1986), 142–43.

19. We believe the motivations of hosts and guests at the Anasazi Chacoan pueblos were complex, as are the motivations of hosts and guests at present-day pueblos. Early treatments of "ceremonial exchange" systems such as the Melanesian *kula* (Bronislaw Malinowski, *Argonauts of the Western Pacific* [London: G. Routledge and Sons, 1922]) gave the impression that such exchange systems featured ritualistic exchange that served

political rather than economic functions. Later treatments, however, have clearly shown extensive intertwining of economic exchange with the ritual and political elements of *kula* (e.g., George Dalton, *Traditional Tribal and Peasant Economies: An Introductory Survey of Economic Anthropology* [Reading, Mass.: Addison-Wesley, 1971], 17–18; Annette Weiner, "A World of Made Is Not a World of Born: Doing *Kula* on Kiriwina," in *The Kula: New Perspectives on Massim Exchange*, eds. Jerry W. Leach and Edmund Leach [Cambridge: Cambridge University Press, 1983]). It is a task (so far largely unattempted) for descriptive ethnography to elucidate the mixtures of economic and noneconomic motivations of modern-day southwestern tourists and the American Indian communities that they visit.

20. Jean-Michel Dewailly, "Sustainable Tourist Space: From Reality to Virtual Reality," *Tourism Geographies* 1, no. 1 (1999): 41–55.

TOURISM, DIFFERENCE, AND POWER
IN THE BORDERLANDS ⌐

SYLVIA RODRIGUEZ

The practice of tourism reflects, shapes, manipulates, and transforms culture and identity in complex and multiple ways structured by power. New Mexico, as a "place" and subnational state, exhibits a configuration of racial and cultural politics that bears the distinctive signature of tourism. There the tourism industry has shaped postcolonial cultures and identities by fusing race, landscape, and architecture into romance and commodity. The case of New Mexico, which represents one node in a regional complex, is striking for its extraordinarily successful mystification of race. It is successful because of the enduring and pervasive power of the iconic triad of Indian-Mexican-Anglo, which continues to structure civil and state discourses of race and ethnicity while simultaneously obscuring real complexity. How this radical disconnect between image and reality is sustained and utilized by the practices and discourses of tourism is—or ought to be—of critical and practical interest.

Three recent books crystallize critical findings and pursue individual analyses of the workings of tourism in the Southwest as well as the global processes of tourism: Leah Dilworth's *Imagining Indians in the Southwest*, Chris Wilson's *The Myth of Santa Fe*, and Hal Rothman's *Devil's Bargains*.[1]

Dilworth illustrates modernist primitivism between 1880 and the 1920s with four case studies. Wilson traces architectural history in relation to tourism development, ethno-class relations, and public ceremony in Santa Fe. Rothman argues that western tourism typifies the colonial impact of the industry and inevitably incurs a fatal "devil's bargain." These works examine the power and creativity as well as the destructiveness of tourism as the quintessential modern/postmodern form or phase of global capitalist development. Rothman's very choice of words makes explicit the peril inherent in tourism development. He is not the first to use the devil as a metaphor for the cultural machinery of capitalism.[2]

Observation and research in Taos and Santa Fe have led me to formulate ways in which tourism constructs race relations, ethnic identity, and cultural politics in the Land of Enchantment. Several processes and consequences have been engendered by more than a century of tourism development in the region. These include bourgeois Anglo Indianism and the objectification and commodification of ethnicity; differential adaptive and strategic ethnic reconstruction by Pueblos and Hispanos; a privileging of the visual; an internalization of the tourist gaze by natives; the commodification of subjectivity; Anglo self-erasure in art and public culture; and hyperethnicity and the intensification of ethnic boundaries, including a recent surge in Hispano ethnopolitical and ethnoreligious mobilizations. My approach has been inspired, corroborated, complemented, and expanded by the works cited as well as writings by Bodine, Weigle, Babcock, Hinsley, Riley, and others.[3]

This essay will look at the question of how tourism interacts with culture and identity in New Mexico through a focus on the problem of race and power. New Mexico exhibits an unusual and extremely effective hegemonic transmutation of the symbolic meaning of race. The intent of this work is to formulate an understanding of the cultural workings of tourism in the U.S. Southwest and to pose questions and issues for future research.

Mystification is a Marxist term that seems to have fallen out of favor in our poststructural, postmodern, postcolonial era. But despite its alleged obsolescence, there are compelling reasons to renew its use. The word wavers between thick description and surrender to the process it names. This essay deconstructs the processes and mechanisms of mystification, or what is sometimes labeled "culture." Poststructural, postcolonial, and feminist analyses likewise deconstruct and expose how culture and ideology embody, enforce, express, resist, manipulate, contest, interrupt, and modify local as well as larger historical agendas of power. Behind this is the optimistically insurgent motive to weaken the bonds of power through insight into how they work. The following will consider the relation between tourism, race, and culture in New Mexico.

Tourism and the Mystification of Race

The most famous process or artifact of the touristic mystification of culture in the U.S. Southwest is bourgeois Anglo Indianism, which Weigle, Babcock, and Dilworth have also likened to Said's Orientalism. Dilworth calls it *prim-itivism*, but the term *Indianism* is used here because it calls attention to the racializing role of this genre of discourse and practice. Indianism is the romantic idealization, appropriation, and commodification of Indians, Indian culture, and all things Indian by white people since before the beginning of the 1900s. This historical process has gone through many phases, beginning with the productions of art colonists, writers, and anthropologists and cul-minating in today's ubiquitous plastering of "Indian" imagery all over the public, commercial, and even private spaces of Santa Fe, Taos, Phoenix, and the rest of the Southwest. The emergence of Euro-American Indianism in conjunction with and in service to the rise of the railroad in the West and the birth of modern tourism can be documented, along with its evolution through subsequent eras of automobile, air, and now virtual travel. But the omnipresence of Indianism cannot be fully appreciated without attention to the set of implicit and explicit contrasts within which the all-important image of the Indian Other is framed. This double set contains the ambigu-ous Mexican on the one hand and the ever more invisible yet pivotal Anglo on the other. Both have been almost entirely elided in art and public dis-course, albeit in very different ways.

Inside what Bodine so aptly named the "tri-ethnic trap," the other side of the Indianism coin is Hispanophobia and anti-Mexicanism. Central to this ideographic (meaning both ideological and graphic-visual) structure is the development of Anglo invisibility. The tourist gaze is a white gaze because the strategy of Anglo whiteness is to erase itself through normalization as national citizenship. In leisure it seeks a state of otherness. Bourgeois white-ness is the organizing principle behind the yearner sensibility that seeks tran-scendence and redemption through union with a spiritually suffused Indian Other, located within a pristine, empty, geologically monumental landscape. This framing of a primordial, nonwhite ethnic Other within a stark desert-mountain wilderness is both modernist and privileged. It belongs to the anti-modernist variety of modernism because it flees the alienation and corruption of industrial civilization, just as Mary Austin and Mabel Dodge Luhan did and as hundreds of amenity migrants attempt to do each year in New Mexico's steadily gentrifying tourist towns. Its privilege entails the power to construct a fanciful racial order in which the downtrodden Indian is elevated to a quasi-supernatural position of spiritual superiority, while Mexicans are relegated to the unclean lower class. Anglos are either exoticized (as cow-boys or "Leatherstockings") or left out of this scenario altogether. Yet the enduring and endearing cliché of New Mexico as a tourist mecca is tricul-tural harmony, which does imply the presence of Anglos.

Invocation of the Indian-Mexican-Anglo trichotomy is meant to problematize rather than affirm it as a construct. Elsewhere in the United States, racial discourse is negative and fixated on a black-white binary rather than on Mexicans and/or Indians. But does lived social reality conform to either a tripartite or a dual racial paradigm? Do not direct observation and experience give the lie to this fiction? Is anyone today purely and exclusively "Indian," "Mexican," or "Anglo"? Many are none of these. Yet civil and popular discourses perpetuate this triadic model despite its manifest untruth. But if untrue it is still very real, because official discourses of difference have the power to define and separate people and to dictate normative relations between them. This process constitutes the hegemonic workings of power.

Scholars have noted how visual the practice and discourse of tourism are—note MacCannell's premise that sightseeing is the core activity in tourism practice and Urry's insight that the tourist gaze is differentiated by class. Pratt, Kaplan, and others have shown how the imperial gaze prefigures the tourist gaze, expressing colonial design, consumerist desire, and global relations of power.[4] A privileging of the visual sensory mode is a key feature of tourism in general, and its predominance in the Southwest is especially significant. It offers escape from industrial-extractive-colonizing capitalism's otherwise pervasive emphasis on words and numbers. The touristic privileging of the visual reigns supreme in an economy where art, especially painting and photography, becomes the cultural coin of the realm. The eye has always been the primary organ of touristic gratification in the West. Painting, photography, and derivative ephemera are the dominant artistic media of New Mexico and the Southwest generally. Although there is also a strong literary tradition, the region remains known most vividly through dramatic visual images.

The tourist gaze in New Mexico issues from a position of middle-class privilege and seeks an experience of "solitude, privacy, and a personal, semispiritual relationship with the object of the gaze." This romantic gaze contrasts with a working-class "collective" gaze, which strives toward common experience.[5] It focuses on a threefold visual semiotic or system of meanings comprised of Indians; a vast, empty, arid landscape; and adobe architecture. Its cornerstone is art. The core whiteness of this gaze lies not only in imperialist nostalgia or antimodern escapism, but, most importantly, in the selectively racialized landscape it projects.

Southwestern art may function as an advertisement to attract tourists, amenity migrants, and investors, but it does not necessarily follow that this is the conscious or cynical intent of those who produce the art. Rather, the power of hegemony lies in its unconscious nature. Like television commercials, much southwestern art manipulates people into complicity with an exploitative system profitable to a few. But unlike television commercials, the art is not deliberately designed to achieve this end. Its goals are loftier and more varied. Because hegemony constantly struggles against the resistance it engenders, not all art succumbs to the dead hand of advertisement. Nor are people blind and passive victims in this complex, dynamic process. Of particular interest is how individual artists, works, and consumers simultaneously enact and resist hegemonic processes. The production and gratification of cultural desire by positioned subjects are complex formations not reducible to rational, economic motive. Yet no serious analysis of these phenomena can ignore the "bottom line."

Tourism and the Indianist commodification of culture created economic opportunities and niches for Indian models, craftspeople, dancers, and artists. It is arguable that bourgeois Anglo Indianism has been a boon to most Indian peoples in the Southwest. As Native American (White Earth Band of Anishinabeg) activist Winona LaDuke put it, she enjoys visiting New Mexico because Indians are treated better there. Art colonists and anthropologists were the first white people who admired and sought to emulate and preserve Indians and Indian culture. Such seekers are usually seen by those they admire as preferable to hostile racists or ignorant, indifferent bureaucrats. One way to underscore the impact of tourism on Indian life in the Southwest is to try to imagine what would have happened had there been no tourism. For one thing, there would have been no "Art."

It is a cherished truism that "true art" transcends race, ethnicity, or other forms of difference to express what is universal. But in New Mexico, what is called art is about little other than race and ethnicity. Consider the fact that just about any painting, sculpture, or other artifact on display in any given art gallery or museum or shop window in downtown Taos or Santa Fe makes some kind of implicit or explicit statement about ethnicity or ethnic identity, including that of the artist. Indeed, it is very difficult to find a work of art, much less any curio or tourist trinket, that does not make some kind of ethnic, pseudoethnic, or metaethnic (reflexively, sometimes ironically, ethnic) statement. This does not mean that ethnicity or ethnic identity is necessarily the original subject matter of the art or artifact in question, but rather that the contemporary context within which the object is viewed, interpreted, and valued imbues it with fundamental and inescapable ethnoracial meaning. This is as true for a Georgia O'Keeffe landscape as it is for a santo, a pot, a rug, a kachina doll, or paintings by Joseph Sharp, Bert Phillips, R. C. Gorman, Michael Martinez, Tavlos, or Fritz Scholder. Each of these art objects may invoke ethnicity in a somewhat different way, while the positionality of each artist reveals a different aspect of the totality. But ethnicity is central to the contemporary meaning and appeal of the object.

Tourism and the Indian art market stimulated the revival and modification of weaving, jewelry, pottery, painting, music, and ceremonialism among southwestern Indians and stimulated what MacCannell calls *reconstructed ethnicity*, or "the maintenance and preservation of ethnic forms for the entertainment of ethnically different others." But ethnic reconstruction notwithstanding, southwestern tribes have tried to use tourism in the service of survival rather than the other way around, and they have actively and passively employed ways to contain, control, exclude, and represent tourists and tourist activity within their sovereign boundaries. The love-hate affair between tourism and the pueblos is bittersweet and complex, like all devil's bargains. "Authentic" Indian behavior, appearance, and cultural products are scripted, performed, and their purity and authenticity policed in touristic settings to protect their market values. At the same time, people manage to subvert tourism-generated cultural, racial, and gender stereotypes, as exemplified by Nora Naranjo-Morse's "Pearlene" figures described by Babcock.[6]

How does the commodification of ethnicity affect identity and subjectivity? At some hypothetical moment the art colonists' Indian models understood for the first time what the artists and other yearners saw or thought they saw in them. This revelation was seductive, painful, and empowering. It offered a remedy to the debased self-image that conquest and colonization perpetuate. Tourism and its gaze compounded the split sense of self subalterns experience between how their oppressors see them and how they see themselves. Internalization of the tourist gaze by its objects represents a new phase in the colonial or postcolonial process and leads to mixed results. It ossifies identity into an image generated in the mind of a conqueror afflicted with imperialist nostalgia. Still, as Rina Swentzell describes, the disparity between the Indian in the painting and the Indian in the street can evoke a sense of inadequacy: "We felt idealized, yet unworthy of that adoration."[7] Virtually everyone in the late twentieth century, ethnic or otherwise, constitutes a modern/postmodern subject who imagines a premodern, traditional, primitive, or authentic Self/Other with a sense of loss. The authentic, pristine indigenous subject is a modern, romantic construct. This construct represents a trap but also a resource for play, irony, creativity, and resistance, all strategies employed by different individuals at different times.

The commodification of subjectivity in a touristic universe constitutes the inner battlefield all ethnics as well as resident "nonethnics" (or "Anglos") experience and struggle over. This is the war of commodification versus something like "tradition" or "integrity." Yet the problem of authenticity has different implications for tourists and the human objects of their gaze as well as for amenity migrants (or "neonatives," as Rothman calls them) who broker their relation. "Authenticity" is least consequential to the casual tourist, who nevertheless is probably in Taos or Santa Fe looking for mystique. Amenity migrants have a stake in perpetuating the features that first attracted them to the place, as experience and as investment.

The iconically racialized landscape of New Mexico is a touristic fantasy that seeks aesthetic alterity far away from banal urban reality. "Vacation" is the momentary escape from the burden of everyday labor. The amenity migrant seeks to convert the enjoyment of vacation into a "more authentic" way of life. Some are able to achieve this through wealth, while others strive through bohemian austerity. For the native Pueblo or Hispano, the problem of authenticity is more complex, but in different ways. For them it involves boundary maintenance and resistance against the threatening incursions of tourism, resort development, and assimilation. But natives too have a stake in tourism, which, apart from government, is the major source of income, direct or indirect, for the area.

Rothman's book shows how in western communities tourism is a devil's bargain wherein the fulfillment of desire becomes the machinery of self-destruction. Commodification of touristic assets ultimately degrades or destroys them. This dilemma and irony at the heart of tourism development is compounded by yet another. Preservationism, whether Anglo, Indian, Hispano, or some combination, does not really counter tourism but can only raise the market value of that which it "preserves." This has political implications for amenity migrants and natives because it turns the fruits of resistance into commodities, thus threatening to commodify subjectivity, the source of resistance.

Tourism and the State

Tourism and the state are two major forces that underwrite, justify, and perpetuate ethnoracial difference. The "state" refers to the entire bureaucratic complex of local, state, and federal structures, agencies, policies, and functions that hierarchically organize national society. Although this essay cannot focus in depth on the relation of the state to tourism, the state's centrality to both tourism development and the persistence of ethnic difference among people living in the region is of fundamental importance. Consider the fact that the very definition and legal status of Indians and Hispanos as distinct populations is sustained by actions and policies of the state operating at a multiplicity of levels. It is the federal government that decides which land belongs to the Indians and which is public domain, as well as who is an Indian, an enfranchised citizen, a prisoner, or an alien. The state monopolizes coercion and asserts, extends, and defends the nation's borders.

Much of the social, political, and economic difference between Pueblo and Hispano-Mexicano peoples flows from their differential statuses vis-à-vis the American state. Indian reservations are held in trust by the federal government, and their lands are inalienable outside the tribe. Spanish-speaking New Mexicans were incorporated into the United States under the same treaty as the pueblos, but males were enfranchised as full citizens from the start and community grant lands were privatized or appropriated as public domain. Today Indian tribes in the Southwest are attempting to reconstruct the meaning of sovereignty while Hispanos, Mexicanos, and other Latinos are negotiating, from different positionalities, the politics of citizenship.

The state and tourism both work to sustain and sometimes to intensify ethnic boundaries. Yet both are usually seen as threats to ethnic persistence and cultural survival. Ethnic identity and mobilization or nationalism are produced by contact, competition, and inequality. The long history of Indo-Hispano interaction that preceded Anglo domination constitutes a shared yet differentiated substratum of interpenetrating histories, senses of place, and identities. Tourism built upon an Indianist version of this drama imaginatively erases the presence or influence of urban Anglos and the industrial conditions they flee. The "impact" of tourism upon Indians and Mexicanos/Spanish Americans in the town of Taos and its surrounding communities differed also by virtue of their individual locales, relations with each other, and relations with Anglos.

Tourism and the state are partners in the ethnicity-commodifying enterprise of enchantment. Both promote, evoke, stimulate, and shape the intensification of ethnic boundaries in New Mexico. *Intensification* refers to increased self-awareness and public assertion as members of a distinct ethnic group with ancestral links to specific places. Boundaries are the markers or "traits" that ethnically differentiate people who are also differentiated by gender, age, and class. Tourism is one face of the global capitalist forces and transnational processes that are variously dissolving and creating states while nations and nationalist movements flow across, resist, or adhere to ultimately transient state boundaries. Tourism intensified Hispano ethnic boundaries by prizing Indian culture, valuating difference, and creating an economy in which certain expressions of ethnicity became marketable assets. Like the Pueblos, Hispanos living in tourism centers such as Taos and Santa Fe have shown diverse responses to the successive waves of resort development during the twentieth century.

Tourism and Boundary Politics

Anthropologists may no longer conceive of ethnic groups as bounded, discrete, territorial, and cultural entities, but most people still speak of Taos and the other pueblos in such terms. Taos Pueblo is described and dealt with by the outside world as an agentive, autonomous, corporate, and sovereign entity. Externally accessible internal accounts of the pueblo are taboo, and the power to suppress information internally appears to reside with an entrenched, all-male, gerontocratic oligarchy. From an internal standpoint, the pueblo, like any small community, represents a force field of structural and contingent inequities interlocked in continuous struggle. From within, Taos Pueblo is heterogeneous, stratified, struggling for unity and at war with itself.

Taos Pueblo's strategy of survival over the past four hundred years has been to exert boundary maintenance along multiple fronts, including territorial defense and hydraulic control, language, endogamy, and secrecy. Secrecy is a long-standing mechanism of internal stratification as well as external boundary maintenance among the Pueblos.[8] It has adapted over the course of successive regimes of domination dating from the inquisitor's gaze to the tourist gaze. While internal secrecy protects tribal hierarchy and minimizes the possibility of significant revelations to outsiders, external secrecy feeds the aura of mystery attached to things Indian, particularly religious matters. Today secrecy enhances Taos Pueblo's touristic mystique by keeping its supreme cultural capital, Native American Spirituality, a scarce commodity.

The question of consciousness and intentionality in the deployment of such a strategy is problematic because while I do not mean to suggest cynical deliberation or manipulation by disingenuous elites, neither do I underestimate the political astuteness of generations of individuals who spent their lives defending pueblo boundaries. Taos Pueblo's canny use of affluent, educated, well-connected Anglo sympathizers to help sustain and advance its sixty-four-year legal battle for Blue Lake as well as other land and water claims and sovereignty issues is well documented and endlessly instructive.[9] This ongoing pragmatism is the result of a dialectic between the intentional and the unconscious; people both know and do not know what they are doing.

Mexicans occupy a very different position in the Euro-American imagination than Indians, just as they occupy very different positions vis-à-vis the state and in the borderlands political economy. The Anglo-Mexican dynamic that pervades the U.S.-Mexico borderlands (Texas, New Mexico, Arizona, California) comprises a kind of transregional binary that assumes a different character in each subregion. Historically, the most openly agonistic and oppressive Anglo-Mexican interface was in Texas. Today anti-immigrant, anti-Latino sentiment seems most virulent in California, yet festers all along the increasingly militarized border.

Northern and southern New Mexico differ significantly in terms of the demographics and character of race relations between Mexicans and Anglos. This discussion focuses on the northern dynamic and how it interacts with tourism. There, unlike any other subregion of the borderlands, Mexican-descent peoples, who may variously call themselves Mexicanos, Hispanos, or Spanish Americans, have a political culture and a tradition of electoral enfranchisement that is generations deep and that exercises considerable local control in Hispano-majority counties. A good percentage of them are still landed, albeit in eroding and ever smaller proportions, and trace their ancestry in the region to pre-American times.

The presumptive exceptionalism or uniqueness of Spanish New Mexico may be a creature of tourism and state policy, but a Hispano sense of ethnic differentiation originated in the colonial relationship vis-à-vis Indians. Spanish American or Nuevomexicano nationalism emerged during the territorial period, seems to have crystallized by the time New Mexico became a state, and was linked to the spread of a Spanish-language press.[10] Like Pueblo people (and, for that matter, "Anglos"), Nuevomexicanos or Hispanos are today the genetic products of centuries of miscegenation. Yet the social boundaries that mark them off from Indians on the one hand and Anglos on the other are sustained by mechanisms that originate internally as well as externally and from above. In a word, structural inequality sustains external, racialized ethnic boundaries, from outside the group and from above. What sustains internal boundaries from within is accounted for by Fredrik Barth's now classic insight that ethnic boundaries can organize access and claim to resources.[11] In short, although ethnic identity (as opposed to the national identity of unmarked or normalized whiteness) carries a stigma, it also confers access to certain resources, ranging from the concrete, such as land and water, to the symbolic, such as acceptance or affective membership in a community.

The motive to express, sustain, and defend ethnic identity is usually subaltern and, paradoxically, resistant by way of compliance, for example, by virtue of conforming to received or imposed images of group identity. Both Pueblo and Hispano communities in the Upper Rio Grande Valley articulate their cultural identities with reference to land bases and specific territories, as well as to features of tradition, culture, language, food, kinship, and religion. Tourism did not invent these ethnic boundaries, but it selectively commodified them. Hispano boundaries developed first in relation to Indian boundaries and then to Anglo boundaries under the U.S. racial order. Both Pueblo and Hispano groups have mobilized ethnopolitically in recent

decades around issues of land and culture. Such intensification or mobilization is caused by global forces beyond and yet not entirely distinguishable
from tourism; in New Mexico, it has been shaped by touristic tastes.

In northern New Mexico economic development and urbanization mostly
take the form of resort expansion and gentrification, processes that have escalated dramatically in Taos and Santa Fe since 1970. Resort development has
generated a major real estate boom in land, water rights, adobe buildings, and
the construction industry. It also raises the cost of living. There has been dramatic turnover in land and real estate ownership along with exponential esca-
lation in their values. Hispanos dependent on modest, insecure incomes from
government or tourism increasingly find themselves unable to hold on to inher-
ited properties or to afford new housing in rapidly gentrifying areas.

Gentrification and the competitive pressure it places on surface and
groundwater has been the primary catalyst for the place-based Hispano ethnocultural mobilizations seen in Taos and other areas of New Mexico over
the past thirty years. These mobilizations take religious and political forms,
both of which are grounded in ancestral claims to resources such as specific
tracts of land and water, including acequia (traditional community irrigation
ditch) systems. The political form is exemplified by protest mobilizations
against large developments that threaten specific water supplies and water
rights. Such movements, prefigured by the Alianza land grant movement of
the 1960s and fictionalized by John Nichols, have in fact been ethnically
mixed, although their power and legitimacy derive from acequia and land
grant association involvement. The religious form consists of ritual revivals,
sacred site restorations, and a generalized intensification of parish- or place-
based folk Catholic religious activity.[12] It is accompanied by a revitalization
of the santero as well as contemporary Spanish arts traditions, which represent the friendly interface with tourism and expand niches for salable art.

Symbolic intensification of Hispano identity has diversified over the past
two decades. Crossing class, generational, urban-rural, and national boundaries,
it encompasses a broad spectrum of Iberian-Mestizo-Indigenous identities.
Hispano-Chicano cultural nationalism ranges in New Mexico from claims to
the enduring whiteness of the conquistadors to Chicano polemics against
the very notion. Most adult native Nuevomexicanos are situated somewhere
between these extremes. The political and religious forms described above constitute their modal expression of collectively mobilized Nuevomexicano ethnic identity. Tourism is part of the local as well as global contexts within which
Hispano and Pueblo mobilizations take place. The role of tourism needs to be
understood with reference to the other major forces at work in this complex
situation, including the state and urbanization. It would be a distortion to claim

that tourism is the sole catalyst for Hispano, Pueblo, or other ethnopolitical and ethnocultural mobilizations, yet no analysis can be accurate that does not place tourism at or near the center.

Tourism can foster ethnic pride and at the same time fan the flames of local resentment against the pressures created by expanding touristic appetites and numbers. Most environmentalists who join forces with acequia communities to fight large developments are amenity migrants whose stake in site preservation is experienced and configured differently from most natives'. In some contexts their interests may conflict with native constituencies', for example, over issues of endangered species versus long-standing subsistence and extractive practices (spotted owl vs. woodcutting, silvery minnow and in-stream flow vs. acequias). Where tourism takes root and grows for many years in already divided places such as Taos and Santa Fe, it not only forges commercial alliances but foments schisms at all levels: between natives and newcomers, tourists and locals, pro- and antidevelopment factions, and, as ever, ethnic insiders and outsiders.

Between 1970 and 1990 Anglos increased from 6 percent to 28 percent of the population in Taos and from 34 percent to 49 percent in Santa Fe. Hispanos in Santa Fe thus lost their demographic majority during this period, going from 65 percent to 47 percent. This growth was due mostly to amenity migration and despite a higher Hispanic fertility rate (the Native American percentage did not change appreciably). During the early 1980s resort expansion became a volatile issue in Taos, where ethnically mixed grassroots coalitions including acequia officers picketed Taos Ski Valley, protested against condominium developments, and succeeded in establishing a grassroots, community-based special rural zoning district subsequently defeated by developers in court. Widespread dissatisfaction with rapid development grew strong enough in 1994 to get city councilor Debbie Jaramillo elected the first woman mayor of Santa Fe. Jaramillo is the first and only Hispanic candidate to run successfully for political office in the state of New Mexico on a platform openly critical of tourism. Her milestone election was followed by four tumultuous years that ended in her resounding defeat for reelection in 1998.[13]

Part of the underlying struggle in Taos county politics is over changing ethnic proportions and their anticipated impact on local electoral politics. Many Hispano politicians feel threatened by the steady growth of vocal amenity migrants who want to change public policy and decision making. This line was crossed long ago in Santa Fe, but not quite yet in Taos. As one local put it, "Raza is just holding its breath waiting for it to happen," referring to the dreaded day Anglos will take over electoral politics. Political control based on demographic majority and land tenure are the two footholds and last bastions of Hispano power in the "Hispanic counties" of northern New Mexico, where the Hispano population is 50 percent or more. Gentrification threatens both. This, in conjunction with the rise of a Hispano middle class, is a catalyst for the defensive ethnopolitical and ethnocultural mobilizations that are occurring.

The town of Taos has become highly gentrified during the past three decades, a process that continues unabated. During the same period town government has been securely in the hands of Hispano businessmen who run a smooth ship and cooperate with resort developers. Mayoral and city council races are in essence uncontested in terms of alternative platforms of any kind. But unlike Santa Fe, there have been no Anglo town officials for many years. County government is likewise controlled by Hispanos but openly embroiled in the struggle between developers and mixed constituencies of amenity migrant preservationists and native resisters. Racial politics operate everywhere in Taos: as a subtext in newspaper coverage of corrupt county politicians; in native resentment of newcomers; in the complaints by Anglos who feel victimized by Hispano racism; in social tensions in the schools; in legal discourse between Taos Pueblo and the town, county, surrounding acequias, and individual land claimants. Race-ethnicity saturates all political, social, and cultural meaning in Taos.

Polarized as they may become in tourist town politics, over time both so-called natives and newcomers will ultimately have in common the experience of being tourists. Tourist, native, and amenity migrant exist as pure types only in the segregated imagination. This is because almost no one born in New Mexico since World War II has not been a tourist somewhere else, if only momentarily, as part of a diasporic experience as worker, soldier, student, or emigrant. Like amenity migrants, natives are modern subjects and therefore by definition, as MacCannell suggests, tourists. Many live and work away for much of their adult lives but aspire to return. Some then commit themselves to cultural-political activism and/or preservationism. But this common ground still does not mean that amenity migrants, natives, and ethnic nationalists are the same—further divided as they are by race, ethnicity, class, and class fraction.

New Mexico's climate of hyperethnicity also affects Anglo identity. Wilson notes how Anglos began to recede from representation in public art and pageantry in Santa Fe around the time they were first called Anglos, an act of naming that made them "into one ethnic group among others."[14] In Taos a similar elision of whiteness and bourgeois Anglos from depiction in paintings and other public representations was concurrent with the growth of amenity migration. Despite their erasure from the iconography (but not the reality) of Enchantment, Anglos have become, by virtue of the term, a marked category. This presents an interesting twist from the standpoint of contemporary race theory, which tends to emphasize how whiteness remains invisible in racial discourse and practice. The (nonsupremacist) marking of whiteness originates with racial subalterns as an act of resistance. Activists and critical scholars have taken up the tactic in order to analyze the construction of whiteness in a sociohistorical context.[15]

Seventy years ago Anglos paraded as Kearney's Army of the West, pioneers, cowboys, trappers, or artists, a spectacle no longer seen on the streets of Santa Fe or Taos (Taos was approximately twenty years later than Santa Fe in expunging such figures from public pageants). They were also comfortable dressing up as Indians or even Mexicans for pageants. But since at least the 1960s this practice has been abandoned, while members of the otherized subaltern groups now claim the exclusive right to self-representation in public discourse. Needless to say this constraint does not hold in the realm of fine art. Nonsupremacist identity-based expressions of ethnic or otherwise inflected whiteness by white people nevertheless does occur in New Mexico as elsewhere. Examples include dressing up like mountain men for trade fair reenactments and the pursuit of a neo-Celtic identity (partly inspired by New Age phenomena plus the River Dance fad). Recent interest in "Crypto-Jewish" identities in New Mexico seems to signal a step away from mainstream Anglo whiteness for Jewish amenity migrants drawn toward this heritage but a step toward whiteness for Hispanos who embrace a rediscovered converso ancestry. It is noteworthy that individuals who are called Anglos in New Mexico often voice resentment of the term because it lumps together very disparate kinds of people—virtually everyone who is neither Indian nor Hispano-Mexicano. The hegemonic, tourism-sustaining triethnic paradigm does violence to everyone, yet people seem oddly powerless to resist it.

The ability to erase and to mark whiteness in public discourse is a measure of power, and the marking of Anglos in New Mexico is largely a function of Hispano political power. Anglos enjoy the power to erase images of themselves from public art and culture, but Hispanos have the power publicly to name Anglos as such. It is another measure of Hispano political power to claim a white identity through emphasis on Spanish ancestry and traditional culture. The most controversial aspect of Nuevomexicano, Hispano, or Spanish American identity is this claim to whiteness, which is internally divisive and denounced by virtually all outsiders, including Mexicans and self-identified Chicanos. The Nuevomexicano claim to Spanish over Mexican identity is influenced but not determined by class position. It is expressed publicly in essentialist metaphors and pageantry where men dress up as conquistadors—such historical figures as Coronado, Oñate, or de

Vargas. Conquistador imagery and reenactments are not popular in Mexico or among most other Mexican Americans. Indeed, the controversy that began during the 1999 Cuartocentenary over a proposed statue of Oñate may portend a downturn even in their New Mexican popularity.[16]

Tourism did not cause the "Spanish phenomenon" in New Mexico but encouraged it by creating a market for Spanish colonial artifacts and other exotica. The quaintness of Spanish American villages was underwritten in the 1930s by government programs and policies including the New Deal. Spanish American identity emerged as New Mexicans became Americans. Their history represents the northern frontier variant of the Latin American colonial context, with its own spectrum between white and indigenous extremes. Today mestizo and other hybrid identities such as Chicano/as and (nouveau) Genízaro and (nouveau) Crypto-Jewish fill the middle ground between purely ideal poles. Nuevomexicano Spanish identity emerged defensively in relation to contrasting categories of whiteness (Anglo) and non-whiteness (Indian and *surumato*, or Mexican nationals).

Difference and Scarcity in the New Century

How can we best formulate the relationship between the contrasting touristic images of Indians and Mexicans in the Southwest, their differential access to tourist markets, and their respective statuses vis-à-vis the state? Can we predict how these relationships are likely to play out in the future? Such questions animate concern with what is happening now and what is likely to occur over the next quarter century.

Two factors loom large that have major implications for the future of tourism and race relations in New Mexico: gaming and water rights adjudication. Both evoke issues of sovereignty. Sovereignty implies a state plus a counterclaim to identity, agency, and autonomy—a condition ripe for conflict. How might gaming and water rights adjudication interact with tourism and ethnoracial relations in the future?

Gaming began in New Mexico when Republican businessman Gary Johnson became governor in 1995. The pueblos of Isleta, Sandia, Acoma, Santa Ana, San Felipe, San Juan, Pojoaque, Tesuque, and Taos now all operate lucrative casinos. Jicarilla and Mescalero Apaches also have gaming enterprises, while opposing sides among the Navajo slowly wrestle their way toward joining them. The casinos create an infinite interior space of eternal night, cigarette smoke, cheap food, and the glitter and jingle of slot machines. There among a river of everyday local faces and total strangers a jackpot or a movie star just might appear. This ambiance inverts the familiar touristic construct of "sun, silence, and adobe." Although it is too early to assess the long-term economic, social, political, and cultural effects of Indian gaming in New Mexico, it seems safe to say that gambling has already empowered the tribes and drawn lines of competing interest among various constituencies over its material costs and benefits. The gaming tribes have become weighty political campaign contributors and a powerful lobby within the state. Dispute between state officials and the tribes has emerged over revenue sharing, for which the legislature imposed a rate of 16 percent in 1997. The Mescaleros and some pueblos, including Taos, claim the high rate is illegal and refuse to pay all or part of the amount. They are lobbying to have the rate cut by more than half while the state attorney general prepares to take them to court. By the late 1990s several casinos were undergoing expansion as part of a development strategy to become destination resorts. Their success has generated income and growth but inevitably intensified competition over limited resources, including consumer dollars and water.

Each case represents a different face of the larger picture. For example, in Taos the proposed expansion of gambling has precipitated division within the pueblo, between the pueblo and the city, and between pro- and antiexpansionist coalitions across ethnic lines. In 1999 Taos Pueblo began negotiations to buy Kachina Lodge, a large motel that sits just inside the municipal boundary between the pueblo and the city of Taos, in order to relocate and expand their casino, started on reservation land in 1997. The proposed deal drew opposition from RISE (Residents in Support of Education), a grassroots organization in the pueblo that questioned the economic soundness of the plan and publicly (in the local media) challenged pueblo officials to be less secretive and open their decision making to community discussion. RISE also questioned the tribal government's minuscule allocation of gaming revenues to pressing educational and senior citizens' needs. The Kachina Lodge scheme departed from the usual pattern of building casinos along highways rather than inside towns. The city of Taos balked at the prospect of having a large tribal casino near its heart and protested on the grounds that the pueblo's environmental impact assessment finding of no significant impact was "completely inaccurate." In December the city and a coalition between RISE and a Taos citizens' group (Coalition for a Better Taos, or CBT) filed injunctions to stop a Bureau of Indian Affairs (BIA) loan that would help finance the motel purchase until a full environmental impact study could be completed. In early 2000 the tribal council and a newly installed pueblo governor reassessed the situation and decided to abandon the plan. The reason given was that the financial risk involved might imperil the tribe's ability to maintain payments on its purchase of a large mountain tract adjacent to the

Blue Lake wilderness. The decision was easily attributed to the leadership's primary commitment to protect tribal religion by protecting Blue Lake.[17]

In its mystique and conflict structure, the Taos case telescopes the major issues at play throughout the region: difference, power, tourism, and scarcity. Inevitably the question arises: can the tribes promote economic development through gaming resorts and still be who they are? What determines who they are? Tourism transmuted difference from a stigma into an asset for Indians in New Mexico. But even though they became the primary objects of the tourist gaze and benefited from this, Indians never controlled the economy to which they were subject. To some, gaming appears to hold this promise, perhaps at best as a transitional phase to a more diversified or stable economy. At present the casinos attract mostly locals, but in order to survive they must capture a tourist market as well. If and how they can accomplish this remains to be seen. Will they decide to specialize and diversify in order to compete with each other? Will they market themselves as a package in order to compete with Las Vegas and other centers? Could the Upper Rio Grande corridor ever become a popular Indian-themed gaming "strip"? Is it possible to attract tourists without capitalizing on identity? Can the pueblos reconcile the mystique of their traditional identity with Las Vegas–style glitz and the massive scale of water consumption required by destination resorts?[18]

Thus we come to the final variable that might portend trouble. This is the limiting factor of water, considered in light of projected rates of demographic growth that promise to exceed an imprecisely known (in terms of actual water supply) environmental carrying capacity within the next half century. Water shortages are already evident along the border, and in each subregion, nation, and state the process will unfold differently, according to a complex configuration of local and global factors. The development, irrigation, and urbanization of the arid West have depended on a massive federal hydraulic infrastructure constructed to divert, capture, and control water. Without this infrastructure many agricultural, industrial, and urban centers would fail; indeed, they would not be there in the first place. A straightforward prognosis for the region suggests that ultimately, a viable human habitat will be sustainable only through population control.

The state and federal water rights adjudication is a lawsuit initiated by the New Mexico State engineer in order to determine the ownership of all non-Indian rights along the tributaries of the Rio Grande. This automatically entails the determination of Indian claims, starting with pueblos situated on tributaries shared by acequia communities, municipalities, and sanitation districts, and other entities and individuals who claim and exercise surface and ground-water rights. Thus the suit opposes each of the pueblos against its closest non-Indian neighbors, starting with the acequias, over water rights. In the Pojoaque drainage the case is known as Aamodt (listing all defendants in alphabetical order) and in Taos as Abeyta. This vast, complex, glacially slow legal process started in 1966 and will probably continue on appeal past our lifetimes. The case has consequences for everyone living in the borderlands because it determines who owns use rights to the region's most vital limited resource. The federal government claims ultimate ownership of water in New Mexico.

Federal water discourse in New Mexico and the West is not merely legalistic discourse but also a racializing discourse, based as it is on an Indian/non-Indian binary. There is no more telling evidence for the existence of a racial state in North America than the fact that American Indian identity and land and water claims are federally determined.[19] This commonplace fact is often taken for granted without anyone thinking about how profound its political implications really are. But some reflection on this leads to the realization that water claims in the West are defined by the state in racial terms. What does this mean? Certainly the matter is too complex to be reduced to a binary of good and evil. Without this federal, postcolonial, racializing apparatus or regime there would be no Indians, no pueblos, and no tourism.

It is ironic that the greatest natural wealth in New Mexico—or the best, oldest, most prior water rights—belongs to the two most impoverished and marginal rural sectors: pueblos and traditional acequia communities.[20] Perhaps, in the ultimate machinations of power, the privatization of acequia water rights and the federalization of Indian water rights will conspire to consolidate the wealth and control of water into the hands of that old married couple, capital and the state. Interests and entities who define themselves as neither must mobilize to protect their claims.

Tourism interacts with culture, identity, and power in complex ways in New Mexico and the Southwest. Along with urbanization and the expanding computer chip industry, resort development and amenity migration exert ever-greater demand on limited water supplies. At the same time, tourism creates markets for ethnicity and fosters ethnocultural self-consciousness, assertion, and pride. Tourism depends upon, fosters, and intensifies the ethnoracial boundaries that demarcate difference and differential access to resources. Here the devil's bargain takes a curious twist. Stay tuned.

Acknowledgments

Thanks to David Weber and Jane Elder of the Clements Center and to the other authors in this volume for their suggestions. I am especially grateful to Chris Wilson for his insightful comments and recommendations.

Notes

1. Leah Dilworth, *Imagining Indians in the Southwest: Persistent Visions of a Primitive Past* (Washington, D.C.: Smithsonian Institution Press, 1996); Chris Wilson, *The Myth of Santa Fe: Creating a Modern Regional Tradition* (Albuquerque: University of New Mexico Press, 1997); Hal Rothman, *Devil's Bargains: Tourism in the Twentieth-Century West* (Lawrence: University Press of Kansas, 1998).

2. See, for example, June Nash, *We Eat the Mines and the Mines Eat Us: Dependency and Exploitation in Bolivian Tin Mines* (New York: Columbia University Press, 1979); Michael Taussig, *The Devil and Commodity Fetishism in South America* (Chapel Hill: University of North Carolina Press, 1980); José Limón, *Dancing with the Devil: Society and Cultural Poetics in Mexican-American South Texas* (Madison: University of Wisconsin Press, 1995).

3. John Bodine, "A Tri-Ethnic Trap: The Spanish Americans in Taos," in *Proceedings of the American Ethnological Society*, ed. June Helm (Seattle: University of Washington Press, 1968); Marta Weigle and Kyle Fiore, eds., *Santa Fe and Taos: The Writers' Era, 1916–41* (Santa Fe, N.Mex.: Ancient City Press, 1982); M. Weigle, "Southwest Lures: Innocents Detoured, Incense Determined," *Journal of the Southwest (JSW)*, Special Issue, *Inventing the Southwest* 32, no. 4 (winter 1990): 499–540; Barbara Babcock, "By Way of Introduction" and "'A New Mexican Rebecca': Imaging Pueblo Women," *JSW* (ibid., 1990): 400–437; Curtis Hinsley, Jr., "Authoring Authenticity," *JSW* (ibid., 1990): 462–78; Michael Riley, "Constituting the Southwest, Contesting the Southwest, Re-Inventing the Southwest," *JSW* 36 (autumn 1994): 221–41. My own work dealing with the effects of tourism in New Mexico includes the following: "Land, Water, and Ethnic Identity in Taos," in *Land, Water, and Culture: New Perspectives on Hispanic Land Grants*, eds. Charles Briggs and John Van Ness (Albuquerque: University of New Mexico Press, 1987), 313–403; "Art, Tourism, and Race Relations in Taos: Toward a Sociology of the Art Colony," *Journal of Anthropological Research* 45, no. 1 (1989): 77–99; "Ethnic Reconstruction in Contemporary Taos," *JSW* 32, no. 4 (1990): 541–55; "The Tourist Gaze, Gentrification, and the Commodification of Subjectivity in Taos," in *Essays on the Changing Images of the Southwest*, eds. Richard Francaviglia and David Narrett (Arlington, Tex.: Texas A&M University Press, 1994), 105–26; "The Taos Fiesta: Invented Tradition and the Infrapolitics of Symbolic Reclamation," *JSW* 39, no. 1 (spring 1997): 33–57; "Fiesta Time and Plaza Space: Resistance and Accommodation in a Tourist Town," *Journal of American Folklore* 111, no 493 (1998): 39–56; "Tourism, Whiteness, and the Vanishing Anglo," in *Seeing and Being Seen: Tourism in the American West*, eds. David M. Wrobel and Patrick T. Long (Lawrence: University Press of Kansas, 2001), 194–210.

4. See Dean MacCannell, *The Tourist: A New Theory of the Leisure Class* (New York: Schocken Books, 1976); John Urry, *The Tourist Gaze: Leisure and Travel in Contemporary Societies* (New York: Sage Publications, 1990); Mary Pratt, *Imperial Eyes: Travel Writing and Transculturation* (New York: Routledge, 1992); Caren Kaplan, *Questions of Travel: Postmodern Discourses of Displacement* (Durham, N.C.: Duke University Press, 1996).

5. Urry, *The Tourist Gaze*, 24.

6. Dean MacCannell, "Reconstructed Ethnicity: Tourism and Cultural Identity in Third World Communities," *Annals of Tourism Research* 11, no. 3 (1984): 375–91; Deirdre Evans-Pritchard, "The Portal Case: Authenticity, Tourism, Traditions, & the Law," *Journal of American Folklore* 100 (1987): 287–96; also "How 'They' See 'Us,' Native American Images of Tourists," *Annals of Tourism Research* 16 (1989): 89–103; Jill Sweet, "Burlesquing 'The Other' in Pueblo Performance," *Annals of Tourism Research* 16 (1989): 62–75; Rodriguez, "Ethnic Reconstruction," 541–55; Barbara Babcock, "Mudwomen and Whitemen: A Meditation on Pueblo Potters & the Politics of Representation," in

Situated Lives: Gender and Culture in Everyday Life, eds. L. Lamphere, H. Ragoné, and P. Zavella (New York: Routledge, 1997), 420–39.

7. Rina Swentzell, "Couse, Art, and Indians" (paper presented at the William Clements Center for Southwest Studies, Dallas, Tex., 1998), 7.

8. Elizabeth Brandt, "On Secrecy and the Control of Knowledge: Taos Pueblo," in *Secrecy: A Cross-Cultural Perspective*, ed. Stanton Tefft (New York: Human Sciences Press, 1980), 123–46.

9. John Bodine, "Taos Blue Lake Controversy," *Journal of Ethnic Studies* 6, no. 1 (1978): 42–48; R. C. Gordon-McCutchan, *The Taos Indians and the Battle for Blue Lake* (Santa Fe, N.Mex.: Red Crane Books, 1991).

10. Philip Gonzales, "The Political Construction of Latino Nomenclatures in Twentieth-Century New Mexico," *JSW* 35, no. 2 (summer 1992): 158–85; Doris Meyer, *Speaking for Themselves: Neomexicano Cultural Identity and the Spanish-Language Press, 1880–1920* (Albuquerque: University of New Mexico Press, 1996); Gabriel Melendez, *So All Is Not Lost: The Poetics of Print in Nuevomexicano Communities, 1834–1958* (Albuquerque: University of New Mexico Press, 1997).

11. Fredrik Barth, "Introduction," in *Ethnic Groups and Boundaries: The Social Organization of Culture Difference* (Results of a symposium held at the University of Bergen, 23rd to 26th February 1967), ed. Fredrik Barth (Boston: Little, Brown and Company, 1969), 9–38.

12. For more detailed discussions of both ritual and political forms of Hispano ethnic mobilization in New Mexico see Rodriguez, "Land, Water, and Ethnic Identity in Taos," "The Taos Fiesta," and "Fiesta Time and Plaza Space"; also, "The Hispano Homeland Debate Revisited," *Perspectives in Mexican American Studies*, vol. 3 (Tucson: Mexican American Studies and Research Center, University of Arizona, 1992), 95–114; and *The Matachines Dance: Ritual Symbolism and Interethnic Relations in the Upper Rio Grande Valley* (Albuquerque: University of New Mexico Press, 1996). An increase or resurgence of public rituals appears to be a global phenomenon, stimulated by the forces of globalization, including tourism; for discussions of this in Europe, see *Revitalizing European Rituals*, ed. Jeremy Boissevain (London: Routledge, 1992); also J. Boissevain, "Introduction," *Coping With Tourists: European Reactions to Mass Tourism*, ed. J. Boissevain (Providence, R.I.: Berghahn Books, 1996), 1–26.

13. For an account of Debbie Jaramillo's election see "This Town Is Not for Sale!: The 1994 Santa Fe Mayoral Election," a video documentary produced by Sylvia Rodriguez, Christine Sierra, and Felipe Gonzales (Albuquerque: Colores Series, KNME TV, 1999).

14. Chris Wilson, "Tourist Commodification and Ethnic Polarization in Santa Fe (A Newcomer's Narrative)" (paper presented at the American Studies Association meeting, Kansas City, 16 October 1996), 5–6.

15. The new "whiteness studies" scholarship on race posits whiteness as an analytic construct, an unmarked category, a set of practices, a structure of privilege. It shifts analytic focus away from the races to the structures and operation of white privilege and implicit or naturalized definitions of whiteness against which all color is located and assigned meaning. A variety of theoretical approaches is emerging within this general framework. Some examples of recent works include Dean MacCannell, "White Culture," in *Empty Meeting Grounds: The Tourist Papers* (New York: Routledge, 1992), 121–46; David Roediger, *The Wages of Whiteness: Race and the Making of the American Working Class* (New York: Verso, 1990); Toni Morrison, *Playing in the Dark: Whiteness and the Literary Imagination* (Cambridge, Mass.: Harvard University Press, 1992); Ruth Frankenberg, *White Women, Race Matters: Social Constructions of Race* (Minneapolis: University of Minnesota Press, 1993); also R. Frankenberg, ed., *Displacing Whiteness: Essays in Social*

and *Cultural Criticism* (Durham, N.C.: Duke University Press, 1997); Theodore Allen, *The Invention of the White Race* (London: Verso, 1994); Vron Ware, *Beyond the Pale: White Women, Racism, and History* (London: Verso, 1992); Karen Brodkin, *How Jews Became White Folks and What That Says About Race in America* (New Brunswick, N.J.: Rutgers University Press, 1998); Noel Ignatiev, *How the Irish Became White* (Cambridge, Mass.: Harvard University Press, 1995); Ian F. Haney Lopez, *White by Law: The Legal Construction of Race* (New York: New York University Press, 1996); David Stowe, "Uncolored People: The Rise of Whiteness Studies," *Lingua Franca* (September–October 1996): 68–77; Mike Hill, ed., *Whiteness: A Critical Reader* (New York: New York University Press, 1997).

16. In 1998 New Mexico celebrated the four-hundred-year or cuartocentenary anniversary of the first settlement colony (1598) in New Mexico. The Albuquerque-based organizers of the celebration planned to erect a statue of colony leader Don Juan de Oñate in downtown Albuquerque. Highly vocal opposition to the statue emerged among a mixed constituency of Native Americans, Chicanos, and Anglos, on the grounds that Oñate had committed terrible brutality against the people of Acoma Pueblo, a crime for which he had indeed been tried and expelled from New Mexico. The controversy over what kind of statue would be acceptable, who should have input in designing it, and where it should be situated brought various intra- and interethnic fissures to the surface and continues into the new century. It heightened awareness among Spanish Americans of others' deeply felt critical attitudes toward the previously unobstructed placement of conquistador imagery in public places.

17. My account of the Taos Pueblo Kachina Lodge casino controversy is based largely on news stories published in the *Taos News* and *Geronimo*, an alternative newspaper that was discontinued only to be subsequently reincarnated as *The Horse Fly* during 1999. The following issues of these publications are especially relevant: *Taos News*, 10 June 1999, 12 August 1999, 10 February 2000, and 17 February 2000, particularly the editorial; *Geronimo*, August 1999 issue; *The Horse Fly*, 15 January 2000.

18. The potential impact of pueblo resort developments on local water supplies is not known because as sovereign entities, they are not legally required to apply for permits from the state engineer to pump groundwater. This means that municipal and regional water planning must proceed without access to or calculation of this crucial information. At least two pueblos in the greater Albuquerque area are building multi-million-dollar deluxe casino resorts: Santa Ana and Sandia. These are each estimated at $80 million, with the former reported by the *Albuquerque Journal* as using possibly up to 1.15 million gallons of groundwater a day and the latter with a 750,000-gallon-capacity wastewater treatment plant. See, for example, "Santa Ana Resort's Effect on Water Supply Unknown," *Albuquerque Journal*, 27 February 1999; "Water Use Will Draw Down Ground," *Albuquerque Journal*, 3 June 1999; and "Spring 2001 Opening a Go: Sandia Casino Work on Track," *Albuquerque Journal*, 3 March 2000.

19. For a theoretical account of the racial state, see Michael Omi and Howard Winant, *Racial Formation in the United States: From the 1960s to the 1980s*, particularly chapter 5 (New York: Routledge, 1986, 1994).

20. This point was made by Legal Services attorney David Benavides at a public forum on water planning held in Española on August 9, 1999.

TOURIST TRAP
VISITORS AND THE MODERN
SAN ANTONIO ECONOMY ⟶

CHAR MILLER

In the midst of a hotly contested reelection campaign in March 1997, Bill Thornton, then mayor of San Antonio, did something curious: he told a truth. In defense of his support of tax abatements for a proposed Sheraton hotel linked to the convention center, he argued that the low-skill jobs the new building would generate were an exact match for the city's large, undereducated workforce. "Unfortunately, there is a great number of adults in our community that are defined as functionally illiterate," he observed, and then cited a pair of studies that estimated its level as ranging from 15 percent to "a staggering, frightening" 34 percent. Given these figures, and the minimal skills associated with this population—illiteracy was defined as anyone with an eighth-grade education or less—Thornton concluded that using tax abatements to lure only high-paying jobs to the Alamo City, as his campaign rivals proposed, was unrealistic. It was "naive to expect much of San Antonio's work force to step into management or technical positions."[1]

With these words, the mayor ignited a firestorm that consumed his political career. Although none of Thornton's opponents directly challenged the accuracy of his insight into the relationship between San Antonio's economic fortunes and its population's education and training, they pounced on the political implications of his arguments; his four challengers pledged to support a moratorium on tax abatements and a revision of the city code so that in the future abatements would be tied to the production of a "living wage." Grassroots organizations turned up the heat. "Yes, we have an undereducated work force," agreed the Reverend Eric Ruggs, a spokesman for the Metro

Alliance, an advocacy group, but Thornton's position was "contradictory, because we are giving money away instead of putting it into education," a retort reinforced in a number of newspaper columns and commentaries. So furious was the response that within a week Thornton appeared to backpedal, proposing an ordinance that would ban tax abatements. "We are not going to do phase-ins for any more hotels," he confirmed. "We are sending a message that we are not in the tax phase-in business." The exception was the already proposed project downtown, the abatement for which the city council approved before Thornton offered to halt the phase-in tax strategy. The mayor's waffling undercut his credibility, and this was partly responsible for his failure even to make that spring's electoral runoff; he came in third in the primary to the eventual victor, councilman Howard Peak. Speaking a truth can have serious political consequences.[2]

Naturally, neither the soon-to-be ousted mayor nor his many critics spoke the whole truth. Or rather, none of them bothered to explain why San Antonio was such a low-wage, cheap-labor town. The key to understanding this is the powerful role tourism plays in the local economy. The city's dedication to servicing an ever-larger number of visitors has depended on the building up of a complex infrastructure that includes historic landmarks such as the Alamo and four other Spanish-era missions, the River Walk and a burgeoning convention center, as well as theme parks, hotels, restaurants, and bars. The investment has paid off in this respect: tourism now contributes more than $4 billion to the community's coffers, a contribution that looms larger still as the once-massive federal spending that flowed through the town's five major military installations has decreased with the close of the cold war. Yet the bargain the city has struck with itself through its focus on tourism comes with a decisive cost—the creation of an increasing number of low-skilled positions that provide necessary entry-level work for those with minimal education but that have done, and will do, little to enhance their economic prospects. Thornton and his opponents were both right, in short, and both were caught in a vicious cycle of their own making.[3]

There is nothing new in this catch-22. Although the city of San Antonio and the state of Texas did not employ tax abatement strategies until the late 1980s, when the legislature passed an initiative that enabled communities to reduce or eliminate property taxes for ten years in so-called reinvestment zones, other cities had had long experience with this fiscal policy. Through its Chapter 353 abatement program, Missouri had been using this mechanism to pursue urban redevelopment projects since the 1940s; Massachusetts had devised a similar program in the early 1950s, through which it underwrote the Prudential Center redevelopment scheme. However delayed in their use of abatements, Texans quickly realized what their national peers had long understood. Politicians have "supported tax abatement not because it was effective but because it was a remarkably easy path to follow," Todd Swanstrom has argued, "one that allowed them to claim that they were mounting a serious attack on the economic problems of the city."[4]

That the Alamo City, along with other tourist towns, has an array of economic problems that need addressing is irrefutable. That many of these cities in dire straits have granted tax abatements to strengthen the tourist infrastructure and thus resolve their pressing needs is just as clear: hotels, resorts, and theme parks are among those construction projects that have regularly secured ten- or twenty-year abatements. Even the opposition that this strategy has spawned has been consistent across time and place. Everywhere citizens have voiced their worries about the social implications and economic consequences of a policy that generates minimum wages; the heated debate in San Antonio over the Sheraton hotel is part of a larger national argument.

The sources of that debate are also local and depend upon a particular historical context. Since the mid-nineteenth century, when tourism first emerged, San Antonians have responded to the interplay between climate and geography, markets and demography—between the people and the landscape they inhabited and reconstructed in ways that prefigure early-twenty-first-century debates about the city's commitment to the tourist economy. For better and worse, and at considerable expense, San Antonio has long catered to its many visitors.[5]

Stock Answers

In the beginning there was a jeremiad, a warning. Appropriately it emanated from a minister, the Reverend John McCullough, who rode into town in 1846 to serve as the city's first Presbyterian minister. He knew he was in for a rough passage. The local population was largely Mexican and Catholic, a fact that led his presbytery to recommend his work fall under the aegis of the Foreign Board of Missions; from these "deluded peoples" McCullough anticipated little support for his religious endeavors. The rest of the community would not pay him much attention either: the outbreak of war with Mexico brought a rush of new population to and economic activity in the city; although his church and home were centrally located on Commerce Avenue, the major east-west thoroughfare, his presence and work were nonetheless lost in the whirl. "Church membership was commonplace neither in the Republic of Texas nor in the early years of statehood," historian Donald E. Everett has observed. "Even so one would expect more than seven names to be added to the church roll in the succeeding eighteen months."[6]

In his disappointments, McCullough knew whom to blame: "You can have no idea of the difficulties of establishing or getting a foothold for the gospel in San Antonio in those early times," he would later write. "I was persecuted, slandered, and insulted. Every effort was made by ungodly Americans to induce me to leave." Among those who tormented him was "a devilish set of men and gamblers" who he recalled had "overrun" the town. They "would gamble and rowdy all night and sleep most of the day," leaving McCullough exhausted: "My nervous system suffered so much that I became excitable and sleepless." He had cause: when he rebuked his tormentors from the pulpit, when he demanded "a Vigilance Committee to execute law and keep order," these "Emissaries of the Power of Darkness" struck back with violence: on two occasions, armed men on horseback rode up to his home and blasted away at it (and him). Wounded physically and drained spiritually, McCullough would leave San Antonio in 1849 and from the greater safety of his new pulpit in Galveston let loose a final shot at the Alamo City: "a dilapidated, and miserable-looking place," it offered up an "'occular demonstration' of desolating war and semi-barbarism."[7]

Ministerial harangues about frontier barbarity were common in the literature of nineteenth-century evangelism; they established a narrative tension between the forces of good and evil that defined the work and gave it meaning. But McCullough's concerns also reflect a complex struggle evident in once-isolated communities such as San Antonio that endured rapid social dislocation. Pitched battles over the moral order were also bound up with intense economic conflicts. Those boisterous and shady gamblers whom McCullough so despised played an important role in the city's exploding economy. They profited from the large number of soldiers marching in and out of town during the Mexican-American War; with peace, their earnings accelerated, for the U.S. Army established a permanent, large post that served as the supply depot for a string of new frontier forts stretching out to El Paso. The wages of sin squeezed from this profitable venture, when paired with those generated in the city's saloons and houses of ill repute, helped create a highly visible, commercially potent entertainment sector. It would only expand with the development of a new industry then just getting its legs. Although the Reverend McCullough apparently knew little of cows and cowboys, and thus his departure from the city to which they would bring so much money and infamy could not have been better timed, the danger and tension he experienced suggested that the emerging order might not be an unalloyed benefit; McCullough would not be the last to warn the city to be careful what it wished for.

What it wanted early on, what it oriented itself around, was cattle, making them San Antonio's first tourists. The city had been an organizing point for Spanish and later Mexican drives to markets in New Orleans; it served a similar role in the 1840s, when locals blazed a trail west to California. More profound was the city's centrality, in the decades immediately following the Civil War, to the great annual cattle drives that moved up from south Texas grasslands and swung past San Antonio on their way north to Kansas railheads. Every new set of thundering hooves reinforced a pattern of behavior that has persisted, regardless of species: the swelling herds rumbled through town at peak season—the winter and spring; they guzzled vast quantities of food and drink; and occasionally they got out of hand, endangering life, limb, and property. Residents, fearing for their safety, complained about the bovines' bellowing presence and filthy habits and worried about their deleterious impact on community values. Yet they also banked on their continued movement along the many trails that converged on the town that hugged the San Antonio River, for the economic payoff of this quadrupedal tourism was considerable.[8]

The cattle themselves were a kind of loss leader; the real money was captured in the spending habits of their human owners and tenders. The drovers and vaqueros spent freely in the many hotels, saloons, and gambling emporia thrown up to meet their needs; in 1892, with a resident population of about thirty thousand, there were nearly three hundred bars. Their suggestive names—the Iron Front, Buck Horn, Bull's Head, Stock Exchange, Western Star, and First & Last Chance, along with the White Elephant and Grey Mule (for African Americans only)—bespeak the city's central preoccupation with hawking its wares to a particular clientele who was just passing through. Selling of sexual favors to this transient population was just as lucrative. Bordellos abounded, and prostitutes and other proprietors did a brisk, and reciprocating, business. The release of sexual energy seems to have whet the cowboys' appetite for material consumption (and vice versa): they came and shopped, but especially shopped, busily purchasing accessories essential to their trade—rifles, revolvers, and bullets; chaps, hats, boots, and spurs; saddles and harnesses. As this commercial traffic developed, it had an important spatial consequence, focusing the trade on the western edge of town in an area that would be called Cattlemen's Square, marking it as the hub of the "Gay Capital of the Mesquite and Chaparral."[9]

Naming that space was part of the process by which San Antonio told the story of its intimate and long-standing relationship with the cattle industry. Local newspapers contributed as well, rustling up anecdotes about cowboy conduct that had long been part of the community's conversational currency. These reminted tales—the hard-won ranching fortunes that vanished with the casual roll of the dice, the flush cowpuncher who soaked in a bath of champagne, the tragic thrill when innocent rubes were cut down in the cross fire between dueling desperadoes—gained new life in the transition from oral narration to the written word, adding luster to the marketing of the late-nineteenth-century city. Visitors added their two bits. Harriet Spofford, for one, swooned over the grizzled rider who "on his way northward with his bunch of cattle, has stopped in 'Santone' for a frolic"; although "unkempt and unshorn, filthy and ragged and very drunk," he could spout a verse of Latin and parse a Greek verb. "The Texan makes no such mistake as to regard these vaqueros, in their big boots and old blouses and rough beards, as mere vagabonds at loose ends," she assured her genteel readers in *Harper's Monthly;* "he knows that it is ten to one that the shabbiest on the plaza will draw his check for $100,000 to-day to pay for the cattle he has just bought to improve his stock." By passing on this bit of gilded frontier lore, Spofford, along with other travel writers, exported the notion of San Antonio as a rough-and-tumble town, set within the Old Wild West.[10]

That it was old suggests this late-nineteenth-century publicity also served as a literary sign of the frontier's passing. An economic signal lay in the collapse of the cattle rush itself. By the late 1870s, early 1880s, due to intense overgrazing of the south Texas savannah, difficulties in transporting cattle to distant urban markets, and the desire for more accessible, cheaper, and greener grass, many of the region's herds, and the capital that had been derived from their production, moved to the northern plains. San Antonio was left in the lurch. Much of the businesses, and attendant infrastructure, built in the boom years to separate trail riders from their disposable income, withered; although the last block from this era, which contained a vaudeville theater, a saloon, and an infamous gambling resort, the Silver King, was not torn down until 1914, most others had long since vanished. Dependency on this kind of drive-by tourism had left the city vulnerable to market vagaries.[11]

It was also left to traffic in nostalgia. As if to signify this transformation, in 1908 *The St. Louis Globe-Democrat* published a tall tale about the loss of San Antonio's legendary past and the rise of its newfound ordinariness. The story began: "In them early days every day was like a cowman's convention in San Antonio. They gathered there from all over the Southwest, an' they was rollin' in money, I'm here to tell you." The piece concluded with this wistful sigh: Once, "if a man had the money and wanted to take a flyer at roulette or any other kind of game, he had plenty of chances to do it," but, "Nickel picture shows is the most excitin' thing they've got there now, so I'm told. I've got a whole dollar to spend in dissipation," the cowboy narrator proudly claimed, "an' I'm a-goin' to take in every durned 5-cent show in town." However embellished, this telling, and others like it, contains a kernel of truth: once a center for a regional form of entertainment, San Antonio had become just another purveyor of the new, mass-culture amusements. That these picture shows were often "western" in theme, allowing San Antonio to offer up a stylized, filmic version of its former self, says a great deal about the correlation between shifting economies and alterations in a city's self-marketing strategies.[12]

Nothing in this synopsis of the heyday of San Antonio's cattle connection, and the secondary tourist economy it generated, is particularly unique. Other cow towns experienced similar economic expansions and contractions, whether on a seasonal basis or in the more pronounced boom-and-bust cycles that rolled across the decades. San Antonio was not alone in its simultaneous love of its visitors' spending habits and its anxiety over their moral turpitude. All towns, more or less successfully, sought to craft a public persona that could be sold to and consumed in faraway locales, a publicity loop designed to stimulate more trade. Manufacturing such a persona, as San Antonio and its western urban peers discovered, was wrapped up in the process whereby a site was converted into a "sight." Successful conversion required the assigning of significance to a location such as Cattlemen's Square that invested it with importance, real or imagined (and sometimes a healthy dose of both), a locale about which a bowlegged cowpoke might speak fondly and an urbane traveler, who hankered to see an authentic bowlegged cowpoke, might visit. Fulfilling fantasies: that is what destination resorts—then and now—are intended to provide and what, in the case of the cattle culture, San Antonio offered up until the late nineteenth century.[13]

TB Tourists

More fantastic was the chimera that impelled other humans to the city who were dying to take advantage of what they desperately believed was the restorative powers of the south Texas environment. Die they would: those suffering from consumption, from tuberculosis, who first trailed into this "frontier health resort" in the late 1840s, were no more cured by the salubrious climate than the thousands who later followed their path; for many, the passage to San Antonio, whether on mule or railcar, was one-way. Yet in their care, and demise, there was money to be made, and the community was not slow in realizing a grisly profit from this trade. There was a catch, of course: when, in the late 1880s, investors funneled considerable capital into the construction of health-care facilities, giving a shot in the arm to an economy still struggling to recover from losses associated with the departing cattle business, they unwittingly gave succor to a set of dire public health consequences that would threaten the commonweal.[14]

At its core, this new form of tourism depended on bad science. The nineteenth-century medical prescription for tuberculosis hinged on a simple environmental determinism: pure air, clean water, and warm climes brought relief to the suffering, most medical practitioners agreed, and might also cure the afflicted. Actually, nothing about this regime enhanced the prospects of the victims of the "white plague," but its very vagueness played into the hands of publicists throughout the Southwest: they touted the region's medicinal weather, hoping to entice those whose lungs and throats were unhappily compromised to Los Angeles, Santa Fe, or El Paso. San Antonio was second to none in the promises it made about the recuperative capacities of its "balmy atmosphere": after a short stay in San Antonio in 1843, George W. Kendall, who would later move to the region, gushed that "if a man wants to die there he must go somewhere else," a miraculous claim that managed to find its way into virtually every piece of promotional literature the community would later publish. What about the region made one immortal? An 1850s convalescent who had dragged himself to San Antonio after years of protracted illness found that within two months he had been revived from the dead because of the weather: "This improvement I attribute to the purer, dry, light atmosphere which prevails here the greater part of the time." He was not completely cured, he admitted—"My improvement . . . has not been as rapid as many others of whom I have heard"—but this qualification was a result of the "difference in the natural strength of constitution," not in the nature of San Antonio. What this environment had was plenty of "ozone." That gas was so plentiful in south Texas, hucksters proclaimed, that it was as much a curative for human lungs as it was for meat; how else explain, one health resort pamphlet from the 1880s declared, "the bodies of hundreds of thousands of dead animals lying on the prairie [which] emit no odor whatever"? Even in death, you would be well preserved.[15]

Promotional agents were not the only ones untroubled by the facts: an uncritical, hacking horde hustled south and west in response to these airy assertions, there seeking release in an Edenic landscape. One of their number was the poet Sidney Lanier. Traveling "as valet to his right lung, a service in which he has been engaged some years," Lanier swung into a stagecoach in Austin in December 1872 and headed for San Antonio, on a day that boded well: "The morning was brilliant, the air was full of a certain dry balm which I think is not known elsewhere in the world." Later he would cast doubt on the stability of the region's weather—"The thermometer, the barometer, the vane, hygrometer, oscillate so rapidly, so frequently, so lawlessly, and through so wide a meteorological range that the climate is simply indescribable"—and thus on "its alleged happy influence on consumption." But he was not immune to the charms of this "growing resort for consumptives," in the care and housing of whom the community was quickly responding by expanding its inventory of health spas, sanatoria, and boardinghouses. With the others "who are sent here from remote parts of the United States and from Europe, and who may be seen on fine days, in various stages of decrepitude, strolling along the streets," Lanier roamed the city, poked around its historic landscape, and indulged in any number of curative potions heavily advertised in the local newspapers. "I have been taking Möller's Cod Liver Oil regularly three times a day for a month," he advised his wife in January, and then as a chaser daily drained "from three to six doses of pure whiskey, (the best, by the way, I have ever seen)." This odd tonic may not have cleansed his ailing right lung before he left town, but surely it gave an elevated tone to the day.[16]

The ready resort to such nostrums was depressing, at least in the eyes of another tubercular-ridden writer who briefly inhabited San Antonio. A "sickly" child who at nineteen had left his North Carolina home to escape an alcoholic and abusive father, William Sydney Porter (O. Henry) hoped Texas would be a source of his redemption. So it was, to judge from the characters who dominated his short stories about the Lone Star State: these tall men and intrepid women, like their literary creator, drew strength from the good and bountiful land. Except, that is, in the Alamo City, where people and motives were more troubling and obscure. "A Fog in Santone" opens with a consumptive, his "white face half-concealed by the high-turned overcoat collar," trying to wheedle additional morphine tablets from a suspicious drugstore clerk. Rebuffed, this "Goodall of Memphis," told he only has three months left, determines the thirty-six pills he already has are sufficient to end his life now, a suicidal impulse brought on with the "gray mist" that earlier had swept up the river, "an opaque terror" clutching at his throat. The death he contemplates with some longing is temporarily put on hold through the kind ministrations of Miss Rosa, a prostitute working one of the saloons Goodall stumbles into that fateful night; with the requisite heart of gold, she cheers this cheerless man with "the menacing flame in his cheeks," relieves him of his cache of drugs, and sends him home with new hope in a sunnier day. The dark, final act in her young life had just begun: in a classic O. Henry twist, the bar girl crushes the morphine into her drink and stirs up the fatal concoction with her hat pin.[17]

This grim end deftly pricks the inflated rhetoric of, and the conceit that underlay, San Antonio's tubercular hustle. "It had been computed that three thousand invalids were hibernating in the town," O. Henry wrote, and that they had traveled "from far and wide, for here, among these contracted riverside streets," to bathe in the "goddess Ozone." In this place, with the "purest atmosphere, sir, on earth," whose purity had been repeatedly and scientifically assessed to "show that our air contains nothing deleterious," the citizenry parroted the promotional literature. They thus easily brushed aside contrary evidence: "Santone . . . cannot be blamed for this cold gray fog that came and kissed the lips of the three thousand, and then delivered them to the cross," O. Henry declared. No, it was not culpable for a night in which "the tubercles, whose ravages hope holds in check, multiplied" to such an extent that many of "the wooers of ozone capitulated." Guiltless it was that on "the red streams of Hemorrhagia a few souls drifted away, leaving behind pathetic heaps, white and chill as the fog itself." O. Henry's sardonic take unmasked the city's pretense, its grotesque willingness to sell TB victims down the river, all for the sake of a buck.[18]

The town criers hastened to repair the damage and in local histories and guidebooks rebutted those who found fault with climate and city. In *San Antonio de Bexar* (1890), William Corner dismissed those who, like Sidney Lanier, disparaged the sharp shifts in weather often associated with northers—storms that barreled down the plains and left a "mortal chill" in the air. "They are easily avoided if an invalid desires to do so," he wrote; "all one has to do is to keep indoors." Should one take the necessary precautions and still fall before the "white plague" on, say, a cold and foggy eve, that was not the community's fault either, but rather a consequence of a dilatory personality. So confirmed The Business Men's Club of San Antonio in a brochure it produced for distribution on the nation's railroads. In extolling "Beautiful San Antonio: the Great Health Resort of America," the text assured travelers that those who died of consumption did so because they "unfortunately put off coming to this healthy climate until it [was] too late for them to be benefited." Speaking with the omniscient voice of a physician, it asserted that "too much stress can not be laid on the necessity of coming to San Antonio for her climatical influence in the primary stage of tuberculosis, as only then a sure cure can be effected."[19]

This breathless claim was not as sure as it appeared. An attendant graph of the city's mortality rate—14.95 deaths per 1,000—contained this important caveat, "based on residents only." The defenders of the sick-tourist trade knew, but were unwilling publicly to acknowledge, the high incidence of death associated with TB; they knew but refused to admit the potential threat this statistic posed to the community's health in general. To break this silence and thus open up a debate about this lucrative business that depended in part on communal ignorance, Dr. Frank Paschal, who was briefly the city physician, and other local doctors went public with the relevant health statistics. The numbers were (and remain) unsettling. Records indicated that of the 775 deaths in San Antonio in 1886, 154 were attributed to "pulmonary tuberculosis," which at 20 percent of the total was well above the national average. In subsequent years the percentage spiked even higher: in 1890, deaths attributed to TB amounted to roughly 40 percent of total mortality, a figure that declined over the next ten years to approximately 33 percent. These alarmingly high numbers, which were more than double the national rates, set up a troubling discrepancy that Paschal and his peers explained was a direct result of the city's long-standing campaign to encourage consumptives to come to south Texas to better their health: of the 325 individuals whose deaths were attributed to tuberculosis in 1894–1895, for example, 220 had lived in San Antonio less than a year. From these visitors, the city was reaping a cruel harvest.[20]

More deadly still was the community's failure to understand or accept that TB was contagious. When Paschal and other medical professionals testified before the city council in the late 1890s about the threat of tuberculosis spreading to the resident population and the related need to regulate spas, boardinghouses, and other facilities in which the terminally ill lived, they were met with some disbelief; should there not already have been evidence of dangerous transmissions? aldermen and editorial writers wondered aloud. The possible economic impact of sanitary regulations immediately arose when local physicians pleaded for an antispitting ordinance to control those they dubbed "circulating carriers of contagion." In his vigorous defense of the rights of "our heretofore welcome visitors from the far-lands" to congregate in Travis Park, a "delightful mid-city retreat," for "rest and expectoration," one politician alleged that the city's bright doctors were dimming their town's commercial prospects; even the mere discussion of possible regulation had led other national health resorts "to advise all tourists and travelers with a cough to avoid this [city] . . . for fear of disagreeable and supercilious police supervision." On this score, he need not have worried: an antispitting ordinance was adopted, but it was only enforced six times in its first thirteen years of existence. Worries escalated, however, when doctors floated a plan that would have wiped out the local business of tending the tubercular—the San Antonio medical establishment, in concert with state medical officials, pressed the legislature to quarantine Texas against "nonresident consumptives." When that failed, they secured authority to toss impoverished visitors out of the city hospital as a signal that San Antonio would "no longer submit to the cruel imposition of the poor and helpless [and] therefore dangerous" consumptives; in addition, they successfully campaigned for the creation of a state tuberculosis hospital to segregate this afflicted population. In sharp contrast to earlier generations of medical practitioners, who had been complicit in the selling of San Antonio as an incomparable health resort, these early-twentieth-century physician-activists argued that the escalating costs of tending to the victims of "white plague" far outstripped the financial benefits to be wrung from their misery; public health mattered more than fiscal well-being.[21]

Visitors' Center

Depending on the illness of strangers and drawing off the trailing of cattle had sustained San Antonio's economy through the first decade of the twentieth century. But the medical assault on the marketing of the city as a place "where consumption and catarrah are cured without medicine" and the prohibitionist impulse that outlawed gambling in Texas in 1907 and alcohol a decade later fundamentally altered the terrain on which future tourism could be built. A shift in the orientation of this portion of the economy, though, only reinforced a pattern already evident: however defined, tourism was one of the means San Antonio employed to move beyond its preindustrial origins to become a postindustrial service center, without ever going through the brutal messiness of the industrial revolution. That trajectory at once offered distinct advantages for the construction of venues for visitors and closed off possibilities for a richer, more substantial local economy. Twentieth-century tourism, like its nineteenth-century predecessor, was simultaneously a boon and a bust.[22]

One of those who recognized this tension, and proposed a resolution for it, was Bostonian Thomas W. Pierce, president of the Galveston, Harrisburg and San Antonio Railroad; the line arrived in 1877 to much fanfare, for it was the first to penetrate this once-frontier town and thus linked it to a well-established national transportation network. While the citizenry celebrated, Pierce, who was well aware of the destructive impact this new engine of progress could have, urged caution. "Not completely given over to modernism," the railroad executive suggested in an interview with a local newspaper publisher that "it would be a great thing if old San Antonio could be left undisturbed with all its ancient quaintness"; to do so would require confining growth to the undeveloped edges, leading to the creation of "an old city and a new city." This spatial segregation, he hoped, would give free rein to, even as it controlled, railroad-induced commercial development that everywhere else had ripped through the historic urban fabric. If successful, it would have spared what Harriet Spofford—whose husband was general counsel for the GH&SA—called the "sinuosities of the countless streets of San Antonio," a maze "through which one may wander a year and yet find intricacies unknown before." These outsiders well knew the touristic appeal of the city's seemingly antiquated charm, its sidewalks "worn in ruts by the tread of many feet," and the beguiling, "serpentine course of the river, crossed by a score of bridges and as many fords," which created "such a confusion and a snare that you never know which side of it you are on." That kind of exotic disorientation only heightened a visitor's fascination, only added to the sense this was a place of "strange and foreign sights." San Antonio's ruins were too valuable to turn into rubble.[23]

Rubble they would become. In proximity to the GH&SA station sprang up a bustling district of warehouses, hostelries, and transportation services; six years later this pattern of development was replicated when the International & Great Northern Railroad laid down its tracks just west of Cattlemen's Square, stimulating the development of lumberyards, hotels, department stores, storage facilities, and residential housing. To facilitate traffic and trade between these two new centers of economic activity, the once-narrow twisted streets were widened and straightened, obliterating an architecture dominated by "flat-roofed, Moorish stone buildings with thick walls, projecting stone water spouts, [and] wide arched entrances." Through this more geometric and Americanized streetscape, mule-powered trolley cars clattered. The effect, newspaper editor James P. Newcomb observed, was "like the intrusion of a flashily dressed, vulgar stranger upon the society of a gen-teel, old fashioned citizen." Offering a less class-based, if equally blunt assessment of this great transformation was Richard Harding Davis, who passed through town in the early 1890s: "San Antonio is the oldest of Texas cities and possesses historic and picturesque show-places which in any other country but ours would be visited by innumerable American tourists prepared to fall down and worship." Few locals showed any interest in genuflecting. "The citizens of San Antonio do not, as a rule, appreciate the historical values of their city; they are rather tired of them." Energized instead by the modernist urge, they encouraged the famed New York journalist to "look at the new Post-office and the City Hall, and ride on the cable road," but his eyes strayed else-where: "The missions which lie just outside the city are what will bring the Eastern man or woman to San Antonio, and not the new water-works."[24]

Others felt similarly. The massive reconstruction of the city's central core, which potentially threatened such landmarks as the Alamo, activated a group of preservationists, cheered on by the *San Antonio Express*, to lobby the state to purchase a portion of the fabled battleground, including the chapel; it did so in 1883, which, when combined with later purchases in the early twentieth century, rounded out the site. These actions established an important connection between the denotation of this space as "historic" and tourism: preserving the "sad glory" that enveloped the Alamo and hallowing the ground on which so much blood had been spilled created a shrine to which any number of good patriots would journey. But they would flock to San Antonio only if its heralded past was protected. Were its monuments to continue to fall to "the storm of progress," the *Express* editorialized in 1912, if the citizenry continued to "be careless custodians of the goose that lays our golden egg," there would be a substantial economic ramification. "The tourist comes because he has heard of San Antonio's fame as a picturesque, historically interesting city. He brings millions of dollars annually." History sells.[25]

Yet what portion of it was being sold, to whom, and why says a great deal about the degree to which the reorganization of Alamo Plaza, designed to accommodate a budding tourist business, also reflected alterations in the contemporary social order. In the 1840s, when the U.S. Army leased the Alamo chapel from the Catholic archdiocese as a supply depot, its presence was a commercial stimulus, so much so that this plaza to the east of the San Antonio River began to supplant the once-dominant western plazas, Main and Military. The Menger Hotel initially serviced army officers and contractors; blacksmith and leather artisans, dry goods merchants, and stables crowded into and around the plaza in response to substantial military procurements. When in the late 1870s the army pulled out to its new base to the north of town—later named Fort Sam Houston—activity in the district briefly slumped, only to be revived with the arrival of the railroad in 1877; additional hotels, boardinghouses, and new stores and shops popped up and were further sustained with the increasing number of visitors who were on a pilgrimage to the Alamo.[26]

What these tourists came to venerate, like the evolving sources of income that had come to shape the plaza's economy—the U.S. Army and later the railroad—illustrated how much the Alamo, a marker of a revolutionary past, had become a "critical symbol of modernity." Breaking from "the social content and spatial logic of the earlier plaza tradition" that the Spanish and later Mexican cultures had brought to life and emerging as "a source of income producing property" intrinsic to late-nineteenth-century capitalism, the plaza ensured "a place in the present, and future, [for] a particular social order." So argues anthropologist Richard Flores, who connects growing Anglo control of the region's economy, politics, and culture with its "remapping of San Antonio around the Alamo." This enabled this new elite "to solidify [its] hold on the local geographic and social terrain" and to advance through the landmark "a particular mythological past of Anglo-American heroism and Mexican tyranny." As such, the Alamo became a "public icon" that represented white Texans "as morally, politically, and socially superior." Richard Harding Davis participated in this "form of reconquest" when he challenged San Antonians to orient their heritage around what "Eastern men or women" found compelling, around a signifier these visitors could claim as their own: "The Alamo is to the South-west what Independence Hall is to the United States, and Bunker Hill to the East; but the pride of it belongs to every American, whether he lives in Texas or Maine." By nationalizing the Alamo narrative and thus excluding the Tejanos who had fought within its walls, Davis and other revisionists freed millions of subsequent visitors to bear witness to the bloody 1836 battle as yet another moment in American triumphalism.[27]

Water Music

Manifest destiny was equally bound up in the various plans floated to reconceive the San Antonio River. They all depended, however, on some of the first words written about the stream. In May 1716, Capitán Domingo Ramón and his company of soldiers, who were marching to present-day east Texas to reestablish abandoned missions, reached the San Antonio area. "On this day I marched to the northeast seven leagues through mesquite bush with plenty of pasturage," Ramón jotted down in his diary on May 14. "Crossing two dry creek beds we reached a water spring on level land, which we named San Pedro," the flow of which led him to conclude with practiced eye that "there was sufficient water here for a city of one-quarter league." This hypothetical community's size increased when Ramón came upon the San Antonio River, a bit farther east. Noting its beauty and cataloging its value—along its banks grew "pecan trees, grape vines, willows, elms and other timbers"—he and his men crossed a ford and trooped along the eastern bank to the headwaters, where they set up camp amidst "beautiful shade trees and good pasturage." Further exploration led Ramón to exclaim anew over the landscape's riches: "Here we found . . . hemp nine feet high and flax two feet high. Fish was caught in abundance for everyone, and nets were used in the river with facility." This well-watered and fertile land could sustain a flourishing agriculture and support a thriving population.[28]

Subsequent Spanish settlement, with its substantial investment in an extensive network of acequias (irrigation ditches), was predicated on Ramón's insights into urban development. So too was the community's activity during the Mexican and Texas Republic eras: without the river, there would have been no San Antonio de Béxar, a conclusion mid-nineteenth-century travelers also reached. In the 1840s, George Kendall, who would become a significant force in the expansion of the region's grazing industry, was convinced that the stream was the city's lifeblood. German scientist Ferdinand Roemer concurred: he was charmed by the "location of the city in the broad valley, watered by the beautiful stream and surrounded by gently sloping hills," and that led him to muse about its future course: "What an earthly paradise could be created here through the hands of an industrious and cultured population." Flowing through these and other travelogues was the assumption that in a semiarid landscape, water was capital.[29]

It was priceless in another sense. Roemer for one was transfixed by a certain recreational use to which the river was put: "It is quite a startling spectacle to see here just above the bridge in the heart of the city, a number of Mexican women and girls bathing entirely naked." Smitten by their fluid grace, Roemer continued to stare: "Several times a few of them were carried near us by the stream then they would dive and reappear again quite a distance below the bridge. If this was done to hide themselves from our view, it was the wrong thing to do, for the water was so clear that one could see the smallest pebble at the bottom." It was not the skinny dipping, but another form of aesthetic pleasure that a decade later led Frederick Law Olmsted to halt in his tracks as he rode across the bridge: "We irresistably stop to examine" the river, he wrote, because "we are so struck with its beauty. It is of a rich blue and pure as crystal, flowing rapidly but noiselessly over pebbles and between reedy banks. One could lean for hours over the bridge-rail."[30]

Capturing the river's sensual quality and meditative character has been central to a series of twentieth-century schemes to integrate it into the tourist economy. That required—as it had with the Alamo—disconnecting the river from its colonial and Mexican heritage, much of which was achieved indirectly: as the city exploded in size in the late nineteenth century and redoubled during the first decades of the twentieth—by 1910 its population was an estimated one hundred thousand—it swallowed up farmlands the acequias once watered and outstripped the eighteenth-century ditches' capacity to deliver potable water to a large number of households. Many acequias were abandoned or buried as new roads were constructed over them and a modern sewage and water system bisected them. By then, the river was no home to bathing beauties cavorting in the buff, and for good reasons. As with most urban river systems, the San Antonio was a convenient dumping spot for garbage, litter, and effluent—clogged, its flow was further impeded as the city began to drill innumerable artesian wells to slake the growing urban thirst; this dried up springs at the headwaters. By 1911, the *San Antonio Express* lamented that although few "cities possess so great a natural asset as a winding, tree-lined stream such as the San Antonio River," and although visitors still cooed over its "sinuous course through the city," it had "dwindled to a sluggish current running through neglected banks over a riverbed covered with slime and silt."[31]

That the river was a mess, paradoxically, allowed the community to debate its place in local development initiatives, free from the past's constraints. Many of the business elite, sick of the river's stench, repulsed by its clotted disarray, and longing to profit from its disappearance, periodically proposed that it be buried, piped underground with streets platted along its former course, generating a new flow of street-level trade; for them, the river *as* a river had no current value, thus justifying its obliteration. For others, its future value far outweighed its present dreary state. City Beautiful reformers at the turn of the century touted a plan to increase stream flow and trim, prune, and dress up the river's banks, turning the eyesore into the central artery of downtown. The economic payoff would come by using the river's new-won beauty (and a confused appropriation of its history) to lure a carefree clientele to its waters: along this "vast park," which at night would be illuminated "by myriad lightbulbs," local Mexicans "dressed in the garb of Aztec Indians will paddle canoes, filled with tourists," who then would stop off "at picturesque mission landings for refreshments." In this lurid vision, the San Antonio River was made into "a bit of fairyland and unlike anything in the world."[32]

The reformers' dreamy notion of the river as a fantasy zone of play and entertainment began to take hold, accelerating the process by which this natural space would become increasingly artificial. One sign of this was a significant shift in nomenclature: in time the river would become known simply as the River Walk. But that evolution took the better part of the twentieth century. Early efforts to spruce up the river's appearance (and smell) were swept away in the devastating flood of 1921. Throughout the next decade, commercial agents redoubled their efforts to funnel the dangerous watercourse underground, an attack on the river that a number of organizations—including a powerful women's lobby, the San Antonio Conservation Society (SACS)—deflected. In alliance with other civic groups and city hall, SACS supported an ambitious riverside design project, known as "The Shops of Aragon and Romula"; as its name suggests, it wrapped mundane commercial enterprise in a patina of Spanish exoticism, establishing a romanticized landscape in which visitors would frolic and through which they would consume. Its final development, originally stalled with the onslaught of the

Great Depression, was reenergized with Works Progress Administration funds and local investment. But its many pathways and staircases, designed to facilitate tourists' movement along the river's banks and up and down between the water and street levels, were strikingly underutilized until the 1960s, when a bold initiative to convert a large portion of the central business district into a tourist haven and convention center surfaced. The planners of Hemisphere '68 recognized that the river was the thread that could stitch together many of the disparate elements of a new urban fabric. With its construction of the aptly named hotel, the Palacio del Rio, the Hilton Corporation demonstrated the degree to which water could bring coherence and focus to a site. Rising up twenty-one stories on land situated between the San Antonio River and a new exhibition hall that postfair would be turned into a convention center, Palacio del Rio opened up in two directions: its elevators and lobbies serve as a corridor for conventioneers, guests, and other visitors to cycle easily between the riverside restaurant, bar, and shops and street-level exhibit space.[33]

This crucial linkage sparked a gold rush: since 1968, many hotels have attempted to replicate this model, perhaps the most immediately successful of which was the Hyatt Regency (1979): its investors purchased and tore down a portion of the Alamo Plaza streetscape to construct Paseo del Alamo, a stairway flanked by a water sculpture that evokes the Spanish acequias and pulls pedestrians from the Alamo down through the hotel's river-level entryway; the 500-room Marriott Riverwalk (1979) and the 1,000-room Marriott Rivercenter (1988) were sited between built Rivercenter Mall (1988) and the convention center. These and other anchors, as well as countless smaller establishments, annually introduce tens of thousands of guests to the River Walk, a rising volume of traffic that supports any number of businesses and dramatically underscores its profound economic impact.[34]

The River Walk's profitability is one reason why the river itself has all but disappeared. To ensure an even, clean flow of water, the city graded, then made concrete, the streambed, which every year is drained and refurbished; in addition, a series of upstream and downstream check dams regulate the water level. Altered too is the river's course: in 1968, a new outlet was channeled east to create a lagoon in front of the convention center, and in the mid-1980s another extension was dug north and east to pool in front of the Marriott and Rivercenter Mall. Added flood control measures—including a three-mile-long, 24-foot-wide tunnel bored 140 feet beneath the river—along with pumps, filters, and recycling processes—have turned the whole into a hydraulic system that is as fully divorced from the original watershed as it is artfully concealed from the casual gaze.

Not all is illusory. As early-twentieth-century activists had hoped, the River Walk has become the communal artery and civic stage, albeit without buff Aztec warriors plying languid waters. Making full use of the paths and river surface are a series of parades and processions that crowd the calendar and embody a mix of cultural, economic, social, and religious values. The oldest is staged by the most exclusive male organization in the city: in 1941, the Cavaliers, whose membership constitutes a small subset of the Anglo elite, launched the first River Parade. The River Art Show followed six years later, and 1957 marked the debut of the Kiwanis Club's Fiesta Noche del Rio, a summer theater production (not to be confused with the club's Fiesta Navidad del Rio, a winter holiday act); in 1969 the first St. Patrick's Day parade pushed down a channel awash with green dye. By far the most crowded set of weeks is those within the Christmas shopping season: Friday after Thanksgiving is the River Walk Holiday Parade (1982), at the start of which seventy thousand colored lights, laced through the overarching trees, are illuminated. Additional wattage is supplied via the two thousand votive candles wedged into sand-filled paper bags, which are fired up during Fiesta de las Luminarias; through their flickering light Las Posadas, a secular-sponsored reenactment of Mary and Joseph's journey to a manger, is performed. More spontaneous celebrations invariably sweep down these same waters: when the troops came home in 1945, they floated through the cheers of a grateful citizenry; when the San Antonio Spurs won the National Basketball Association championship in 1999, 250,000 packed the banks and yelled themselves hoarse. The River Walk is not just for out of towners.[35]

Yet for all its cultural significance and dramatic space and despite the billions of dollars it generates, the River Walk has not been a windfall. San Antonio has long been, and remains, one of the poorest large cities in the United States, vying with Detroit for that dubious distinction. But its poverty—the median income hovers in the mid-$20,000 range, about 30 percent less than the national average—comes conjoined with a remarkably low level of unemployment. What accounts for this seemingly anomalous situation? Tourism, a point of some pride to its local representatives. A 1999 study the San Antonio Area Tourism Council underwrote concluded that tourism was responsible directly and indirectly for the creation of more than seventy-eight thousand jobs (approximately 12 percent of the workforce) and for the generation of nearly $2 billion in wages. These figures reflect the industry's robust health, concluded council president Carol O'Malley, "and we need to make sure it stays that way."[36]

Its strength, critics retort, is predicated on the continued immiseration of its workers. That is why in the mid-1990s an ad hoc coalition of grassroots activists and labor organizers began to attack the city's ready resort to tax abatements to subsidize the construction of downtown hotels. It was this issue that helped topple Mayor Thornton in 1997 and that in 2000 troubled his successor's final year in office. Howard Peak had used tax abatements as a wedge issue in the 1997 campaign and a year later helped pass legislation calling for their use only if the corporations receiving them provided a substantial number of "living wage" jobs. But two years later, by arguing that an exception should be made for the same 1,200-room Sheraton hotel project that had derailed his predecessor's political ambitions, the mayor sparked a furor. Its crescendo came on March 23, 2000, when six hundred demonstrators packed council chambers to berate His Honor and the council; after two hours of blistering testimony, the politicians voted to delay consideration of the Sheraton tax abatement proposal. Although the protesters congratulated themselves for winning a temporary reprieve, theirs was but a minor victory. As with the mayor, they refused to question the dominant place of tourism in the city's economy and the dependency that this situation has produced. Conceded another archfoe of the tax abatement project, *Express-News* columnist Carlos Guerra: "San Antonians don't dislike tourists, the tourist industry or the thousands of jobs it provides." That has always been the trap.[37]

Notes

1. Chris Williams, "Thornton Champions Abatements," *San Antonio Express-News*, 12 March 1997, p. 1A (hereafter *E-N*).
2. Travis E. Poling and Chris Williams, "Mayor Says No More Hotel Tax Abatements," *E-N*, 21 March 1997, p. 1A.
3. Aissatou Sidimé, "Study Measures Tourism's Impact," *E-N*, 12 January 2000, p. 1E; the study concluded that "visitors directly spent $2.001 billion in San Antonio in 1998, including $631 million at lodging facilities"—the impact on work totaled more than seventy-eight thousand jobs and accounted for an estimated $900 million in wages.
4. Daniel R. Mandelker, Gary Felder, and Margaret R. Collins, *Reviving Cities with Tax Abatement* (New Brunswick, N.J.: Rutgers University Center for Urban Policy Research, 1980); Robert R. Weaver, *Local Economic Development in Texas* (Arlington, Tex.: Institute for Urban Studies, University of Texas at Arlington, 1986); Todd Swanstrom, *Crisis of Growth Politics: Cleveland, Kucinich, and the Challenge of Urban Populism* (Philadelphia: Temple University Press, 1985), 145; I am grateful to my colleague Heywood Sanders for sharing his insights into this tangled aspect of urban development and city politics.
5. Hal K. Rothman, *Devil's Bargains: Tourism in the Twentieth-Century American West* (Lawrence: University Press of Kansas, 1998).
6. Donald E. Everett, *Adobe Walls to Stone Edifice: A Sesquicentennial Pilgrimage of the First Presbyterian Church of San Antonio, Texas, 1846–1995* (San Antonio, Tex.: First Presbyterian Church, 1995), 8–9.
7. Ibid., 9–15; Kenneth W. Wheeler, *To Wear a City's Crown: The Beginnings of Urban*

Growth in Texas, 1836–1865 (Cambridge, Mass.: Harvard University Press, 1968), 20–46; Carland Elaine Crook, "San Antonio, Texas, 1846–1861" (master's thesis, Rice University, 1964), 77–120; McCullough's departure in 1849 was also brought about by the death of his wife in the cholera epidemic of that year.

8. On the growth of the tourism/hospitality spending relative to military spending, see Sidimé, "Study Measure's Tourism's Impact," pp. 1E, 8E.

9. Donald E. Everett, *San Antonio Legacy: Folklore and Legends of a Diverse People* (San Antonio, Tex.: Maverick Publishing Company, 1999), 1–2; Anne Butler, "The Frontier Press and Prostitution: A Study of San Antonio, Tombstone, and Cheyenne" (master's thesis, University of Maryland, 1975); Caroline Mitchell Remy, "A Study of the Transition of San Antonio from a Frontier to an Urban Community from 1875–1900 (master's thesis, Trinity University, 1960), 3–7.

10. Remy, "Transition of San Antonio," 7–10; 15–18; 39–47; Marilyn McAdams Sibley, *Travelers in Texas, 1761–1860* (Austin, Tex.: University of Texas Press, 1967), 61–65, 119; Harriet Spofford, "San Antonio de Bexar," *Harper's Monthly*, February 1877, 849.

11. Char Miller, "Where the Buffalo Roamed: Ranching, Agriculture, and the Urban Marketplace," in *On the Border: An Environmental History of San Antonio*, ed. Char Miller (Pittsburgh: University of Pittsburgh Press, 2001), 56–82; Everett, *San Antonio Legacy*, 39–47.

12. Everett, *San Antonio Legacy*, 15–18; for an earlier and equally arch depiction of San Antonio's "decline" into respectability see Alexander E. Sweet and J. Armory Knox, *On a Mexican Mustang through Texas: From the Gulf to the Rio Grande* (St. Louis and Houston: Y. N. James and Company, 1884), 354–56.

13. Dennis R. Judd and Susan S. Fainstein, eds., *The Tourist City* (New Haven: Yale University Press, 1999), 4; James E. Sherow, "Water, Sun, and Cattle: The Chisholm Trail as an Ephemeral Ecosystem," in *Fluid Arguments: Water in the American West*, ed. Char Miller (Tucson: University of Arizona Press, 2001), 141–55.

14. Carland Elaine Crook, "San Antonio, Texas, 1845–1861" (master's thesis, Rice University, 1964), 177.

15. William Corner, *San Antonio de Bexar: A Guide and History* (San Antonio: Bainbridge and Corner, 1890), 58–61; Remy, "A Study of the Transition of San Antonio," 124–26; Billy M. Jones, *Health-Seekers in the Southwest, 1817–1900* (Norman: University of Oklahoma Press, 1967), 23–122; John E. Baur, *The Health Seekers of Southern California, 1870–1900* (San Marino, Calif.: Huntington Library, 1959), 1–53.

16. "Letters from Texas," in *Sidney Lanier: Florida and Miscellaneous Prose*, centennial ed., vol. 6, ed. Philip Graham (Baltimore: Johns Hopkins University Press, 1945), 187–90; Corner, *San Antonio de Bexar*, 202, 235–39; Remy, "A Study of the Transition of San Antonio," 125.

17. Miran McClintock and Michael Simms, eds., *O. Henry's Texas Stories* (Dallas: Still Point Press, 1986), vii–xxviii, 33–42.

18. Ibid., 33–34.

19. Sidney Lanier to Mary Day Lanier, 15 January 1873, quoted in Remy, "A Study in the Transition of San Antonio," 126; Graham, *Lanier*, 187–90; Corner, *San Antonio de Bexar*, 58; "Beautiful San Antonio" (San Antonio: The Business Men's Club of San Antonio, 1905), 24–25, 38; Jones, *Health-Seekers in the Southwest*, 123–50.

20. George H. Paschal, Jr., "The Public Service Aspect of the Medical Career of Dr. Frank Paschal in San Antonio, 1893–1925" (master's thesis, Trinity University, 1956), 1–17; Pat Ireland Nixon, M.D., *A Century of Medicine in San Antonio; The Story of Medicine in Bexar County, Texas* (San Antonio: privately published, 1936), 154–56.

21. Paschal, "Public Service Aspect of the Medical Career of Dr. Frank Paschal," 17–35; 114–35; "An Answer to the Doctors," *San Antonio Express*, 9 December 1895, p. 6; "They Say It Is Contagious," *San Antonio Express*, 10 December 1895, p. 5; "Texas and Its Climate," *San Antonio Express*, 1 July 1900, p. 15; Nixon, *A Century of Medicine*, 154–56.

22. The U.S. Army and U.S. Air Force were essential in the development of the city's service economy. David R. Johnson, "The Failed Experiment: Military Aviation and Urban Development, 1910–1940," in *The Martial Metropolis: U.S. Cities in War and Peace*, ed. Roger W. Lotchin (New York: Praeger, 1984), 84–108; Char Miller, "Sunbelt Texas," in *Texas Through Time: Evolving Interpretations*, eds. Walter Buenger and Robert Calvert (College Station: Texas A&M University Press, 1991), 279–309.

23. James P. Newcomb, "Passing of the Chili Stands," *San Antonio Daily Express*, 9 June 1901, p. 15; Spofford, "San Antonio de Bexar," 836–87; Lewis F. Fisher, "The Preservation of San Antonio's Built Environment," in Miller, *On the Border: An Environmental History of San Antonio*.

24. Newcomb, "Passing of the Chili Stands," 15; Richard Harding Davis, *The West from a Car-Window* (New York: Harper and Brothers, 1892), 15–16. The city's spatial redesign is discussed in Miller, "Where the Buffalo Roamed."

25. *San Antonio Express*, 12 July 1912; Lewis F. Fisher, *Saving San Antonio: The Precarious Preservation of a Heritage* (Lubbock: Texas Tech University Press, 1996), 37–60.

26. Wheeler, *To Wear a City's Crown*, 20–46; Thomas T. Smith, *The U.S. Army & the Texas Frontier Economy, 1845–1900* (College Station: Texas A&M University Press, 1999), 27–33.

27. Richard F. Flores, "Private Visions, Public Culture: The Making of the Alamo," *Cultural Anthropology* 10, no. 1 (1995): 110–12; Flores, "The Alamo and the Spatial Terrain of Dominance" (paper presented to the NACCS, spring 1996), 15–16; Flores, *Remembering the Alamo: Memory, Modernity, and the Master Symbol* (Austin: University of Texas Press, 2002). Flores focuses on the late nineteenth century as the moment when Anglo commercial activism and social customs began to dominate San Antonio, but in truth, military spending, the emergence of a German mercantile elite, and other economic developments during the Antebellum Era undercut the status and financial clout of the Mexican population. See Char Miller and David Johnson, "The Rise of Urban Texas," and David Johnson, "Frugal and Sparing," in *Urban Texas: Politics and Development*, eds. Char Miller and Heywood Sanders (College Station: Texas A&M University Press, 1990), 3–29, 33–57; nor were these changes solely centered on Alamo Plaza: the wool exchange facilities, dry goods stores, livery stations, and banks that grew up on Military Plaza at the end of the Civil War, as well as the nearby and substantial catering to the cowboy trade, were also controlled by Anglo-Americans. See Char Miller, "Where the Buffalo Roamed," 70–72; Davis, *The West from a Car-Window*, 15–17.

28. Ramón quoted in Karen E. Stothert, "The Archaeology and Early History of the Head of the San Antonio River," Southern Texas Archaeological Association, Special Publication Number Five, 1989, pp. 53–54.

29. Jesús F. de la Teja, *San Antonio de Béxar: A Community on New Spain's Northern Frontier* (Albuquerque: University of New Mexico Press, 1995), 8, 32–36, 76–79, 86–89; Paul H. Carlson, *Texas Woollybacks: The Range Sheep and Goat Industry* (College Station: Texas A&M University Press, 1982), 36–41; Dr. Ferdinand Roemer, *Texas with Particular Reference to German Immigration and the Physical Appearance of the Country* (San Antonio, Tex.: Standard Printing Company, 1935), 124, 133.

30. Roemer, *Texas*, 124–25; Frederick Law Olmsted, *A Journey Through Texas; Or, a Saddle-Trip on the Southwestern Frontier, with a Statistical Appendix*, reprint (New York: Burt Franklin, 1969), 149.

31. *San Antonio Express*, 5 February 1911, p. 1A; 18 May 1913, p. 1A. The most complete discussion of the river's revival is Fisher, *Saving San Antonio*, 181–216, and his *Crown Jewel of Texas: The Story of San Antonio's River* (San Antonio, Tex.: Maverick Publishing Company, 1997).

32. Fisher, *Crown Jewel of Texas*, 26–27.

33. Fisher, *Saving San Antonio*, 181–216.

34. Ibid., 85–89.

35. Ibid., 89–96.

36. Carlos Guerra, "Boondoogle Details Are Emerging," *E-N*, 12 March 2000, p. 1B; Sidimé, "Study Measures Tourism's Impact," p. 1E.

37. David Anthony Richelieu, "Hotel Tax Deal Delayed," *E-N*, 24 March 2000, pp. 1, 12A; Carlos Guerra, "Hotel Deal Shows City's Bad Priorities," *E-N*, 26 March 2000, p. 1B; "Will Workers Get Stiffed in Hotel Deal?" *E-N*, 24 March 2000, p. 1B; "Boondoggle Deals Are Emerging," *E-N*, 12 March 2000, p. 1B; "The Mother of All Hotel Giveaways II," *E-N*, 12 February 2000, p. 1B.

CULTURAL TOURISM AND THE FUTURE

WHAT THE NEW LAS VEGAS TELLS

US ABOUT OURSELVES ➤

HAL ROTHMAN

For much of the brief life of the First City of Entertainment, the idea that Las Vegas might represent a dimension of cultural tourism would have galled any self-respecting university professor. Las Vegas was a sham, a fraudulent city devoted to sin, the worst of American society. It was degrading, a shame, a place that pandered to the worst instincts of the human race. Americans went there to cast off their sins, to escape reality, not to find meaningful experience. Las Vegas was something Americans looked down their noses at in disdain—but scampered to when no one else was looking.

The new Las Vegas is different, a function not only of the change in the city itself but in the mores, manners, and values of Americans. Since the late 1970s, Las Vegas has moved away from gaming and toward entertainment, not necessarily cutting-edge entertainment but a broad combination of mainstream and high culture, with a little bit of avant-garde thrown in. You can't find Tony Orlando in a Las Vegas showroom anymore, but you're as likely to find Blue Man Group, works of Picasso, Monet, Gauguin, and the like, first-run musicals like *Rent* and *Chicago,* and since hotel impresario Sheldon Adelson has had his way, satellite Hermitage and Guggenheim museums, not quite Bilbao, but certainly something special.

At the same time, American society underwent a remarkable shift. The old rules and standards of neo-Victorian culture were tossed out and new ones, defined through media, evolved into prominent positions in a world without clear cultural distinctions. Experience has become currency, and entertainment has replaced culture. Authentic and inauthentic have blurred;

it's not that people can't tell the difference—they can. But in a culture without a dominant set of values or a commonly shared base of premises, with a strong twist of relativism thrown in, it's hard to communicate why authentic is better. "Better" morphs into a description of preference, and people do as they please, encouraged by talk shows, self-help books, and twelve-step programs. When the value is on the self, when people rationalize their pleasure as socially useful, when it's all "me, me, me, now, now, now," what pleases them is Las Vegas.

Fundamental changes in American society began the long road of making the pariah a paradigm, of bringing Las Vegas to a broader American mainstream. The cultural liberalization of the United States—from a place where Baptist preachers piled rock-'n'-roll records on Friday night bonfires and Elvis Presley could be shown on television only from the waist up to the far more individually oriented culture of personal choice of the cusp of the new century—created the context for the rise of leisure and the transformation of socially unacceptable "gambling" into recreational "gaming." The Microchip Revolution played a significant role, for Las Vegas had perfected the colonial service economy long before the rest of the nation began to encounter it. The rise of entertainment as a form of commodity increased the cachet of the city. From Frank Sinatra and Sammy Davis, Jr., to the Hard Rock Hotel, Las Vegas became more sophisticated at reflecting the desires of the public back onto it, at creating a script for visitors that placed you—any you—at the dead center of all that you saw.

In this sense, Las Vegas is the true core of new culture, "Nobrow" as John Seabrook has labeled it, a self-defined media-created version that is real to the people who come to see it.[1] I'd venture that more people who'd never had any exposure to great works of art saw them in Steve Wynn's Bellagio Hotel's first year than ever would elsewhere. Putting them in a casino took away the arrogance of high culture, the reverence people feel they're supposed to experience in a conventional museum setting but that makes them so uncomfortable, and brought high art to them on their own terms. Steve Wynn narrated; the gallery-goers held the telephonelike wands that picked up fixed position radio signals. It was art, it was in a museum, it was in a casino, and it spoke to ordinary viewers on their own terms. Welcome to the future of cultural tourism.

—

A New Yorker once said to me: "New York has magic moments. You stand in Yankee Stadium and look out at Joe DiMaggio's centerfield and Babe Ruth's short rightfield porch, you're by the Rockefeller Center and the light hits you just right, you catch Central Park at just the right moment, when the ducks are swimming and the glaze of the frost is beginning to melt and it'll take your breath away. In New York, you can get those magic moments. You just have to put up with a lot of shit in between. You're living in shit, hour after hour, day after day, and you live for the magic moment. Poof! It's there. Then back to the shit." He cocked his head. "Las Vegas gives you the moment without the shit, over and over. It's magic, alchemy. It's better than real." This hard-bitten cynic, twenty-plus years from the New York of his youth, hit the nail on the head. What Las Vegas does better than anyplace else on the planet is plane off the rough edges of a visitor's experience and make the traveler, however lame or pathetic, the center of the story. A Hollywood actor passing through town observed the same phenomenon: "I've never been anywhere except here where they give you the stage and the setting, the cast of supporting characters and let you write the script with yourself as the star!" Here's the secret to Las Vegas in a nutshell: it can always be whatever you want it to be as long as you're willing to pay for it.

In an age when faux beaches and resorts captivate tourists, Las Vegas appears no more inauthentic than anyplace else. What's the difference? The real New York is where little old ladies look the two hundred pounds of ol' linebacker that is me in the eye and smack into me like I'm not there—I was raised not to bump them back—where everyone is always yelling, "Fugetaboutit, getouttamyway," and a whole array of indecipherable epithets that I think are in English and I'm sure aren't very nice. Las Vegas is where the state flag is a ten-dollar bill and people know where their bread is buttered. Give me purposefully inauthentic in a heartbeat! New York, New York, the casino hotel that mimics the Big Apple, creates a New York experience that is almost bearable for me. In Las Vegas, the change cages that look like subway ticket kiosks are cute instead of threatening. The people manning the mobile change dispensers painted like Yellow Cabs speak English, and the streets are safe. I'm not even the dorkiest person walking around. Look, this way, New York ain't all bad, even for a small-town kid.

It took me a while to get New York, New York. I couldn't figure out why anyone would go to a hotel that offered you the experience of a city where people are rude, the streets are noisy and dirty, everything is expensive, and everyone tawks funny. Local cynics figured the hotel would flop: the change people wouldn't speak English, the waiters and waitresses would ignore you, the service would suck, and everyone would yell, push, and shove. People would flee New York, New York; after all, enough of them fled the real thing to populate the desert three times over.

When I saw the place, I finally got it. It wasn't the New York of my lifetime they were selling, the one filled with crime and grime. It was the world of Frank Sinatra and *On the Town*, the city you can see "from Yonkers down to the Bay, in just one day." New York, New York gives that great postwar burst of energy when no other city in the world could compete. If you're in your sixties, it lets you go back to a mythic moment when all was right with the world, when Americans finished making the world safe for democracy and were back to the business of their own lives, when nightlife was fun instead of tawdry and dangerous and the streets were filled with young white people on the make, back when everything had promise. You can almost hear them whistlin' "New York, New York," and everyone can see in their mind's eye Frank Sinatra and Gene Kelly in uniform.

If you're younger, New York, New York offers a romantic stage full of mythic characters, a place you never knew but surely heard about and/or have seen on TV. Here it is—or is that "was"?—reconstructed so that you can share what was in essence a cross-generational experience. You could feel the New York you never saw, you could feel the charm of Coney Island before the gangs took it over, get a shave in the Euphoria Barber Styling Shop—I didn't have the nerve to see if they used a straight razor—and eat in a faux Little Italy without worrying about getting gunned down. Never mind the tinytown of Bleeker Street and Greenwich Village abutting Columbus Circle and the Upper West Side; the Statue of Liberty was holding her skirt down à la Marilyn Monroe! Even the Motown Café—"didn't Motown used to be Detroit?" a baggy-pantsed, shaved head queried a pal. "Yeah," his friend answered, "but so what? Who cares?"—didn't ruin the image. The month it opened, The Moments, faux Temptations and faux Supremes, broke into the DJ's act and sang live songs about once an hour, occasionally dragging people from the audience to dance with them. The people, especially women in their thirties and forties, were really into it. I watched one get so into her dancing that when she realized everyone at the seventy or so tables was watching her, she blushed a full crimson. Here she was, Dolores from Ottumwa, or more likely Ashley from the Valley, living her dream—onstage for just a second with the Temps and Supremes. She was the star, the center of the script, and for a minute it all seemed possible. And no wonder. One faux Supreme and one faux Temp were . . . white! How much more inclusive can you get?

New Yorkers hated New York, New York, disparaging it from the moment it opened, but residents of other copied cities found Las Vegas doppelgangers less objectionable. Before the Paris Las Vegas hotel/casino opened in the fall of 1999, the hotel ran a series of commercials: as a catchy French tune played in the background, a truck pulled up, workers hopped out and snatched tables from French cafés, art and statuary from French parks, and finally even French apparel from a store, crated it up, stamped *Las Vegas* on the side, and headed the material essence of France directly to the desert. The commercial ended with a toppled Eiffel Tower astride a flatcar with a desert sunset behind. The effect was cute—we're fake, we know it, but we know what we're doing. It isn't France, but you'll like it anyway. The few French hanging around Paris when it opened just before Labor Day 1999 found themselves charmed by the illusion. "We feel like we're in France," Claude Ayache told a reporter. "We're afraid people won't come to France," Celine Moliere agreed, "because there's a little part of France here." Then again, the French like Jerry Lewis. Under a kitschy sign advertising Le Jacque Pot, with three legs of the Eiffel Tower anchored in the casino, the illusion was complete—if you could suspend disbelief. So what if you spoke French to one of the attendants and after *"bonjour,"* the response was: "Uh, my name is really Eric and I'm from Orange County." Tiny town and fake accents not withstanding, Paris offered audiences France as they would like it—without the rudeness and condescension Americans so expect that when you see it in *National Lampoon's European Vacation*, it isn't even funny. At Paris Las Vegas on the Strip, the faux French act like Americans and offer Las Vegas–style service. What more could the real city have to offer a wide cut of humanity?

Las Vegas is the most malleable tourist destination on the planet. It holds up a mirror to visitors and asks: "What do you want to be, and what will you pay to be it?" When you ask for your dreams and fantasies, the only object is the cost. Las Vegas is in the tourism business, selling the experience you want, not trying to teach you, indoctrinate you, offer you curiosities or illustrate the real past. That's why implosions are sport in the desert. In Las Vegas, the past is truly prologue. Nowhere in American society does who you were or what you were yesterday make less difference. The Strip is a skin, to be shed at will, when culture, custom, or capital change.

In the past decade, the themes on the Las Vegas Strip have undergone a transformation as great as any in the history of the city. As major global corporations pumped bewildering sums of money into palaces of play, they built a new facade, an edifice that perfectly mirrored American and world culture as the twentieth century drew to a close. Every city is defined by its downtown skyline: *Dallas* showed us the Sun Belt boom against the hard Texas sun; *L.A. Law* gave us Bunker Hill, both visions of steel-drenched commerce and competition. Seattle has used the Space Needle to highlight its identity for more than a generation. Las Vegas gives us . . . Venice, New York, and Paris. Its engine is . . . everywhere and nowhere, not here and not there. The desert is gone, moved to Italy. The Bellagio is the Italian Riviera, nicer than it could ever be; the Venetian gives you the canals and gondolas of Venice without the stench and the pigeon poo. What's next? What could be next after Oscar Goodman, the criminal defense attorney who along with pornographer Larry Flynt, one of the few remaining defenders of the First Amendment in the United States, was elected mayor of Las Vegas? The next hotel might be a Mob knockoff; Chicago, Chicago, Al Capone's town. The bellmen will wear pinstripes and speak in gravelly voices. They'll carry faux tommy guns. "Your room is over there, sir," the concierge will say. "Mr. Luciano"—he waves for the next bellman in line, using the name of the *capo di tutti capo* Charles "Lucky" Luciano—"will take you for a ride."

The malleability makes it possible. After sixty years of never-ending growth, there is no base population to rely on, no fixed core identity that the town sells. Las Vegas is about options, nearly infinite, a choice of packages that are admittedly false but that allow you to be the center of the experience. This isn't Santa Fe, which claims one exotic moment out of the past as its authenticity, or even San Antonio, with the Alamo and all its baggage. It isn't Key West, with its paean to Hemingway, or New Orleans and the Vieux Carre, or even Fisherman's Wharf in San Francisco Bay. In Las Vegas, nothing is real and you know that. But instead of being fake, it's better than real. Las Vegas is how it should be, how it would be if you told the story and it really was about you. Everything you need to see in Las Vegas has been built so you'll experience it on your own terms. Las Vegas is the script: you write it, you pay to produce it, and it's yours to do with as you please.

⸺

Still sporting the golden boy good looks that made him a 1970s teen heart-throb, an older but only slightly subdued David Cassidy strode to the podium to introduce Smokey Robinson, recipient of a lifetime achievement award at the 1999 EATM, Emerging Artists and Talent in Music, convention in Las Vegas's Mirage Resort. Looking out over a lunchtime audience of almost a thousand music industry representatives, musicians, media, and others, Cassidy declaimed that Las Vegas "is now the entertainment capital of the world." Cheeky for certain, Cassidy's pronouncement rattled few cages. After all, it wasn't exactly coming from someone standing at the pinnacle of the industry. The same statement resonated considerably more when issued from the mouth of Rod Essig of Creative Artists Agency (CAA), a shaper of musical talent for more than two decades and the man who brought the world not only Jim Croce and the Red Hot Chili Peppers but countless other acts of all stripes. What some attendees thought of as tongue-in-cheek hyperbole from an aging teen star took on the ring of reality coming from Essig.

Las Vegas's claim to be the city of entertainment is new but formidable.

This isn't Sonny and Cher's Las Vegas anymore, a town where entertainment was often cheesy and lame, where the lounge singer, an icon so often parodied as an image of all that was wrong with the universe, originated. Entertainment was always a part of the Las Vegas package: from Jimmy Durante and Rose Marie at the Flamingo in 1947 to Frank Sinatra, Sammy Davis Jr., and the Rat Pack, to Elvis Presley, who sold out the theater at the Las Vegas Hilton a record 837 consecutive times between 1969 and 1976, to Wayne Newton, Las Vegas simultaneously epitomized the hip and the trite, the edge and the kitsch. "Viva Las Vegas" so many sang, caustically, tongue in cheek and straight from the heart as well. Now the desert metropolis has charted a new course, and music is a crucial piece of that process. The old proverb that if you stand in one place long enough everyone you ever met will come by is just a little different in Las Vegas: you don't have to stand still for long to see every act you ever saw in the 1970s, 1980s, and 1990s and all the ones competing for your heart in the next century.

Entertainment in Las Vegas had long been a throw-in, something that came along with the prerogatives of gambling. It started as center stage, with Jimmy Durante opening the Flamingo, the Moulin Rouge's brief moment at the pinnacle of cool, and finally peaked in the early 1960s with Oceans Eleven and the Rat Pack. Then Las Vegas stumbled: instead of cutting edge it became middlebrow before the concept really existed. Las Vegas belonged to Wayne Newton, a place where entertainment placated and did not challenge, a place so unhip that it was bound to become a caricature of whatever it intended. Tony Orlando and Dawn headlined 1970s Las Vegas after they got booted from television.

In the 1990s, the desert city once again reinvented itself, this time as the first city devoted to the consumption of entertainment. Once a town of roadhouses—"carpet joints," the old Mobsters used to call 'em—not far removed from illegal gambling, Las Vegas became a casino town, a place where Americans could engage in a legitimate recreational choice with only overtones of shadiness. Gaming too had its limitations, and as the Mirage Phase took shape, impresarios reached for a broader market and transformed the town into a family destination. As casino gambling spread, Las Vegas needed ways to broaden its reach and further distinguish itself from places that offered comparable—well, not comparable—games. The influx of corporate dollars granted the flexibility to experiment.

The opening of the Mirage in 1989 provided the signal moment in the transformation from gaming to entertainment. It has become a cliché to call Steve Wynn a genius and a visionary, but as the revolution he inspired comes to an end, it is equally easy to underestimate the vision of his conception and the boldness of his execution. The Mirage cost fully $500 million more than any previous casino/hotel operation. It required a daily net profit—a "nut"—of $1 million just to break even. But the Mirage wasn't put together on a wing and a prayer. Almost two decades of development preceded the opening of the hotel and the creation of the Mirage Phase.

Wynn clearly saw something that neither the old-time gamblers—the Benny Binions and Sam Boyds—nor the new corporate owners quite grasped. The gamblers were, well, gamblers. It was about the game to them, and everything else was a frill. The corporations that owned hotels by the 1980s were well endowed with cash but lacked imagination. They weren't entertainers, they were hotels, and they followed . . . each other around in a circle. The mopes who built the two towers at the Flamingo in 1972 and 1977 typified the breed. Architecture critic Alan Hess says architects Rissman and Rissman's 1972 addition "could have been taken for an office building anywhere in the country." With the second tower, Bugsy Siegel's pool, the pinnacle of his bizarre idea of class, was in the shade all day long. The gamblers were idiosyncratic. The corporations standardized and normalized, but they weren't very exciting. It took real stones to think up ways to keep an increasingly corporate town interesting.

Wynn fused three things that none of his predecessors possessed in abundance: access to capital, verve, and an understanding of the changing nature of the American public. With E. Parry Thomas, the most important financial figure in Las Vegas prior to Howard Hughes, behind him, Wynn parlayed a small piece of land into control of first the Golden Nugget in downtown Las Vegas, then bought the Strand Motel on the Boardwalk in Atlantic City and parlayed that into the Mirage and, in 1998, the $2.1-billion Bellagio. Even though critics thought Wynn was in over his head before the opening of each hotel—especially the Mirage—he'd read the nation and indeed the world just right.

Wynn's hotels were like no other. The Mirage opened with a $30-million volcano that erupted every thirty minutes. David Hersey of *Cats* and *Les Misérables* did the lighting. Wynn made Siegfried and Roy into household names; he introduced the nouveau circus Cirque de Soleil to the nation. The elegance and mystery of the Mirage drew them in; the culture and shopping of the Bellagio, with the art collection, a $10-million Dale Chihuly glass canopy in the lobby, and a formal conservatory, created the right touch. Wynn understood the public's emotions. The gamblers understood their wallets and the corporate hotels their business needs.

Wynn's inventiveness spurred imitation by corporations. During the Mirage Phase, an unparalleled spate of construction changed not only the themes and look of the city but its very purpose. All of a sudden Las Vegas became a place to eat out and to shop, to take the kids to a roller coaster or theme park. All of a sudden Las Vegas became upscale. Local restauranteurs dueled with their James Beard awards. All of a sudden, cachet meant Sephora in the space that the All-Star Café vacated when the chain folded, FAO Schwarz in the Forum Shops, Prada at the Bellagio, and much more. Enormous high-end shopping malls graced the last Mirage Phase gargantuans, the Aladdin and the Venetian. The Desert Passages mall at the Aladdin offered another version of shopping as entertainment. Even the Grand Canyon came to Las Vegas—the third phase of Showcase included the Grand Canyon shops. Now Las Vegas had two grand canyons, the Grand Slam Canyon theme park at Circus Circus and the Grand Canyon shops. For the adventurous, roller coasters sprang up atop the Stratosphere—which also sported an attraction where the really foolhardy strapped themselves to a jet pack and were rocketed to the very tip of the tower, more than 1,100 feet above the street below—and at the Sahara and New York, New York. The MGM added an attraction called the SkyScreamer, where people dropped in free fall in something like a pendulum, for reasons only they could understand.

The roller coasters and theme parks were themselves only a prelude to another in an ongoing series of reinventions. In this latest, Las Vegas is becoming the city of entertainment. It has become a place where, as in Doug Liman's 1996 hit film, *Swingers*, the young and hip come to play. There's no limit to what properties will do to bring in young hip spenders, and an entire ancillary industry has sprung up to serve them. Peter Morton's Hard Rock Hotel gets much of the credit. "If the house is rockin', don't bother knockin', c'mon in," the inscription above the entry there reads, and like Stevie Ray Vaughn, from whom the quote is taken, the place rocks. It's a shrine to rock-'n'-roll, a place to which people make pilgrimages. Where better to dive from a second-story hotel room balcony into the pool than the Hard Rock? What more powerful iconography could there be for the rock-'n'-roll generation?

By 2000, Las Vegas had developed an even more envied nightlife than ever before. Nightclubs like the RA at the Luxor, C2K at the Venetian, Baby's at the Hard Rock Hotel, and the reprise of Studio 54—did we really need this?—at the MGM are one dimension. Las Vegas was touted as one of the hottest club scenes in the country. Impresarios like twenty-seven-year-old John D. Guzman, progenitor of Naked Hollywood, a high-end takeoff of the sinfully exquisite mansion parties of Los Angeles packaged for nightclubs that seek to offer the titillation of the old Las Vegas, thrive. Musicals like *Chicago* presented another dimension, and of course, the staples: Siegfried and Roy, Cirque de Soleil, Mystère, O, EFX, Splash, and their kind. Las Vegas is filled with dance clubs like Utopia or Drink and raves at the Candy Factory, and to cap it all off, there are more venues for live music than even the most die-hard fan could get to in a lifetime. The proliferation of venues for national acts, as well as an emerging club scene ranked among the best in the country, gave Las Vegas one of the most exciting and viable music scenes as the new century began.

In the late 1990s, music venues transformed the landscape of the town. "Four to six years ago, there was no place except Caesar's," Essig observed in front of an audience of musicians in 1999. "Basically there were Vegas shows in the showrooms." With fifteen arenas, outdoor stages, and showrooms of 1,500 or more seats, Las Vegas now has an unequaled capacity to present music of all kinds. On any night, a major headliner or three is playing somewhere in Las Vegas. A typical two-month period bookended by Tom Petty's August 21, 1999, show at The Joint at the Hard Rock and his October 15 return to the MGM Grand Garden included Little Feat and the Neville Brothers, the Righteous Brothers, the Bolshoi Ballet, Donna Summer, LeAnn Rimes, Alice Cooper, Night Ranger, Styx, Dwight Yoakum, a Los Angeles Kings–Phoenix Coyotes exhibition hockey game, *NSYNC, Linda Ronstadt, Alanis Morissette and Tori Amos, Alan Jackson, Dennis Miller, the Beach Boys, Jeff Beck, George Carlin, Ray Charles, Lenny Kravitz, Sting, and dozens of others. There's something for every taste, every day. A real music fan need never stay home.

The battle to bring clientele in the doors has changed the meaning of entertainment. "In the old days, shows used to be a loss leader," Las Vegas native Pat Miller, the grandson of an entertainer, observed. "Now the owners are laughing all the way to the bank." They have read postindustrial Americans perfectly and made entertainment into a culture the public understands and embraces. Formed from popular music, film, television, and increasingly the Internet, this new culture more than competes for the attention of the American public. Because it markets at the same time, it has come to define the liberal consumerist age of the new century.

For pure grandiosity, nothing quite matches the MGM Grand on the Las Vegas entertainment scene. Since it opened in 1993, the resort has billed itself as the "City of Entertainment," featuring such behemoth events as the Rolling Stones No Security tour show. The MGM's various venues have hosted title fights and rock extravaganzas, as well as countless other giant acts. Mike Tyson and Evander Holyfield fought there, and Barbra Streisand came out of hiding to grace its stage to kick off her six-city 1994 tour and to play the New Year's Eve 2000 show. None of this is accident. The MGM offers the consumer a complete experience, one-stop shopping for entertainment: countless top-rated restaurants, gaming, and a whole range of other options for a night on the town are there to be plucked on the way to and from a show. The 650-seat Hollywood Theatre; Catch a Rising Star, the premier comedy club; Studio 54, modeled on New York's hot dance club of the 1970s; and EFX, a stage extravaganza featuring Tommy Tune, fill out the entertainment options. A theme park offers another form of entertainment.

Tall and powerfully built, Mark Prows exudes the confidence of a man who knows his business. The vice president in charge of the MGM Grand Arena, Prows is one of the strongest voices to claim that Las Vegas is the entertainment capital of the world, now and in the future. "It's a five-sense experience we provide," he said over lunch at one of the many fine restaurants at the MGM. "You see, feel, smell, taste, and hear."

The MGM Grand Garden was the first major hotel/casino arena in Las Vegas. Before its opening in 1993, the Thomas and Mack arena at the University of Nevada, Las Vegas, which doubles as the home for the UNLV Runnin' Rebels, who won the NCAA basketball championship in 1990, was the only venue with more than ten thousand seats. Prows calls the T&M, where he once worked, a "stand-alone" venue: the only sources of revenue to support its acts are the Big Four of the entertainment industry—tickets, parking, concessions, and merchandise. Casino venues have other sources, but other constraints.

When the MGM Grand Garden first opened, many of the events it booked were boxing matches, long golden in casino eyes for the way they draw gamblers. It helped that the person in charge, Dennis Finfrock, once the athletic director at nearby UNLV, was a big boxing fan. Barbra Streisand's dramatic public reappearance at the MGM on New Year's Eve, 1994, and a changing market helped transform Las Vegas entertainment. The debut of the Hard Rock Hotel in March 1995, with its 1,200-seat venue, The Joint, opened a long closed niche. Las Vegas had never really catered to the young—not since the days of Oceans Eleven and the Rat Pack in the early 1960s. The Joint served a smaller version of the market that interested the Grand Garden, and with its success, the idea—and attendant competition—took shape.

The primary theater in Las Vegas had long been the Aladdin Theater for the Performing Arts at the Aladdin Hotel. The seven-thousand-seat venue booked everything: "One week, it was *Joseph and the Amazing Technicolor Dreamcoat*, the next it was Mötley Crüe," Prows observed. "It was all over the place." Without a clearly defined mission and short a few thousand seats to make the biggest acts pay, the Aladdin could not really dominate the market. The theater was a cultural center for a town that had not yet defined itself, a B-level stop on most tours, a purveyor of a combination of what passed for sophisticated popular culture and what the rowdy public demanded.

The Joint opened a new niche, one that deftly melded popular culture with desire. The Hard Rock Hotel was a museum—you could see Keith Richard's guitars, Prince's clothes, Bob Dylan's hat, and countless other pieces of rock-'n'-roll memorabilia in the walkway around the casino floor. Here was an iconography for the rock-'n'-roll generation and their younger siblings, a culture—yes, a culture—of their own making that reflected their lives. Enough of Thomas Jefferson and Abraham Lincoln, of D day and VJ day. Here was a culture that talked about the times of the baby boomers, that made their experience significant and fun. Here was nostalgia masquerading as culture for a new generation, much as World War II did for their parents.

The music itself is a catalyst. Las Vegas is an "excuse market," Prows suggests. "People are looking for an excuse to come here, and music can provide it." If you live in Los Angeles and want a weekend away, what better opportunity than your favorite band at a big Las Vegas hotel? Not only do you see an act you've longed for, you can stay in luxury, eat at a fine restaurant, and maybe play a little too. As I waited for a flight the morning of the Rolling Stones' MGM show in April 1999, the airport in Tucson was clogged with concertgoers; the anticipation was thick. Dressed in their Stones wear and ready for twenty-four hours of partying, they were stoked. The next morning, on an 8 A.M. flight back to Tucson, they were satiated. The ones who were awake talked about the show. Music was one more variation on the oldest theme in modern Las Vegas's history.

"Well, the joint was rockin', goin' round and round," Tom Petty belted from the stage at The Joint, the 1,200-person-capacity hall at the Hard Rock Hotel in August 1999. "Yeah, reelin' and a-rockin', what a crazy sound, and they never stopped rockin' till the moon went down," and the 1,500 people who paid $100 a head for a general admission ticket rocked along. The crowd was a mix of vacationers and excuse travelers—I met a fan who came from LA, liked the Hard Rock, and felt that he needed a weekend off—locals and rock-'n'-rollers, button-downs and aging Harley enthusiasts. Such is the audience for a band with twenty years of hits and a grating, almost antisocial edge. Petty came on late—he had a fight with his girlfriend, the scuttlebutt insisted—and put on a two-and-one-half-hour show that had the entire place moving. In songs like "Free Falling," the entire crowd chanted the chorus.

Even in his late forties, Petty is still an edgy guy, prone to bite the hand that heaps caviar onto his plate. The Hard Rock displays guitars, clothing, and other rock-'n'-roll memorabilia as if they were religious icons. "If you see any of my shit up there," Petty tersely told the cheering crowd, "you have my personal permission to rip it down and take it with you!"

Still, $100 for general admission seemed like a lot, especially for a band that made its rep in part by fighting the commercialism of rock-'n'-roll. A few months before, the Rolling Stones' No Security tour played the eight-thousand-seat Grand Garden at the MGM Grand. Top ticket price reached $300, but at least the seats were reserved. Sugar Ray opened, bringing the ordinary punk club sound of their bar show to accompany the ballads like "Every Morning" that made them famous. Their excitement at opening for the Stones—following the legions so anointed, from Ike and Tina Turner to Rage Against the Machine—was palpable. Front man Mark McGrath couldn't contain himself. He couldn't believe that he and his little Orange County band were opening for the Stones in Vegas. The Stones came out and rocked as they hadn't in a generation. In the end, it was one of the best rock-'n'-roll shows I've ever seen—and I've seen thousands. But $300? When the Stones' last tour, Bridges to Babylon, peaked at $75?

The price of live music has gone through the roof in the 1990s. *Rolling Stone* called 1999 the year of the three-digit ticket, something Las Vegas had experienced for at least five years. As rock-'n'-roll audiences have gone gray and affluent, they've been more selective about what they see and more willing to pay to see it on their own terms. The days of waiting in line for days to get premier seats are over for anyone in their right mind over the age of twenty-five. Call a broker and pay to sit where you want. No one wants to fight the crowds, the noise, the parking, and the endemic violence for a glimpse of their youth. They'd rather pay to be transported as spectators, be able to drink champagne or Absolut and tonic and sit in comfort as the memories roll over them.

More intimate venues were an aging rocker's dream, a fulfillment of the prerequisites of postindustrial culture. If you weren't going to two shows a week—and you weren't—and you were there to hear the music rather than make new friends, what could be better than a two-thousand-seat hall, an eight-thousand-seat theater, or even a faux beach? The environment worked better, these were rock-'n'-roll clubs, so they expected you to boogie—no more cries of "down in front" with general admission or theater seating—and you could always stay in your seat and see pretty well if you didn't want to boogie. The drinks were expensive, but you had your choice: no need to drink swill if you didn't want to. The smaller venues felt more like a party than a concert, more like the Stones were playing your fiftieth birthday party instead of going to a concert with the masses.

—

It might chill the blood of Jacques Barzun, but the pattern is clear. Culture no longer means the collected layers of human experience on the planet. Instead there is a cultural disconnect in American society, a break point that I unfairly attribute to the appearance of MTV on the airwaves in 1982. People who came to maturity before that point understood the world in primarily textual terms. They read to get information. Many of them were raised with television, more with TV and the movies, but they still placed a primacy on information acquired by reading—whether it was the newspaper or Kafka. Those who came after that fictive moment were visual. They learned by watching, as spectators of a screen. The remote control was their tool. They learned from an image-based culture that claimed to offer them everything they needed to know. In the process, they discarded the signs and symbols of textual culture as irrelevant to their experience and especially their needs.

Las Vegas is one of the pinnacles of this new culture—for better and worse. It excels in providing this new audience what it wants and, as Steve Wynn proved at the Bellagio, even could bring the visual images of older culture to audiences it had never before reached. In this way, Las Vegas has become a center of cultural tourism, not the cultural tourism of historic preservation—Las Vegas is after all the town that implodes its past—but of the new American culture of me, me, me, now, now, now. By refracting a self-referential public onto itself, Las Vegas has become an icon of a new society that not only doesn't respect its past, but also doesn't even know it exists.

—

When Elvis Presley first came to play Las Vegas in 1956, he was still young, ripped, and taut, not the blimplike caricature he later became. The booking came about at the last minute, and Elvis found himself in the Venus Room at the New Frontier, a thousand-seat venue, he and his band backed by Freddy Martin and his orchestra. Elvis's new manager, the wily Colonel Tom Parker, took the credit; Parker had previously booked Eddy Arnold, the first mid-South country singer to reach Las Vegas, and he recognized that his new phenom had real crossover reach. Even by March, 1956 had already been a good year for Elvis, and the neon city of excess in the desert promised more. In pure Las Vegas style, a twenty-four-foot-high cutout of the twenty-one-year-old stood in front of the hotel. Even then, Las Vegas could recognize a star.

Elvis bombed. For two weeks, he, guitarist Scotty Moore, bass player Bill

Black, and drummer D. J. Fontana played Las Vegas. At the opening, they were, according to Elvis biographer Peter Guralnick, "a very nervous, very out-of-place hillbilly quartet."[2] Elvis even introduced one of his hits as "Heartburn Hotel." They were just the wrong fit, too eccentric for the older, staid if somehow frisky Las Vegas audience. A guest of the hotel vice president bounded up from a ringside table and screamed that it was too loud. He headed back to the casino. Elvis was the fringe, and Las Vegas never did well with the fringe. Then he came back in 1969 as a star for his record seven-year stay and performed 837 sold-out shows in a row beginning in the first month at Kirk Kerkorian's International Hotel and remained after Hilton bought the property. After the army, after the rock-'n'-roll revolution, in the midst of the Vietnam War, Elvis was a Las Vegas act. The years, the weight, and the changes in society conspired to make him an anachronism on the cutting edge but perfectly right for Las Vegas in 1969.

Las Vegas doesn't create entertainment. It packages music, art, and, like it or not, culture to a wider audience than those concepts could otherwise reach. The millions of people who saw real Monets, Gauguins, Renoirs, and Matisses at the Bellagio were never likely to grace any conventional museum. Certainly more people saw Elvis in the showroom of the Las Vegas Hilton than anywhere else in the world. But what they saw in the fading star was a memory, a package, a wrapper for desires they once held or to which they aspired. In this sense, its claim to be the City of Entertainment rings truer at the box office than in the coffeehouses. Las Vegas takes mutable forms and fixes them, makes them palatable. As for Elvis in 1956, the stamp of Las Vegas—positive or otherwise—signaled his emergence from the ghetto of hillbilly and his arrival in the larger market. But it cost him something too, both immediately and in the long term. After two and a half years of girls screaming, he'd finally reached a little Waterloo, a place where his act didn't fly, where the audience turned him back. Although Scotty Moore thought "people that were there, if you'd lifted them out and taken them to San Antonio, the big coliseum, they'd have been going crazy," he was probably wrong.[3] A Las Vegas audience in 1956 wasn't made up of teenagers, didn't hail from the Bible Belt, and wasn't entertainment starved.

Elvis loved Las Vegas. There was plenty to do, and a guy who didn't sleep much didn't have to worry about the town closing. He also intuited a future in Las Vegas, a way to reach the audience that was ambivalent toward him in 1956 a decade or more down the road. Elvis's intuition was always precise. This failure with a future became the paradox and promise of the City of Entertainment. Las Vegas doesn't nurture entertainment; it only buys it. An artist can hold the town, can become it and be it, but Las Vegas will push you as an artist and compromise you at the same time. It's a model for the culture of the world of the future, a place where authentic and inauthentic are purposefully indistinguishable.

Notes

1. John Seabrook, Nobrow: *The Culture of Marketing, the Marketing of Culture* (New York: A. A. Knopf, 2000).
2. Peter Guralnick, *Last Train to Memphis: The Rise of Elvis Presley* (Boston: Little, Brown, and Co., 1994).
3. Ibid.

INDEX ➤

Note: Page numbers followed by *f* or *n* indicate the presence of figures or notes.

abundance, culture of, 74–75
acequias, 195, 202, 220, 221
Acoma Pueblo, 178–79
action plans, 181
Adams, 27*f*, 27–28
adventure travel companies, 161
affordability, 153–54
Aladdin Theater for the Performing Arts, 239–40
Alamo, 218–20, 222–23
Alaska cruise tourist industry, 160–61
Albuquerque, 12–13
amenity migrants, 196, 197
American Orient Express, 1–3
Anglo Indianism, 186–87, 189
Anglos: Adams mural, 28; business suits, 22–23, 23*f*; California annexation, 53–54; hyperethnicity, 197–98; ignoring Indian problems, 67; mission incongruity with, 42, 43*f*, 44; New Mexico invisibility, 187, 198; New Mexico population, 196; playing Indian, 81, 83*f*, 95*f*, 95, 107; San Antonio (TX), 219–20, 227n. 27; tourism as boon, 189; wealthy Taos, 68; whiteness studies, 204n. 15

appropriate cultural tourism, 141
Arizona, tourism success, 141
art: commercialization, 69; identifying pieces, 138n. 22; Indian approach, 69–70; Indian models, 190; inheritable Indian tradition, 111; power of hegemony, 188–89; Pueblo peoples, 70; race and ethnicity, 189–90; representational, 69; tourism benefits, 181; values and attitudes, 68–69
arts and crafts: authenticity signified, 105; documenting, 35n. 12; federal laws, 109–10; history, 14–15; markets, 106–7; movement, 81; New Deal, 24, 26–28; New Mexico, 20–22; pottery, 20–22, 36n. 15; pottery revival, 167; Santa Fe, 15
authentic experience, concept of, 137n. 6
authenticity: adventure and, 130–33; commercialization, 164; cultural tourism, 164; ethnic implications, 190–91; Indian, 110–11; "Indian" experience, 119; Indian-made goods, 130; Las Vegas (NV), 231; postmodern, 229–30; sanitized experience, 156–57; scripted, 190; social construction, 164, 182n. 2; souvenirs, 109

wage labor, 106
water issues, federal discourse, 202;
    gentrification, 195; pueblo resorts,
    205n. 18; San Antonio (TX), 220–25;
    shortages, 201–2
whiteness. *See* Anglos
wilderness experience, 90
Wild West, 86, 87f, 93; cowboy economy,
    209–12; frontier barbarity, 208–9

women, clothing, 23–24
Woodcraft League of America, 80–81
World War II, 4–5
World Wide Web, 118
Wynn, Steve, 235–36

Zuni Pueblo, 171–72